# ACHING FOR LOVE

# ACHING FOR LOVE

## The Sexual Drama of the Adult Child

*Healing Strategies for Women*

Mary Ann Klausner
and Bobbie Hasselbring

*1817*

Harper & Row, Publishers, San Francisco

New York, Grand Rapids, Philadelphia, St. Louis
London, Singapore, Sydney, Tokyo, Toronto

They counted on silence
and they were wrong . . .

To the tender child
cringing in the dark closet
who could not prevent
the horror.

To the brave girl
callously disgarded—
thrown over
the sun-filled mountain.

I remember
and dedicate *Aching for Love.*

Mary Ann Klausner

ACHING FOR LOVE: *The Sexual Drama of the Adult Child.* Copyright © 1990 by Mary Ann Klausner and Bobbie Hasselbring. All rights reserved. Printed in the United States of America. No part of this book may be used or reproduced in any manner whatsoever without written permission except in the case of brief quotations embodied in critical articles and reviews. For information address Harper & Row, Publishers, Inc., 10 East 53rd Street, New York, NY 10022.

FIRST EDITION

Library of Congress Catalogue Card Number: 89-045236

ISBN 0-06-250482-7

90 91 92 93 94 **HAD** 10 9 8 7 6 5 4 3 2 1

Every life and every childhood is filled with frustrations: we cannot imagine it otherwise, for even the best mother cannot satisfy all her child's wishes and needs. It is not the suffering caused by frustration, however, that leads to emotional illness but rather the fact that the child is forbidden by the parents to experience and articulate this suffering, the pain felt at being wounded. . . . Children are not allowed to reproach their gods—their parents and teachers. By no means are they allowed to express their frustrations. Instead, they must repress or deny their emotional reactions, which build up inside until adulthood, when they are finally discharged, but not on the object that caused them.

Frequently, parents will not be aware of their child's narcissistic wounds; they do not notice them because they learned, from the time they were little, not to take them seriously in themselves. It may be the case that they are aware of them but believe it is better for the child not to become aware. They will try to talk her out of many of her early perceptions and make her forget her earliest experiences, all in the belief, that this is for the child's own good, for they think that she could not bear to know the truth and would fall ill as a result. That it is just the other way around, that the child suffers precisely because the truth is concealed, they do not see.

As I have repeatedly stressed, it is not the trauma itself that is the source of illness but the unconscious, repressed, hopeless despair over not being allowed to give expression to what one has suffered and the fact that one is not allowed to show and is unable to experience feelings of rage, anger, humiliation, despair, helplessness, and sadness.

Pain over the frustration one has suffered is nothing to be ashamed of, nor is it harmful. It is a natural, human reaction. However, if it is verbally or nonverbally stamped out . . . then natural development is impeded.

—Alice Miller, Ph.D.
*For Your Own Good*

# Contents

# Preface

For those of us who grew up in alcoholic families, the taboos around talking about our sexuality and the pain we feel about it run deep. We were raised in families with the alcoholic "no talk" rule that prohibited us from reaching out to others about the confusion and sadness surrounding our childhoods. Some of us suffered sexual abuse from relatives or friends of our alcoholic families. Many of us received inaccurate and distorted messages about intimate relationships and sex.

As adult children of alcoholics (ACOAs),* our unhappiness around our intimate relationships and our unfulfilling sex lives can be traced back to our chaotic alcoholic childhoods. Our alcoholic families severely impacted our sense of self—who we are as individuals—as well as our self-esteem, our body image, our ability to be sexually and emotionally vulnerable, and our ability to trust and share our innermost thoughts and feelings with others.

You demonstrate great courage in reading this book. Perhaps for the first time, you are breaking the silence and confronting the secrets that surround your childhood and your sexuality. One hundred courageous women broke the silence about their own alcoholic families and their sex lives to bring you *Aching for Love: The Sexual Drama of the Adult Child*. For many of them, it was the first time they had shared the intimate details of their lives and the process proved both painful and therapeutic.

Each woman came forward to discuss her childhood, adolescent, and adult sexual attitudes and behaviors. In *Aching for Love*, her poignant words describe in detail the sexual messages she received from her parents as she was growing up, the caregiver changes that occurred in her family, and her early feelings of attachment and loss. She further defines the sex-

---

* Throughout this book, we will use ACOA as a shorthand reference for adult children of alcoholic families.

ual relationships she has developed, maintained, and ended in her adult years. She speaks about what she has done sexually, what she feels about what she has done sexually, and about what changes she desires in her sexual life. She demonstrates through her words the many ways in which her sexual life is affected today by having been raised in an alcoholic family system.

As a sexologist and clinician, I believe that we are all sexual beings from the time we are born until the time we die and that we are entitled to enjoy and celebrate our sexual selves*. I believe the development of sexual identity and sexual relationships are affected by being raised in an alcoholic family system. I believe sexual healing and the integration of that healing process into the rest of our emotional, physical, and spiritual recovery is vital for all adult children of alcoholics who want to have full, joyful lives. I believe that the ability to heal sexually depends upon the willingness to disclose to ourselves and to others our sexual life histories and the feelings associated with them.

The women who participated in this research were willing to come forward to share their sexual life histories with Karen Howell, M.A., and myself. Talking explicitly about alcoholism and sexuality is not easy. For some research participants, this was the first time they had ever shared this information with anyone. We clearly recall how the women took care of themselves in the process.

One participant walked into the office with a paper bag and indicated she had brought with her something from home that might assist her in relaxing and being more centered during the interview. She first pulled from the bag an old photograph of herself as a child of four years and found a spot in the room to place it. Having put it on top of a desk facing her, she said, "I have an idea that these questions might be a little difficult. You said that you would ask about childhood and adulthood. I wanted to bring that picture of myself so that I could remind me of what I looked like and felt like back then. I wanted to let the child in me know that I would not forget her, that I would tell the truth about what happened to her." She then removed a soft stuffed animal, placed it on her lap, and wrapped her arms around it. She said with a soft smile, "I'm ready whenever you are."

This adult child of an alcoholic respected the child within her and created a climate of safety for that child throughout the interview. She knew what would assist her in the process of examining her sexual life history and respected herself enough to provide it. We ask that you take

---

* Throughout this work, the first-person pronoun will always refer to May Ann Klausner.

your own needs for safety as seriously by providing the nurturing care that you need in order to examine this area in your life.

The material presented in *Aching for Love* is explicit and involves descriptions of the sexual intimacy and sexual pain of real people. Sometimes their stories are heartbreaking. What they share may cause old feelings or memories to surface for you. It is important that you are able to discuss your feelings with someone you know and trust. You may want to write down your emotional and physical reactions as you progress through the book. We suggest you share what you learn about yourself from your reading with your therapist, with Twelve-Step program members you know and trust, or with empathic friends. Sharing can help you reduce the feelings of anger, fear, shame, and isolation which may develop. Examining and sharing with others your childhood and sexual experiences can be the first step in healing the sexual wounds from your past.

Conducting this research has been a privilege. Karen Howell and I recall sitting across from each woman as she spoke with us about her life. Many women broke years of silence in describing what occurred to them in their alcoholic families and in their subsequent intimate relationships. We were touched by their candidness and felt honored and enriched to have been able to hear, witness, and document their shared histories.

Our goals for you in writing *Aching for Love: The Sexual Drama of the Adult Child* are many:

- To introduce you to the most current research in sexuality and chemical addiction.
- To offer a theoretical framework from the fields of child development, object relations, and family systems from which you can interpret and understand your sexual life history.
- To provide you with a summary of the findings from our sexuality research with one hundred ACOAs.
- To help you become familiar with the process of developing your own sexual identity which includes your biological gender, social gender roles, sexual orientation, body image, and sexual "scripts."
- To suggest sexual relationship strategies that require both an examination of your family system and the development of your separate "self."

It is our hope that this book contributes to the process of your sexual healing.

# Acknowledgments

The process of conducting this research and of writing this book has been one of personal integration. Contributors to this project have been numerous and generous. I extend my special appreciation to all who have given of themselves in this effort, to all who have believed in this journey toward truth:

To Katinka Matson, Agent, at John Brockman and Associates, New York. To Thomas Grady, Editor, Kevin Bentley, Editorial Assistant, and Terri Goff, Production Editor, at Harper & Row, Publishers, San Francisco. To California Family Study Center for my introduction to Family Systems therapy. To J. Kenneth Davidson, Sr., Carol A. Darling, and Colleen Conway-Welch of the University of Wisconsin – Eau Claire, for permission to use questions from their research instruments, "Self-Perceptions of Female Sexuality" and "Perceptions of Female Response Patterns." To Lee Cordrey, Ph.D., Dean of Educational Research at Fullerton College, for consultation on research design and development of the computer program. To Pam Borst, Brenda Kenne, Jean Littleton, Marilyn Martin, and Candace Higginson for their cooperative team effort in transcription, editing, and input of original research, and manuscript preparation. To Cynthia Cooley, M.F.C.C., Stephanie Covington, Ph.D., and Sue Saperstein, M.A. for their insight and application of treatment modalities. To Mary Hammond, M.A., Brian Killen, M.A., Stephanie Miller, M.A., and Anne Weaver for their review of the manuscript and for their encouragement to persevere. To current and former individual, couple, and group clients for their continued willingness to risk and trust the process. To participants in Twelve-Step Anonymous programs of recovery for direction, fellowship, gratitude, serenity, and spirituality. To Martin Chess, Michael Castleman, Cynthia Cooley, Jim Dedic, Brenda Kenne, Elizabeth Pearce, Brian Killen, Jane Williams, and Jerry Diller for their ongoing friendship, encouragement to trust self, and for their personal and spiritual support. To Carmen Stukas, R.N., M.A., for being a compassionate passenger and witness. To Karen Howell, M.A., for her professional skills in conducting sexual interviews, analyzing data, and applying clinical and treatment knowledge to the research findings, and for coauthoring the original research which led to this book. "There are no accidents." To Jeff and Lynn Nichols for their patience, support and assistance throughout this project. Most especially, to Stuart Dedic, Erich Pfeifer, and Luke Dedic, each for being exactly who they are, and in celebration of our family recovery. And lastly, to our research participants for their courage, candor, and inspiration.

*Mary Ann Klausner*
*Bobbie Hasselbring*

The examples presented in this book are based
on true case histories, but the names and
identifying details have been changed to
protect the identities of the people involved.

# CHAPTER 1

# In Search of ACOA Sexuality

If you are an adult child of an alcoholic (ACOA), you may be dissatisfied with your sex life, with your relationship partner, and/or with yourself. You know sex should be exciting and emotionally fulfilling, yet something is missing for you. Perhaps sex with your partner leaves you dissatisfied. You may have trouble becoming sexually excited and experiencing orgasm. You may have physically satisfying sex with many partners, yet never really feel loved. You long for closeness, but you cannot seem to let yourself get too close to anyone. What contributes to your sex life being less satisfactory than you want? What creates your difficulty in achieving intimacy and security in your most committed relationship(s)? Why does it seem so difficult to have a close, loving relationship with someone while still holding onto your own life goals, personal friendships, and your self?

You are not alone in your feelings and frustration. Many women and men raised in alcoholic families report feeling conflicts in their sexual lives. Like you, they long for answers and solutions which can contribute to their sexual healing.

## The Search for Answers

As a college instructor teaching classes in human sexuality and chemical addiction, I realized how little we really know about the impact growing up in alcoholic families has on our sexuality.* Could growing up with alcoholics later affect who we choose for sexual partners? Could it explain why so many of us have difficulty trusting others and becoming sexually and emotionally intimate? Do our alcoholic "family systems" continue to dictate how we relate to our sexual partners even after we have grown up?

* Throughout this work, the first-person pronoun will always refer to Mary Ann Klausner.

Therapist Karen Howell, M.A., and I decided to investigate these questions. Using a variety of interviewing tools and techniques, we asked one hundred women ACOAs about their experiences growing up in alcoholic families and about their adult sexual relationships. We have described in detail the study design and the participant sample in Appendix One and encourage you to review it closely.

The results of our research were enlightening. Despite obvious differences in the women's lives—including differences in sexual orientation—their stories and their issues were remarkably similar. We began to see patterns emerge. The patterns of problems faced by the women were so consistent and so similar that we realized it is likely that many ACOAs—and probably most of you reading this book—experience similar issues.

Take a moment and look at the following list of questions devised from issues commonly faced by the ACOAs we studied. You might want to note those that apply to you.

−I choose partners who are sexually, physically, or emotionally unavailable to me.
−I stay in unhealthy relationships.
−I have difficulty defining, maintaining, and receiving intimacy.
−I am unable to trust myself or others in intimate relationships.
−My relationships are often plagued by poor communication.
−I have problems identifying and protecting my personal boundaries.
−I have experienced sexual abuse as a child, adolescent, and/or as an adult.
−I feel the need to control my sexual relationships.
−I am full of grief because of the many losses I have faced as a child, adolescent, and as an adult, yet I cannot express it.
−When I was growing up, my parents gave me inaccurate and unhealthy messages about sex.
−I often use drugs and/or alcohol to enable me to be sexually intimate.
−I feel confused about whether I am heterosexual, homosexual, or bisexual.
−I do not really know what a healthy relationship is or what sexual satisfaction entails.

We suggest that you take this quiz twice—now and after you finish reading this book. We suspect your awareness about your sexual life will grow and that your answers may change.

## A Conceptual Framework

Throughout this book, we provide you with a conceptual framework through which to view your experiences. Theories, ideas taken from experience and observation, can help you interpret the meaning and significance of your sexual experiences. A theoretical orientation can help bring order to the chaos and confusion of your life. Theories can enable you to make sense out of how you and your family feel, think, and behave. They can help you see the patterns in your family's interaction. They can clarify your relationship with your self.

We use three basic theories in interpreting the sexual lives of ACOAs: child development, object relations, and family systems.* While no one theory adequately explains our sexuality, each provides pieces of the puzzle that make up our intimate lives. The questions we asked during our interviews with the women in our study, how we interpreted their answers, and the solutions for change we offer in this book all depend heavily on these three theories. In addition, we use information from the fields of human sexuality and chemical addiction. Here we offer a very brief sketch of each.

The field of human sexuality describes sexual function and dysfunction, assesses sexual satisfaction, examines the development of sexual self-esteem, explores effective sexual decision-making, conducts research on sexual behaviors and attitudes, provides sexual education, reviews conditions of sexual health, and creates guidelines for sexual therapy and treatment.

Chemical addiction focuses on assessing chemical dependency, intervening in the addiction process, and providing treatment ranging from therapy to Twelve-Step programs of recovery.

The fields of child development and object relations explore how and when a sense of "self" develops, examine bonding and how early childhood experiences impact adult functioning, and describe the ways in which early emotional and physical attachments and losses affect the ability to be intimate with others.

Family systems therapy provides techniques for examining factors which govern family myths, family rules, and family roles and for discovering interactional patterns that have been passed down over generations.

## Making Sense of It

As we mentioned earlier, although theories can help us better understand how our childhood experiences affect us as adults, none of these theories alone is adequate. When we step back and view our families as systems, it helps us see how such a system and its rules, roles, and myths

---

* See Appendix Two for an important, in-depth review of each theory.

have affected us. While we are each part of a system called family, we are also separate and unique. While we join with others, we are still separate. For the healing of a sexual relationship to occur, we must seek change from within ourselves and from within our family system. It is from this self-family orientation that we present solutions for change for you as readers.

### Working from a Case History: Kathleen S.

The following case history of Kathleen, a forty-two-year-old ACOA, illustrates how the sexual life history of an ACOA is affected by her alcoholic family system.

*My biological mother left me when I was eighteen months old. I only saw her four times until I was thirteen. After that, I didn't see her again until I was twenty-one.*

*I lived with my paternal grandparents from eighteen months until I was four. My grandfather was an alcoholic. Then from four until I was thirteen, I lived with my alcoholic dad and my stepmother. Like my grandfather and my father, my stepmother was an alcoholic.*

*When I was thirteen, my father died from the liver damage caused by his alcoholism. My stepmother then entered a mental hospital. They said it was for her nerves. I thought things were getting better. She didn't drink for six months after leaving the hospital. Then she started drinking again and continues to drink alcoholically even today.*

*My first intercourse experience was at age fifteen when I was raped by my boyfriend's friend. When I told my boyfriend about it, he blamed me. He said I'd been seductive and that I'd been in the wrong place at the wrong time. He refused to believe that it wasn't my fault. He said his friend would never do that kind of thing.*

*At sixteen, I became pregnant. The same year, my grandmother died. I felt close to my grandmother and I really missed her. You know, from the time I left my grandparents at age four, I've felt alone. No one was ever there for me.*

*Unmarried and pregnant, I had the baby when I was seventeen. That same year, I married the baby's father. He was an alcoholic and a drug addict. He spent most of our first year of marriage in jail on drug charges, leaving me alone with our son.*

*While my husband was in jail, I had an affair with another man and became pregnant. Of course, my husband knew he couldn't have been the father. I carried the pregnancy full term and then decided to give the baby up for adoption at birth. The child was a son. I've never seen him and I have no idea where he is today.*

*When my husband got out of jail, he continued doing drugs. Periodically, he'd physically abuse me. One night after he'd beaten me again, he left the apartment and I packed his bags and put them out on the steps. He came back and broke through the door. He was like a crazy person. He was really different when he used drugs. My son, who was then four, came out of his room to see what all the yelling was about. I did what I had to do to take care of the situation. I had oral sex with my husband. I was afraid and I didn't want my son to see the violence. I did it to protect myself from being hit again. I felt very degraded. We divorced the following year.*

*I remarried at twenty-five and had another son. We've been married for seventeen years. My husband isn't an alcoholic or a drug addict, but he's a compulsive worker. He travels extensively on his job. During my first marriage, I had three affairs. During this marriage, I've had five affairs, all within the past seven years. One of those affairs lasted for two years, another for one year, one for six months, one for three months, and one was a one-night stand.*

*My current lover is addicted to cocaine. He looks and behaves a lot like my father. He's a rock singer and very exciting to be around. I know I'm playing with fire, but I want to be with him every minute. Even though I don't use drugs, I know I could be arrested for being around his drugs. I could jeopardize my marriage. I'm careful though, and so far my current husband hasn't discovered any of my affairs.*

*I'm the pursuer, the initiator in all of my affairs. Like in two of my other affairs, my current lover is married. I like to pursue the unattainable. The challenge is exciting to me. At the beginning, it is always so charged. Then my affairs become settled, comfortable, routine, and the sex becomes very predictable. I lose interest and then initiate a new affair.*

*My husband isn't exciting. He's a responsible, traditional man. He's more concerned about the order in the house than the people in our house. He rarely initiates sex. I have to do it all. He gives me no emotional after-play. After intercourse, he rarely says anything. He just gets up and walks into the bathroom. We live in the same house, raise children together, have sex, yet remain emotional strangers.*

What is Kathleen saying about her relationship with herself, with her family of origin and with others? How is her sexual history like that of so many other ACOAs? Kathleen's history encompasses many of the patterns and themes that emerge in the sexual lives of most adult children of alcoholics:

- Multiple caregiver changes.
- Numerous ungrieved losses.
- Sexual abuse.
- The selection of unavailable sexual partners.
- The need to exert sexual control within relationships.

· The inability to recognize and leave unsatisfying relationships.
· The damaged self-esteem and limited sense of self.

These themes are repeated over and over in our lives as ACOAs.

As you examined Kathleen's sexual history, perhaps you found your-self remembering your own sexual experiences and intimate relation-ships with others. This book can help you explore your intimate relationships by encouraging you to examine your history of emotional bonding, attachments and losses, family of origin dynamics, and your sexual past and present behaviors and attitudes.

In the following chapters, we explore relationship issues shared by most ACOAs, highlighting them with the sexual life histories from women in our study. We suspect you will see portions of your own life reflected in their words. Suggested solutions come from my own training and clinical experience with ACOAs, from the research of others, and from three selected therapists who work with ACOA individuals and groups: Stephanie Covington, Ph.D., coauthor of *Leaving the Enchanted Forest, The Path from Relationship Addiction to Intimacy;* Cynthia Cooley, M.A., director of Chemical Dependency Studies, California Family Study Center, North Hollywood, California; and Sue Saperstein, M.A., a therapist in private practice in San Francisco.

We present several types of suggestions for sexual relationship healing ranging from long-term individual therapy to self-help techniques. Different strategies work for different people. None of the solutions are "quick fixes." We all come to the problems in our sexual lives over a period of years. It takes time to heal the wounds suffered as an adult child of an alcoholic. It takes time to discover and learn to celebrate your sexual self. You deserve and are entitled to sexual healing. Your sexual healing is possible.

# CHAPTER 2

# I Love You
# Because I Can't Have You

Several years ago, a group participant expressed to other group members feelings of total exasperation, frustration, and despair. She chronicled her relationship history by saying *I first married an alcoholic. I suspected a drinking problem but was convinced that I could make my husband want to quit—even though I'd never been successful with my father that way. We divorced after he lost job after job because of his drinking.*

*Within one year after the divorce, I intentionally married a guy who didn't drink or use drugs. It took me a couple of years before I discovered that he was having sex any time he could get it with other women. He compulsively lied to me about the affairs, promising that each would be his last. When he seduced my son's elementary school teacher, I finally divorced him.*

*Seven months ago, I got into a new relationship with a man I met at a church dinner. He's a teetotaler and is adamant about the two of us being monogamous. Even with this, something feels so familiar. He spends twelve to fourteen hours a day on his job, reads reports at home long into the night, travels often to conferences out of state, and just seems gone to me. He talks, eats, and sleeps his job. I have no idea what he even feels. Our sex life is practically non-existent. He's very responsible financially, but is so remote. It's like I'm in a relationship with no one. What am I doing wrong?—Martha C.*

Can you identify with the discouragement of this ACOA? Like her, you may feel disappointed or dissatisfied with your current lover or spouse. Your needs may never seem to get met. You may always seem to be giving more than receiving. Maybe your partner physically or emotionally abuses you. If you've been in an unsatisfying relationship that has ended, you've probably formed a new relationship, one that has let you down again. Strangely enough, you seem to attract the same type of partner over and over.

ACOAs continually ask, "Why do I keep getting involved with this kind of partner?" The answer is that those of us who grew up in alcoholic or other dysfunctional families tend to select partners who are *unavailable* to us sexually, physically, and/or emotionally. In other words, we tend to select partners who are simply not there for us, partners who cannot meet our sexual, emotional, spiritual, and affectional needs.

Every ACOA in our study—except one who'd never experienced a sexual relationship—said she'd repeatedly selected unavailable partners. Ironically, we say we want emotional and sexual closeness. However, by selecting partners who are unavailable, we prevent such intimacy. Not only do we select unavailable partners, we tend to be unavailable partners ourselves.

By choosing unavailable partners and being unavailable to our partners, we wrap ourselves in a cocoon of unavailability. We're safe from having to experience sexual or emotional intimacy with ourselves or with others. We're safe from being vulnerable. We believe we're safe from being hurt.

## Sexual Unavailability

You or your partner can be sexually unavailable for one another in a variety of ways. You may dislike or avoid sex. You may have sex infrequently, and you may have lost your desire for sex with your partner.

You may have difficulty becoming sexually aroused or, if you become aroused, you may have difficulty maintaining your arousal. In men, sexual unavailability may manifest as difficulty in achieving or maintaining an erection, premature ejaculation, or diminished sexual desire. Among women, unavailability may appear as a lack of sexual desire, an inability to achieve orgasm, or less commonly, vaginismus, an involuntary tightening of the vaginal muscles on penetration.

*Third-Party Sex.* Bringing a third person—perhaps a friend, an acquaintance, or a stranger—into your couple sexual relationship can render you and your partner sexually unavailable to one another. Three-way sexual arrangements allow partners to be sexually intimate with others while keeping emotional and sexual distance from each other. Lisa M. says she wants to bring a third person into the sexual relationship with her husband. *I tell my husband all the time I want a three-way. It can be with a man or a woman, I don't care. I think I'd like it to be with my best girlfriend. We've been friends since we were in grade school. I wonder what it would be like to have sex with her?*

Lisa may begin to decrease or refuse sex with her husband until he agrees to bring in a third sex partner. Then she may experience sex with this new partner with her husband present. With the third person in the sexual relationship, she may allow herself to feel more sexual with her husband and/or with her new partner. For some ACOAs, sex with a primary partner is only possible with the inclusion of a third person. Relating one-to-one is too frightening. Without the third partner, the couple may chronically avoid sex with one another.

At times, a husband may arrange for a prostitute to enter a sexual relationship with his wife. He may pay the prostitute to have sex with him, with her, or with both of them. They may select a third person each has sex with while they avoid being sexual with one another.

Including a third sexual partner can conceal or decrease a couple's "intimacy conflict." Such sexual arrangements can allow the couple to maintain a safe emotional distance from each other under the *illusion* of being close.

*Gay Partners.* Some of us maintain our emotional and sexual distance by selecting partners who are confused about their sexual orientation or whose sexual orientation differs from our own. If we're heterosexual, we may select homosexual or bisexual men as partners. If we're homosexual, we may select as partners heterosexual men, heterosexual women, or people who are clearly ambivalent about their own orientation. Sexual orientation confusion can easily make us or our partners less available for a fully intimate relationship.

Several women in our study revealed that they'd selected partners they later discovered were homosexual or bisexual. Other women in our study whose true orientation was homosexual said they became sexually involved with men because they were not convinced they were homosexual or because they thought they "should be straight." These women said they felt guilty about having sex with men while fantasizing about women.

While few of us intentionally choose a partner with a sexual orientation different from our own, this type of partner unavailability often creates a crisis resulting in loss of intimacy. Although it's possible to have sex and to orgasm with someone with a sexual orientation different from our own, deep sexual intimacy is most likely to occur when our sexual behavior coincides with our true sexual orientation.

*Sexual Addicts.* Another way some of us avoid being sexually available in our relationships is to engage in sexually addictive behaviors or choose a partner who is sexually addicted. The sexual addict, always obsessing about the next sexual conquest, is unable to be fully present to a partner.

6

n and feelings of remorse caused by the illicit sex creates dis-
the partners in the primary relationship. Joan F. talks
psychological distance affected her relationship. *When I
out about John's compulsive affairs with women, I felt humiliated and
ashamed. I confronted him with evidence about the affair and he admitted it,
apologized, and promised it would never happen again. But I continued to find
new letters and cards. There were strange phone hang-ups and sudden business
trips. Over and over, I'd break my denial, confront him, hear the apology and the
promises. In a matter of months, it would start all over again. Each time it happened, my ability to trust or even to care seemed to decrease. The codependent
behaviors I used to "catch him in the act" only lessened my self-esteem. I was constantly on the watch for the next lie, the next affair. How could either of us feel
close when we were together sexually?*

If you or your partner engage in sexually addictive behavior with people outside your relationship, you may still have sex together. But physically having sex doesn't mean the sexual addict is "sexually present."
Theresa W. provides an example of this with her sexually addicted husband: *David has been having sex outside our marriage since it first began. We
pretend that I don't know. Our sex together is infrequent, impersonal, and
usually over the minute he comes. I think the only reason he's sexual with me is
to keep me from becoming suspicious about his affairs. We may have sex together
but he's never really with me. I've never confronted him because I feel so hurt and
embarrassed.*

*Secretive Sex.* Like many of the women in our study, you may avoid
physical and emotional closeness with your partner by having "secretive
sex." This often takes the form of secret extra-relationship affairs. Lorna T.
says, *I'd been married seven or eight years when I met a single guy at a party and
we had sex. I'd known him casually for two years. It was very exciting. My husband never learned about it. I think of it often and get a kind of rush of pleasure.*

Many ACOAs say their sexual intensity is greatest when sex is secretive. Sex with our husbands or primary partners may be limited and
unfulfilling. We may find that with our secret lovers, sex can be passionate and exciting. Joanne Y. says, *When I was a teenager, for two years I had sex
with Larry behind his girlfriend's back. Our secretive sex was always filled with
passion. Years later, when I was married to someone else, I began fantasizing
about Larry. I found out that he also was married. We had sex several times. It
was much more intense than with my husband. For me, it seems that sex is
always more intense when it's with someone who "belongs to someone else."*

What factors from the alcoholic family system contribute to the belief
for many of us that secretive sex is more stimulating? Secretive sex is
arousing and seductive to many of us because we learned to keep secrets

as children in our alcoholic families. We learned to keep secrets about our family's drinking, the fights, the abortions, the suicides, the institution-alizations, the premarital pregnancies, the sexual abuse, the physical bat-tering, the divorces and separations, the multiple job losses, the financial difficulties, and the bankruptcies. The "no talk" rule dictates that we must never tell things to certain family members or to those outside the family. In our alcoholic families, we protect our history with secrets. Fam-ily members learn to lie, to excuse, to minimize, and cover-up what they consider to be shameful secrets from others.

If your alcoholic family was like most, an abundance of energy was generated around secret-keeping. The chaos, confusion, and collusion that surround family secrets create a chronic state of crisis and tension within the family. You and other family members who generated or held and protected the secrets may have felt special and included.

This same feeling attracts us to secretive sex. Our secretive affairs often make us feel special and included. The chaos of keeping the secret feels simultaneously exciting, familiar, and comfortable.

If you're an ACOA incest survivor, you're particularly susceptible to keeping sexual secrets. As children, you kept silent about the sexual inva-sions of family members. Misplaced loyalty and fear combine to keep generations of compulsive sexual behaviors silenced. As an adult in inti-mate relationships, you are likely to feel a particular emotional attraction, a pull to participate in secretive sexual encounters. For some of us, our entire sexual lives have involved secretive sexual encounters.

The problem is that secretive sex keeps us from being fully intimate with our partners because we often spend our time fantasizing about our secret lovers, even during sex with our partner. Keeping the secret takes our time and energy and it drives a wedge between us and our partners, preventing us from being really close and vulnerable with them.

## Physical Unavailability

We can also avoid being intimate with ourselves and our partner by choosing someone who is physically unavailable such as one who com-pulsively overworks, lives in another town or state, is ill, or compulsive with food.

*Compulsive Workers.* Workaholics are physically unavailable to de-velop couple intimacy because so much of their time and energy is tied up with business-related travel, night and weekend appointments, and projects completed during home hours, which can all contribute to sexual avoidance. Tony Schwartz, author of *Acceleration Syndrome: Does Everyone*

*Live in the Fast Lane Nowadays?*, describes lives that are in a state of constant overdrive. The day-to-day lives of compulsive workers have been aided by the development of cellular car phones, fax machines, portable stock-quote machines, and laptop computers. Compulsive workers share an urgent need to engage in several activities at the same time and a belief that "rest" is laziness. While reporting feelings of excitement and stimulation, compulsive workers in recovery admit to working as many as thirty-four days consecutively, to years of work without a vacation, and to compulsively sacrificing the unstructured time it takes to nurture relationships. The compulsive worker, ever distracted by lists and deadlines, has little time for affection, sensual exploration, or sexual experimentation with his or her partner.

*Long-Distance Lovers.* Many of us fear losing personal autonomy if we become involved in a committed relationship. By selecting a partner who lives far away or someone who works a different shift from our own, we provide ourselves with an *illusion of safety*. If someone from a more functional family learns she or he is attracted to someone who lives out of town or out of state, it's likely she or he would be cautious and even discouraged about expanding the relationship further. An ACOA, however, might become more interested in pursuing it.

*Ill Partners.* Sometimes we're drawn to partners who are physically unavailable because of chronic illness or hypochondriacal fears, aches, pains, and symptoms. One ACOA we interviewed who worked as a nurse became intimately involved with a man suffering from terminal cancer. Following his death, she developed a relationship with a man recuperating from a severe heart condition. In both relationships, she spent so much time and energy driving the men to and from the hospital and caring for them at home, that there was little opportunity for any sexual intimacy. Concern over medical costs, prolonged hospitalizations, extensive bedside caretaking, and the sexual side effects of medications can all contribute to our partners' unavailability.

*Eating Disorders.* To avoid intimacy, you may develop an eating disorder or select a partner who is unavailable due to anorexia, binge-vomiting, or compulsive overeating. In her book, *Fat Is a Family Affair*, Judi Hollis says that people with eating disorders use food to become who others need them to be. They lose a sense of their inner true self. They often suffer conflicts about distance, anger, control, achievement, pleasing others, unmet nurturance needs, and intimacy and autonomy. Because they choose the secret comfort of food over the unpredictable comfort of others, people with eating disorders are unavailable for truly intimate relationships. They live in denial, are dishonest with themselves and with others, and seek to be nurtured through food without having to become emotionally vulnerable to another person. They are often governed by a false sense of control, feel protected from the need for love, and find a safer, more intimate, relationship with food than with a lover. Like chemical addiction, eating disorders are diseases of isolation. They sedate feelings, mask needs, and conceal the true self. If you or your partner suffer from an active eating disorder, you are most likely unable to relate honestly and intimately to a lover.

### Emotional Unavailability

Perhaps more subtle than sexual or physical unavailability, selecting partners who are emotionally unavailable is a common way many of us avoid intimacy. If you are with someone who is simply not "emotionally there" for you, there's little risk of becoming vulnerable, exposing yourself, being rejected, trusting and being abandoned, or becoming too attached and "losing yourself" in the relationship.

Although emotionally unavailable partners may not satisfy our needs, for many of us, emotionally aloof relationships feel "safer" than trusting and getting close. Such is the case with ACOA Rachael T., who says, *There are days that my lover is just gone, disappeared, completely unresponsive. Her face is like a statue. I ask her what's going on and she says she doesn't know. I ask her what she feels about what I've just shared with her and she shrugs her shoulders. She seems so deep inside herself, yet so unable or unwilling to let me into her world. I feel shut out by some invisible barrier. We have sex regularly but I don't honestly know who I'm with.* Although Rachael's partner is sexually and physically available to her, she's emotionally unavailable.

Nancy R. has a similar emotionally unavailable partner and she copes by withholding her sexual responsiveness from him. *Orgasm is always on my husband's mind*, she says. *I block my sexual feelings because I know he'll come quickly and then disappear. My husband is a five-minute man in every way. Our sex is so mechanical. He never savors the moment. I miss the feeling of being cherished by someone. I don't think my husband knows how to be tender, how to nurture me.*

*Emotional Battering.* For many of us, our partners are not only emotionally unavailable, but they actively emotionally abuse and batter us. Emotional battering includes telling lies, criticizing, blaming, making put-downs, breaking promises, fault-finding, name-calling, giving double messages, making unreasonable demands, throwing temper tantrums, creating periods of stony silence, or invading another's privacy. Lynn K. describes the emotional abuse in her long-term lesbian relationship by saying, *I was with someone who was as emotionally unpredictable as my mother. I'd do anything to make things okay. My lover was a successful real estate agent and when we'd have a fight, she'd put a "For Sale" sign in front of the house. If I said anything wrong or failed to anticipate her needs, she'd fly out the door and list the property. I'd always try to make it okay again and eventually the sign would come down. I'd apologize and do whatever she wanted me to do.*

### Addicted Partners

If you and/or your partner are addicted to drugs and/or alcohol, you are unavailable for true intimacy in your relationship. Addictive drugs make partners emotionally, sexually, and often physically unavailable. Researchers in chemical addiction have found that alcohol severely depresses sexual desire and responsiveness. In men, alcohol decreases testosterone (a male hormone) and increases the level of estrogen (a female hormone). To achieve and maintain an erection, male genitals must be supplied with adequate levels of testosterone. As the disease of alcoholism progresses in men, they often experience shrinking of the testicles (testicular atrophy), chronic low sperm count, loss of body hair, and decreased sexual desire. In women alcoholics, vaginal lubrication decreases and the greater their intoxication, the longer it takes them to achieve orgasm.

ACOA Tanya K. told us about her addicted partner: *John used Percadan, Elavil, Valium, and codeine throughout our marriage. He was abusive and violently jealous.* Why would Tanya or anyone stay with an addict like John? The answer for many of us, and perhaps for you, is that choosing an addicted partner means being able to avoid the intimacy we fear and it allows us to maintain emotional and physical distance.

### The Pattern Repeats

If you've decided to end an unfulfilling relationship, chances are that you'll select another partner who is equally unavailable, but unavailable in a different way. For example, Teresa B., married a practicing alcoholic who physically abused her for several years. After divorcing him, she married a compulsive eater who suffered frequent bouts of deep depression and isolation.

Joan G., a lesbian ACOA, was involved with an alcoholic who drank daily, had been fired from her past three jobs for alcohol-related incidents, and who had several tickets for driving under the influence and disturbing the peace. After ten years, their relationship ended abruptly.

Her next lover was a binge-alcoholic—she'd go for months without drinking and then with no warning, she'd get drunk at home during a weekend, become abusive, and then be unable to recall what occurred the next day. It took Joan three years to recognize that she was once again involved with an alcoholic, only this time with one whose addiction looked very different.

None of us, including the women we studied, *intentionally* chooses partners who abuse, reject, abandon, and humiliate us. We are, however, seriously influenced by growing up with unhealthy relationship role models. We watched our parents and stepparents engage in destructive, unsatisfying relationships. We vowed as adults to develop more loving, meaningful, and sexually satisfying relationships. Much to our dismay, we repeatedly select unavailable partners and relate to them in ways that replicate our painful childhood family dynamics. *We end up creating the same unsatisfying relationships that we feared and rejected as children.*

Our process of selecting sexual partners is far from random, accidental, or coincidental. Therapist Cynthia Cooley sums it up this way, "It's too scary for ACOAs to be with someone who is available. If someone is totally emotionally available, most ACOAs can't handle it. They like to dream about the ideal of emotional and physical closeness. This is especially true for ACOAs who were extremely isolated as children. When they grow up, they live a romanticized fantasy of how they'd like their lives to be. They yearn for the unavailable."

Understanding the alcoholic family system can help us begin to recognize and break these unhappy relationship patterns. In her book, *Another Chance*, author Sharon Wegscheider says the alcoholic family is a closed system with rigid rules and roles which govern the behavior and feelings of family members. These unrealistic rules discourage honesty with self and with others and dictate what can be discussed and what is secret. They encourage secret alliances between certain members and inhibit family members from assertively expressing their feelings.

As children who grew up in the alcoholic family system, we develop an attraction to the "alcoholic lifestyle." We select partners who adhere to the alcoholic family rules and roles we know and feel comfortable with.

Therapist Claudia Black, author of *It Will Never Happen to Me*, suggests that, as children, we adopt rigid rules within our families to gain a sense of much-needed control. The alcoholic family's prescribed roles and behaviors teach us, as children and later as adults, how to be. We take on the traits that support our rigid, prescribed family roles.

From observing and participating in family interactions, the child in the alcoholic family system learns:

- To control.
- To lie.
- To act helpless.
- To deny.
- To isolate.
- To abuse self.
- To remain emotionally remote.
- To blur boundaries between self and others.
- To physically and emotionally abuse intimate partners.
- To become paralyzed when disappointed in the behavior of a loved one.
- To assume all or no responsibility for problems within the relationship.

- To smother.
- To distrust.
- To doubt.
- To rescue.
- To distance.
- To blame self and/or others.
- To fear commitment.
- To disapprove of self and others.
- To expect inconsistency from others.
- To establish unequal relationships.

Most of all, we learned to *simultaneously long for and avoid closeness with others*. These learned behaviors and defenses guide and influence us when we choose intimate partners. The same traits that helped us survive the alcoholic family as children now interfere with our ability to have intimate relationships. They prevent us from achieving the real emotional and sexual closeness we desire.

We've learned our lessons well from our alcoholic families. So well, in fact, that most of us don't know what healthy skills and traits we need to develop in order to choose available partners and have satisfying relationships. Dolores Curran in *Traits of a Healthy Family*, says functional families promote and encourage the development of:

- Autonomy.
- Effective risk-taking.
- Compromise.
- Consistency.
- Active listening.
- The ability to problem-solve with others.
- The development of trust.
- Mutual sharing of vulnerabilities.
- Flexibility within family rules.
- Commitment to self, to others, and to the relationship.
- The ability to define, maintain, and protect appropriate emotional, physical, and sexual boundaries.
- The ability to give and receive affection.

· Sharing honest feelings and opinions.
· The use of a pattern or ritual of reconciliation after conflict.
· Shared relationship power.
· Responsiveness rather than reactiveness.
· The expectation that one will be heard.
· Acceptance and respect of individual differences.

There's no question that developing these kinds of skills and qualities takes time, practice, and patience for those of us who didn't learn them as children. The promising news is that we *can* change. With support, we can begin to develop new skills, begin to change basic characteristics, and unlearn old family patterns. Attending Twelve-Step meetings and developing relationships with other recovering ACOAs can provide us with the tools and encouragement to help us begin this healing process.

## Families of Shame

To heal our ACOA wounds, we also need to understand how shame about our alcoholic families interferes with our being able to reach out to others for the help we need. Shame is something shared by all of us from alcoholic backgrounds. It plays an integral part in our repeatedly selecting unavailable and addicted or compulsive partners. According to researchers Merle Fossum and Marilyn Mason, authors of *Facing Shame,* people from "shame-based" families are more likely to select partners who abuse themselves with drugs or alcohol, who overexercise, or compulsively over- or undereat. They may select partners who abuse themselves or others through compulsive sexuality, exhibitionism, voyeurism, rape, incest, pornography, or obscene phone calls. The partner's compulsion may center on money itself, shopping compulsively, shoplifting, hoarding or overspending money. Or the compulsion may be found in physical or emotional abuse of children, partner, or self. According to Fossum and Mason, *shame-based ACOAs unknowingly and repeatedly seek compulsive partners from other shame-based families.*

Recognizing the patterns of selecting unavailable partners can help us begin to break the pattern. Take a moment and think about your past relationships. How many of your partners were from alcoholic or other shame-based dysfunctional families? Do you see any patterns in the type of partners you select?

The rules of the shame-based family help guide us to select partners with similar dysfunctional patterns of family interaction. Fossum and

Mason find that we internalize and later act out eight shame-based family commandments:

1. Be in control of all behavior and interaction.
2. Be perfect. Always be right and do right.
3. If something doesn't happen as planned, someone is to blame—either another, yourself, or both.
4. Don't expect reliability or constancy in relationships.
5. Never bring transactions to completion or resolution.
6. Never talk openly and directly about shameful, abusive, or compulsive behaviors.
7. When shameful, abusive, compulsive, or disrespectful behaviors occur, deny, disqualify, or disguise them.

When we follow such shame-based family rules, we're *unconsciously* drawn to people who subscribe to the same behavioral guidelines. These rules and the unhealthy, compulsive behaviors they encourage, foster the selection of unavailable partners.

### Unresolved Family Issues

Another clue about why and how we select unavailable partners can be found in genograms, which record the interactional dynamics, the roles, and the relationship patterns of families over several generations. In her book, *Genograms in Family Assessment*, Monica McGoldrick shows readers how to record pertinent facts about their families for three previous generations. She instructs people to trace family members' ages, names, occupations, births, deaths, marriages, divorces, sibling positions, geographical locations, educational levels, religious affiliations, and drug and alcohol histories. Genograms can show who is and has been emotionally close and who has been distant in the family, repeated family triangles, cut-offs, patterns of conflict, and financial, emotional, and sexual over- and underfunctioning of family members. By examining outlines of your own family's history, you can begin to see how unmet needs and unresolved issues in the pasts of family members may influence your current selection of partners.

It may surprise you to discover that problems you may have in your current relationship are frequently repetitions of emotional themes that existed earlier in your own or your partner's childhood family. More often than not, we choose to remain in relationships that feel *familiar* to us and with partners with whom we can either work through or react to problems from our past.

California Therapist Stephanie Covington, Ph.D., says she uses a genogram-like process to help ACOAs learn from their pasts. "I have clients do relationship charts in which they examine their relationships with their mother, father, stepparents, siblings, friends, and lovers, and then evaluate the qualities of those relationships," she says. "What are the costs and benefits of various relationships? What role did they play? How has chemical usage affected them? They start to see patterns emerge. Once you begin to see a pattern and have some awareness, you can choose to change those patterns. You can see the people who are trigger people for you and read the clues you receive but have tended to ignore."

**Dance of Distance.** Such a working out of past problems can be seen in the "distance dance" that more than three-quarters of our research participants said they experienced with their partners. Perhaps you'll recognize this dynamic from your past or current relationships. Described as the "rejection-intrusion relationship dynamic" by Family Systems Therapist Augustus Napier in 1978, it involves one partner (the "rejector") feeling suffocated, stifled, and imprisoned by the relationship while the other partner (the "intruder") feels rejected, abandoned, and seeks more emotional closeness.

Both partners in such a situation are suffering psychological pain. The stifled partner wants free of the confines of the relationship. The abandoned partner wants reassurance that the relationship will continue. As one retreats, the other chases and clutches more tightly. Each partner blames the other for the problem. "If she'd only give me space." "If he'd only be closer." Both believe that if the other would change, the relationship would improve.

Neither partner realizes each is reenacting old childhood conflicts. Intrusive partners seek "oneness" with their partner—based upon the childhood desire for closeness with the parents. They want a relationship in which there are no boundaries between them. Their own identity is based totally on being *in relationship with* their partner, rather than on a separate identity of self.

While intruders want to blur appropriate and healthy relationship boundaries, rejectors strive to limit intimacy by clearly marking off relationship boundaries. Rejectors often divide space, time, materials, activities, hobbies, and even friends into "mine" and "yours." They fear a loss of their identity if they become too close in a relationship. Some rejectors maintain their distance by participating in secretive sexual affairs.

To the outsider, it often appears that the intruders are desperately trying to achieve emotional intimacy and the rejectors are running terrified from emotional contact. The truth is that *both want closeness and both fear intimacy.* They select partners who keep them emotionally safe — partners who provide the distance they are familiar with from their early childhood.

While the intruders complain about their partners' inability to express feelings, they actually fear psychological intimacy. They select partners who permit them to deny responsibility for the lack of closeness in the relationship. The partners who seek more distance in the relationship fear rejection and abandonment and have a secret need for closeness. By selecting intruders for partners, they satisfy their need for closeness while avoiding awareness of their fear of rejection.

This mutual distancing by ACOA couples can be seen clearly when roles suddenly reverse. Now the once-rejector initiates closeness while the once-intruder flees the advances of the rejector. This role reversal creates the same psychological distance between them. The basic level of intimacy remains unchanged. They each protect themselves from the pain they believe true intimacy would bring. Some ACOAs protect themselves by exhibiting engulfing or abandoning behaviors, while others engage in both types of behavior.

Let's examine a distance-dancing ACOA couple. Anna K. always complains that her boyfriend, Bill W., never shares his feelings with her. Although Anna is eager to have Bill share her new house and likes them to buy things together, Bill prefers to maintain his own apartment and isn't fond of sharing material things or friends. When Bill's younger brother suddenly dies of a heart attack, Bill undergoes a change of attitude about his relationship with Anna. Suddenly, he wants to be more emotionally close. He wants to spend every evening with Anna and pressures her to set a date when he can move into her house. In a quick reversal which maintains their emotional distance, Anna decides she's really not ready to share her house. In fact, she tells him, the relationship is starting to stifle her and perhaps they should date other people for a while.

In most cases, this distance-dancing dynamic has its origins in past family relationships. The unhealthy characteristics which produce the distancing usually have existed in most of our families for at least two or three generations. Each subsequent generation simply passes on the dysfunctional interactional traits, and we continue to select partners who are physically, sexually, or emotionally unavailable to us.

### Choosing Available Partners

One of the first steps in breaking our pattern of selecting unavailable partners is to begin to recognize in what ways we and our partners are unavailable. Think about the various ways we've discussed being sexually, physically, and emotionally unavailable. In what ways is your partner unavailable to you? How are you unavailable to your partner?

Consider developing a genogram to examine your past. Encourage your partner to do the same. What conflicts or relationship dynamics from your past are influencing your relationship? What similar family patterns do you and your partner share? Which shame-based family rules dominate each of your family's interactions?

The most critical key to selecting intimate partners who are more available to us and more able to meet our needs, according to Stephanie Covington, Ph.D., is to develop a stronger sense of "I," what therapists call a sense of self. "Often in an unhealthy relationship, the person becomes exclusively focused on the 'we' and loses the sense of 'I,'" she says. "We need to be intimate with ourselves in order to be intimate with others." Intimacy with self, she says, involves getting to know who you are, your thoughts, your feelings, your beliefs, what makes you tick. It also means coming to understand family dynamics and how they impacted you as a child, seeing how you carry the roles of your childhood into your adult life, and beginning to realize you can make some changes.

Becoming intimate with ourselves takes time. The process, however, contributes to our ability to be intimately available to others and to select partners who can more often be emotionally, physically, and sexually available to us.

# CHAPTER 3

# I'm Unhappy, But I Can't Leave

*When I was eighteen, I became pregnant by a twenty-five-year-old man I wasn't in love with. He didn't want to marry me, but his mother forced him. After we married, I had two more children, but our sex life was terrible. While getting ready for bed, he'd go into the bathroom for up to two hours. I could never imagine what he did in there all that time. When he came out, I'd be asleep. He'd run his penis along my back. That was the signal that he expected to have sex with me. He'd turn me over and just put it in.*

*After years of this, when he'd want sex I'd pretend to be a log because logs can't feel—or kill. I'd lay there with him in me and say to myself, "I'm a log." I'd actually envision that. Finally he got the hint and began initiating sex only every six months or so. We never talked about the infrequency of our sex.*

*I tried self-help books to improve our sex life. I learned about my clitoris and one night I seduced him. In the morning, he told me I was a whore. Another time I wore a sexy negligee, but he criticized me for it. I went into the bathroom and ripped it to pieces with scissors. After that, I just gave up. It finally dawned on me that I wasn't the only problem. From then on, we just stopped having sex. I stayed with him for eleven more years and finally divorced him.—Dana P.*

In our research with ACOAs, we found the second most common theme to emerge is the inability to leave unhealthy, unhappy relationships. Often, we know we're unhappy and dissatisfied, yet we can't seem to leave. Many of us stay in these relationships for years after recognizing our needs aren't being met. Even when our friends, acquaintances, and family see the abuse and disrespect we endure and advise us to leave, many of us are never able to escape our unhealthy relationships.

## Alcoholic Relationships

One of the most common problems we face as ACOAs is becoming intimately involved with and/or marrying alcoholics. You might think that growing up in a chaotic, alcoholic family would ensure we'd avoid alcohol and anyone who abuses alcohol. However, the opposite is true. Many of the women we interviewed said they were or had been involved in alcoholic relationships. We seem drawn to the same kinds of people and relationship dynamics we grew up with as children in alcoholic families.

In some ACOA-alcoholic relationships, the partner is alcoholic and the ACOA is sober as is the case in Trudy W.'s marriage. *My husband, a practicing alcoholic, is in total denial,* she says. *I'm angry that just like my first marriage, I'm involved again with an alcoholic. He hasn't initiated sex for the past two years. I feel unloved by him.*

Your ACOA-alcoholic relationship may take other forms: you may be alcoholic with a sober partner; both you and your partner may be practicing alcoholics; or you and your alcoholic partner may be in the process of recovery separately or together. Regardless of who drinks alcoholically in your relationship, if you're like the ACOAs we interviewed, you find it difficult, if not impossible, to terminate these familiar, alcohol-related relationships. The question is why is it so difficult for us to leave unhealthy—and often unhappy—alcoholic relationships? Understanding the stages and dynamics of the alcoholic relationship may help us find an answer.

## Stages of Alcoholic Relationships

In their book, *The Responsibility Trap,* authors Claudia Bepko and Jo Ann Kreston describe three distinct stages alcoholic relationships can go through: *presobriety, adjustment to sobriety,* and *maintaining sobriety.*

*Presobriety.* During presobriety, one or both partners drink abusively and compulsively. ACOA Cara R. says of her presobriety relationship: *I was with a recovering alcoholic who'd "slipped" back into booze. While I cut down on my drinking, I kept up with my pills. When we were both using, it seemed we could relax more with each other. There were fewer fights when we both got loaded. There was no communication in our relationship, no discussion, no problems that ever got worked through. We were together for eleven years, separating several times, but always coming back. She finally found someone else. I felt relieved. I remember thinking, "Now that she's found someone, I can move on."*

If both you and your partner are practicing alcoholics, chances are you stay in the relationship because each one's drinking feeds each other's denial of the addiction. Each cooperates with the other to prevent recognition or treatment of the disease. Often one alcoholic partner excuses, covers, and minimizes the irresponsible behaviors of the other. Getting drunk together becomes the relationship's bonding—the only way they can be close. They get drunk together and later recuperate together. Both collude to prevent each other's recovery.

In alcoholic drinking, the alcoholic maintains a compelling and intimate "relationship" with alcohol. Some alcoholics have no motivation to divorce or end an unhappy relationship because their partner emotionally or physically encourages the addictive drinking, allowing them to continue to be "intimate" with alcohol, their true primary relationship.

While codependence can occur when both partners are alcoholic, it can also occur in relationships in which only one partner drinks alcoholically. If you're involved with an alcoholic and you don't drink addictively, it's likely that you are codependent and that your "helping" behavior enables the addiction to continue.

Codependent behavior supports and minimizes the negative consequences of the partner's alcoholism. Feeling responsible for her alcoholic partner's feelings and behaviors, the codependent "overfunctions" for the "underfunctioning" alcoholic. She protects the alcoholic's feelings. She may make many of the family's decisions, pay the bills, and maintain the only income-producing job in the family.

Even when the relationship is unsatisfying for the alcoholic, she or he often stays for the comfort and protection offered by the codependent partner. Because the codependent takes care of and protects the alcoholic and the alcoholic behavior carries fewer negative consequences for the alcoholic, it becomes difficult for the alcoholic to recognize her or his addiction. The codependent often feels "needed" and important in this protector role and is reluctant to objectively confront how damaging the codependent behavior is to herself and to her partner.

If you're like many codependents, you stay in your unhappy relationship because you feel "sorry for" or "responsible for" your alcoholic partner. ACOA Carol F. says her sexual and emotional feelings for her husband are now dead, yet she stays with him. *He's emotionally dependent on me*, she says, *When I say I'm going to leave, he threatens suicide. I feel nothing for him, but how can I leave him like this? It would be my fault if he hurt himself over my leaving.*

If you're codependent like Carol, you probably focus all of your attention on your alcoholic partner's problems. This allows you to avoid taking responsibility for and dealing with *your* goals and feelings. In a symbiotic way, both you and your alcoholic partner benefit from remaining in the unhealthy relationship.

*Adjustment to Sobriety.* The second phase of the alcoholic relationship, adjustment to sobriety, occurs when one or both partners become sober and begin to participate in a recovery program such as Alcoholics Anonymous. While you might expect the beginning of sobriety to end your relationship problems, adjusting to sobriety can throw your relationship into crisis.

During this phase, the recovering alcoholic begins to feel hopeful that life may become better, that losses in family, career, and relationships may be regained. The untreated codependent may feel lost, unimportant. The codependent partner may feel rage, resentment, and bitterness over painful memories and events from the alcoholic past. At this point, the codependent may be at risk for developing some addictive disorder of her or his own such as an eating disorder, or addictive use of drugs or alcohol.

The newly recovering alcoholic partner is caught off guard by the codependent's reaction to her or his new sobriety. As the codependent becomes more and more dissatisfied with the relationship, she or he may attempt to sabotage the partner's sobriety and the newly recovering partner may relapse.

This shift in health by one partner causes tension and stress in the relationship because it has disrupted the former balance, or "homeostasis," of the relationship. Even if the alcoholic relationship wasn't healthy, it was balanced with each partner filling her or his prescribed role. The new sobriety renders the relationship unstable and unpredictable and the codependent may try to undermine the healthy changes taking place in the formerly addicted partner.

Even under this new crisis, the relationship often continues. While unhappy with the partner's new sobriety, like many codependents, she or he may stay in the relationship out of "duty" or "guilt." Harriet K. says her recovering alcoholic husband was *very angry and immature like a little boy. I was never sexually attracted to him and I'd wanted to leave him for several years. But I couldn't inflict pain on him. I knew he couldn't stay sober without me.*

Harriet, like many other codependent ACOAs, fears that a separation might cause her alcoholic partner to relapse into drinking. Just as she assumed responsibility for home, family, and finances when her partner was actively drinking, she now assumes responsibility for his sobriety.

*Maintaining Sobriety.* This third phase of the alcoholic relationship finds many alcoholic partners realizing they want their relationships to end. With alcohol gone from the relationship, some recovering alcoholics discover how little they have in common with their partners. They feel little sexual interest or love. However, like the codependent, recovering alcoholics often superstitiously believe that leaving the relationship would mean losing hard-won sobriety. They believe that they can only remain sober *within the relationship where they first got sober.* A separation or divorce might "jinx" their recovery. As a result, the unhappy relationship continues.

If you're involved in an alcoholic relationship, both you and your partner need help to recover. The addicted partner needs an individual program of recovery such as Alcoholics Anonymous. The codependent partner can find help through programs such as Alanon or Adult Children of Alcoholics. When each of you begins to focus on self, rather than on controlling the feelings and behavior of the other, your relationship has a chance to recover.

## Physical Abuse

All too commonly, physical abuse involving beatings or threats of violence is a regular part of many unhappy ACOA relationships. Our study participants reported having been kicked, bitten, hit with fists or objects, or threatened or abused with weapons. In some cases, the women said their partners or they themselves physically abused their children. For some women, violence is a daily occurrence. For others, it is sporadic and unpredictable.

Physically abused ACOAs often share two common denominators: *the desire to leave the abusive relationship* and a *tremendous fear and anxiety about leaving.* Janette H. explained her fear about leaving her abusive marriage to a man twenty years her senior. *He was a heavy drinker when we met. I got pregnant immediately and married him. But he beat me. When I finally decided to divorce him, he wouldn't let me out of the house. The day I left, he tore up my driver's license. Two cops had to hold him down while I drove away.*

In violent alcoholic relationships, violence often occurs during all phases of the relationship—during presobriety, during adjustment to sobriety, and during the maintenance of sobriety. Many ACOAs are disappointed to find that even when alcohol is no longer a part of their relationship, the physical abuse continues and, in some cases, even escalates.

More than two-thirds of the physically abused women in our study said they'd seen their parents physically abuse one another. Those of us who've witnessed violence as children often recreate the same violence in our own adult relationships, as victims or as abusers. ACOA Donna C., who married a man who beat her, says she remembers her alcoholic father regularly hitting her mother.

Several ACOAs told us their parents never separated or divorced—"no matter how bad the beatings were." At times, they said this with a real sense of pride. To them, leaving their own abusive partner seemed like a betrayal of their parents who were unable to escape their own relationship's violence.

If you're in an abusive relationship, you may have a variety of other reasons for staying: fear, isolation, economic problems, alternating hopefulness and hopelessness that the situation will improve, and a sense of powerlessness to act in your own behalf. On a deeper level, you may feel you "deserve" the abuse you receive. You may even hold yourself responsible for the abuse—somehow it is *your* fault. Often such beliefs stem from the emotional and physical abuse we received in our childhood alcoholic homes. Like many ACOAs, you may have learned early that people who love you hurt you. You might come to expect abuse in your intimate relationships. Abuse simply "comes with the territory."

Nyla G. says her reason for staying in her abusive relationship is fear of more violence. *My husband is very jealous. He's moody, angry, paranoid, unpredictable. He uses pot daily. He's abused me before. He moves into panic and rage in a second. I stay because I don't trust what he'll do if I leave.*

Louise G. says insecurity keeps her in an abusive lesbian relationship. *There is physical violence—pushing, slapping, pulling each other's hair. She doesn't let me have my own space. But I stay because I feel insecure. I mean, who else would want me?*

Sometimes physical abuse takes the form of sexual abuse. You may be forced or coerced into participating in sex that makes you feel degraded or ashamed. *I participated out of insecurity, not because I liked it*, ACOA Bonnie E. recalls. *He demanded I wear corsets, boots, leather, high heels, nipple rings. He made me watch porn movies with him and then I'd have to hit him and put him into restraints. He told me exactly what to say while I was doing this. It made me sick doing those things to him.*

Like many other sexually abused ACOAs, you may judge yourself harshly for participating in sex which violates your values. These feelings of inadequacy or "badness" contribute to your isolation and decrease the likelihood that you'll get the outside support you need to end your unhappy relationship. Staying in the abusive relationship contributes to an endless downward spiral of self-esteem that further keeps you unhappy and in the relationship. You can't leave because you feel bad about yourself; you feel bad about yourself because you can't leave.

## Emotional Abuse

The abuse you suffer in your relationship may also be emotional — lies, broken promises, acts of humiliation. In emotionally abusive relationships, partners rarely openly or directly express their true emotions. Among the women we interviewed, most *denied* or *minimized* the extent of emotional abuse in their relationships. While some believed that extreme physical or sexual abuse *might* be reason enough to end a relationship, most said that emotional abuse wasn't reason enough to leave their relationship, regardless of how unhappy it made them. Toni D. recalled her emotionally abusive marriage to an older man: *He was a friend, a father figure. I never felt sexual towards him. But our relationship threatened me — I felt absorbed, criticized to my core, taken over. He sapped all my emotional strength. I doubted my own perceptions. I didn't have the energy to leave — he'd never let me go.*

The emotional abuse in your relationship may take the form of neglect, extreme loneliness, and little sex or affection. ACOA Gail K. says, *Tom is a truck driver and I knew that when I got involved with him. Sometimes I see him only a couple of days every month. When he finally comes home, he's often too tired to be affectionate or make love. I try to get him to take local routes or less work, but he says we need the money. What good is money when I feel like I'm dying inside?*

Like many of the ACOAs we interviewed, you may choose to remain in your emotionally abusive relationship for personal security — the possessions and finances you've acquired with your partner may make you feel stable and secure, perhaps for the first time in your life. Divorce or separation, while it would mean an end to your unhappy relationship, might also significantly decrease your income, your status, and your possessions. If you come from an impoverished family, you may fear returning to poverty. Ending your relationship, you may believe, would sever your tenuous hold on material security. Many of us are unwilling to risk losing this *illusion of security.*

If you're like many ACOAs who are unable to leave physically, sexually, or emotionally abusive relationships, you may have extra-relationship affairs as a way to cope with your unhappy primary relationship. *I've been having an affair for five years with an attorney,* says Faith E. *Our sex is exciting. My husband doesn't suspect I have affairs. He thinks I just take his physical attacks on me as if they have no effect. When I'm with the attorney, I feel as if someone in this world cares about me. If he died or left me, I don't think I could continue one day longer with my husband.*

Extra-relationship affairs can function to "take the heat off" your own intimacy issues. By focusing on a third party, you may be able to temporarily avoid your own feelings and problems. A secretive affair may make you feel desirable and loveable. The truth is that affairs prevent any real intimacy between yourself and your lover.

### Denying the Abuse

Our research clearly indicates that most of us who grew up with alcoholics repeatedly involve ourselves in abusive relationships that make us unhappy. Like many women we talked with, you may not recognize that your relationship is abusive. You may use the same denial which surrounded the physical, emotional, and sexual abuse in your childhood family to deny, excuse, or rationalize the abuse within your relationship.

In her book, *Getting Free: A Handbook for Women in Abusive Relationships*, Ginny NiCarthy talks about the denial and the difficulty many women have in recognizing the abuse in their relationships. We encourage you to use NiCarthy's abuse list to assess the presence of physical, sexual, or emotional abuse in your intimate relationship(s).

Has your lover/spouse ever done any of the following things to you? Have you done any of these things to your lover/spouse?

- Pushed, shoved, kicked, slapped?
- Bite, pinched, hit, choked, scratched?
- Prevented you/your partner from leaving or locked you/your partner out of auto, home, or office?
- Thrown things at you/your lover?
- Driven recklessly or left you/your partner in dangerous places?
- Refused you/your partner medical attention when ill, injured or pregnant?
- Raped you?
- Threatened with or used a weapon?
- Told anti-woman jokes or treated you/your partner as a sex object?
- Been jealously angry or very critical about your/your partner's sexuality?
- Minimized your/your partner's feelings about sex?
- Insisted on unwanted touching or withholding touch?
- Called you/your partner sexual names such as "whore"?
- Had affairs while in a monogamous relationship?
- Forced sex or forced you/your partner to watch others?
- Forced unwanted sexual behaviors?

- Forced sex after physical abuse?
- Forced sex with objects or weapons to hurt you/your partner?
- Committed or participated in sadistic sexual acts that you/your partner didn't want to engage in?
- Ignored feelings or ridiculed and insulted your/your partner's race, class, beliefs, heritage?
- Been continually critical, insulting, humiliating?
- Refused to work or share money, or kept you/your partner from working?
- Made all of the relationship decisions?
- Took away car keys or money?
- Regularly threatened to leave or told you/your partner to leave?
- Punished or neglected children or stepchildren when angry at partner?
- Abused pets when angry at partner?
- Manipulated with lies, blaming, contradictions?

How frequently do such events take place in your relationship? How has the frequency of abuse been changing? Some of these acts are more dangerous than others. Some are life-threatening. All are disrespectful and all are attempts to control. Emotional abuse can be particularly difficult to define. Its subtleties and frequency can make you feel slightly injured or tremendously humiliated. NiCarthy cautions that if you feel you deserve to be abused because you are also abusive, you are mistaken. Any abuse that is allowed to continue in the relationship threatens your sense of self and threatens the whole relationship. The first step in healing an abusive relationship is being able to define abuse as abuse.

## What Prevents Your Leaving?

What contributes to our staying when we're unhappy in our relationships? While we may be able to readily identify many obvious reasons such as fear, lack of money, and codependency, most of us are probably unaware of powerful, underlying reasons for staying that can be traced back to our alcoholic family system.

We stay in unhealthy relationships because we develop a false sense of loyalty, because of untrue beliefs we harbor, and as a way to prevent "abandonment depression," a concept that we will later define. Therapist Cynthia Cooley, M.F.C.C., says, "I think ACOAs know when they're in unhealthy relationships, but it feels really normal to them. It isn't that they do not know that they're unhappy. It's that unhappiness becomes normal. They just don't know that it doesn't have to be that way."

*ACOA Loyalty.* The alcoholic family system teaches us and demands that we remain loyal to keeping the secret of addiction. If a child in an alcoholic family breaks this code of silence and tells others about the oftentimes bizarre, dangerous, and sometimes life-threatening family behaviors, the bond of secrecy which holds the family together is broken. No child can risk losing her or his family, no matter how unhealthy it may be. So we learn to be steadfastly loyal regardless of how unhappy it makes us.

This loyalty teaches us to deny, protect, and cover up to maintain the family secret. As adults, that same loyalty continues—we deny the abuse and unhappiness in our adult relationships. Since we believe it's disloyal to discuss our family secrets and our pain, we effectively prevent ourselves from getting the healthy outside feedback and support we need in order to leave.

Children in alcoholic families learn loyalty through the incredibly powerful process of *intermittent reinforcement.* Psychologist B.F. Skinner was the first to demonstrate that human behavior can be shaped by various types of reinforcement. In "continuous" reinforcement, for example, a child performs a particular behavior and receives a reward or reinforcement. If the positive reinforcement is removed, the child eventually stops the behavior.

In "intermittent" or random reinforcement—the kind often found in alcoholic families—the child is rewarded *sporadically.* When the child behaves in a particular way, sometimes she is rewarded, other times she is not. There is no predictability or rationale for the rewards. With intermittent reinforcement, the child continues to perform the behavior even without receiving the reward because she develops an *expectation* of reward.

An example of how this powerful reinforcement works in the alcoholic family is the daughter whose alcoholic father alternately abuses and cares for her. When he drinks, he yells, throws things, and hits her. When he's sober, he laughs, plays, and affectionately hugs her. Confused by this intermittent reinforcement, the child tries to behave in ways that control her father's alcoholic behavior. However, her behaviors don't always work—sometimes what she does evokes her father's smiles and affection. Other times the same behavior is met with drunken, hostile responses. She tries over and over to adjust her behavior in ways to control her father's drinking.

Occasionally, she receives a smile or a kind word from her father; then she desperately tries to figure out which of her behaviors worked. Since her behavior is intermittently reinforced, the child remains ever hopeful of reward. She "hangs in there," always trying for her father's loving, affectionate response. Sometimes she tries new behaviors when old ones fail to work. She'll continue to try long after her father stops reinforcing her. Her efforts may continue for years or for a lifetime. Her patience and persistence are remarkable—and sad—to witness.

If she received continuous reinforcement, she'd be much more likely to reject her father's behavior and abandon her quest for his affection. Instead, the intermittent reinforcement continually keeps her off balance, waiting, hoping for reward.

As adults, our childhood reinforcement for loyally trying to control the alcoholic's behavior and being intermittently rewarded for it continues in our unhappy intimate relationships. Many of us say we remain in our abusive relationships because we see "potential" in our mates. We see this potential when our behavior appears to bring about a positive reward from our partner. Because we're occasionally positively rewarded—sometimes our partner is sensitive, affectionate, loving, interested, or sexually satisfying—we continue to hope that the right combination of our behaviors will bring lasting rewards.

We must learn that we cannot control the reinforcement which comes from our partner. Nor can we control our partner. Settling for occasional positive attention while tolerating abuse depletes our spirit, our self-respect, and our self-value.

*Old Beliefs.* To fully understand why we stay in unhappy relationships, we have to look further at the belief systems we inherit from our dysfunctional alcoholic families. This erroneous belief system, which profoundly affects our relationship decisions, is acquired and passed on from generation to generation. These powerful, paralyzing beliefs, first identified by Physical Abuse Researchers Peter Neidig and Dale Friedman in their book, *Spouse Abuse, A Treatment Program for Couples,* include:

- "My partner is psychologically, physically, or emotionally ill and only I know how to take care of my partner's needs."
- "My partner may commit suicide if I leave and others will blame me."
- "I would never be allowed to leave. If I tried to leave, my partner would chase after me and never leave me alone."
- "I deserve abuse and/or the abuse is my fault."
- "Separation and divorce are always wrong. My parents and siblings would consider me a failure."

- "My children need and deserve this person in their life."
- "I can't survive without someone to support me."
- "Now that this most recent attack is over, things will change for the better."
- "This relationship is the best I have a right to expect and/or all intimate relationships are like this."

It's easy to see why such beliefs serve to keep us in abusive, unsatisfying relationships. How many of these beliefs do you hold? Without challenging and replacing these "learned helplessness" beliefs, it's unlikely that we can end our abusive relationships.

*Avoiding Abandonment Depression.* You may not end your relationship because you don't believe you have the "right" to inflict pain on yourself or your partner. Like many ACOAs, you've probably seen great pain and trauma around ending relationships in your childhood family. To avoid the possibility of having to "refeel" those early childhood separations, abandonments, and divorces, you may choose to stay long past the time you know your relationship must end.

According to Therapist Margaret Mahler, all of us as children need to learn—with support from our parents or other primary caregivers—how to separate from our caregivers and develop an individual sense of self. In *Search for the Real Self*, author James Masterson says that if we're denied such support for our emerging self we experience *"abandonment depression," a combination of intense feelings of rage, panic, guilt, emptiness, depression, and hopelessness.* While as young children we cannot understand such powerful feelings, we do begin to develop an intricate system of defenses designed to prevent the feelings of abandonment depression from recurring. This defense system comprises our "false self," which functions to protect us from reexperiencing the original abandonment depression. As adults, the false self tries to convince us that we're not unhappy, that ending our relationship would cause us more pain than staying. To cope and convince ourselves that we're happy in our unhappy relationships, we often develop addictions to food, alcohol, drugs, sex, work, or other compulsions.

## Unhappy Endings

Although some of us are able to end unhappy intimate relationships, we often use methods that result in excessive pain and leave behind much unresolved hurt. We often use three common, generationally repeated methods of ending our relationships: *attack, self-deprecation,* and *extinction.*

In the *attack method*, the partner desiring to leave the relationship attacks the other with blaming "you" statements. "You never give me what I want." "You're always getting drunk." "You are so selfish that you can't even recognize there is someone else in this relationship besides you." "You look like shit these days." "Sex with you is like no sex at all." "You've never said an interesting thing in your life." These attacks antagonize and shift the "blame" for ending the relationship to the other partner. The indirect message is "I want to leave you."

Sometimes the partner wanting to end the relationship completes the tirade of blaming with a statement that the relationship is over. In this case, the attacker, while blaming the partner for "causing" the relationship to end, takes some responsibility for wanting to leave the relationship.

More commonly in the attack-style of ending relationships, the attacker only *hints* that the relationship is over. She or he might say something like, "I can't understand how you stay in this relationship since you seem to be as disinterested as I am. What's holding you up?" The attacker who wants out of the relationship bypasses any guilt about ending the relationship. Regardless of who ultimately ends the relationship, the attack method of leaving deeply wounds everyone involved with its sarcasm, exaggeration, accusations, violence, and fault-finding.

With the *self-deprecation method*, ACOAs put themselves down, portray themselves as unworthy of the relationship. The person wanting to leave the relationship tries to convince the partner to leave for someone "better." "You are so unhappy with me. I let you down in so many ways. I continually disappoint you. Many people would be interested in you. But I just screw things up. You deserve someone who can be there for you like you want. I can really understand why you'd think of leaving me."

Like with the attack method, the person using self-deprecation to get out of a relationship refuses to take responsibility for ending the relationship. Instead, she or he hopes the partner will take the "hint" and leave. Since many of us have seen the attack method in our alcoholic childhood families and have felt the pain it causes, we opt for the self-deprecation method as a "kinder" or "less hurtful" way of ending. However, if our partner doesn't take the hint and leave the relationship soon enough, often we become impatient and indignant, and resort to the attack method.

The *extinction method* of leaving usually leaves the recipient feeling confused, doubting her or his own perceptions, and feeling or acting "crazy." With extinction, the partner desiring to leave gradually withdraws sex, energy, time, affection, and self-disclosure from the relationship. When the other partner eventually confronts her or him and asks what's causing the changes, the withdrawing partner denies any change while continuing to pull away.

A typical exchange between partners undergoing extinction might go like this: "You seem distant. You say nothing has changed, but it *feels* different. We don't do the special things we used to. You don't tell me what you're thinking or feeling anymore. We don't even cuddle at night. I *know* something is wrong. Don't you love me anymore?" The partner wanting to leave responds, "Oh you're so sensitive. You're always worrying about nothing. I've just been busy with work."

Extinction takes place over a period of time, usually punctuated with indirect comments and gestures intended to allow the lover to recognize the increased distancing. As with the attack and self-deprecating methods, the goal is to manipulate the partner into making the final decision to end the relationship. Sometimes the unhealthy process of extinction occurs over several years. Occasionally the partner desiring an end becomes impatient and moves from the extinction method to attacking.

Most of us who use extinction to end our relationships believe that it is a more gentle way to say goodbye. In fact, extinction, self-deprecation, and attack are all dishonest methods of communicating and only serve to produce hurt, fear, guilt, and rage.

## Learning to Leave

We rely heavily on these destructive tools for ending our unhappy relationships because we've seen these methods used by our parents, stepparents, grandparents, and our sisters and brothers. We use what we know. Few of us have ever seen a healthy, assertive method of ending relationships.

How can we learn to end relationships that are no longer healthy for us? An assertive way to end relationships includes:

- Being direct and honest.
- Speaking with "I" statements rather than "you" statements.
- Stating clearly what we want the change to be.
- Expressing feelings we're experiencing in the present.
- Assuming personal responsibility for the change.
- Deciding the level of physical and emotional intimacy we want with the person.
- Acting in a responsible fashion by establishing and adhering to agreed-upon timelines for when changes should occur.

An assertive method of ending a relationship does not include sarcasm, degradation, humiliation, or blaming self or others. If you decide to leave an unhappy relationship and use this assertive method, it provides no guarantee that your partner won't harbor hostile, depressed feelings about the change. While you cannot assume responsibility for your partner's feelings and reactions, you can reassure them and yourself that you are being honest and that it is not your intention to demean, devalue, or degrade them.

Ending a relationship in an honest, assertive way can increase your self-esteem because it enhances your sense of "entitlement," your feeling of being deserving. In *Treatment of Adult Survivors of Childhood Abuse*, Eliana Gil says that entitlement means being able to identify, protect, and assert your personal rights. She writes, "Abused children have not been taught that they have a right to be seen, heard, respected, valued, cared for, and treated in safe ways with dignity." As you come to believe and accept a sense of entitlement, you'll be less likely to stay in situations or relationships where your rights and your self are violated. An assertive method of terminating relationships reflects both a respect for yourself and your partner.

# CHAPTER 4

# I Don't Know Where ᵻ. and I Begin

*My mom and my alcoholic dad divorced when I was fifteen and I lived with my mom until I married at seventeen. Two years later, my mother married another alcoholic and she and my new stepfather had terrible fights. She'd come and stay with my husband and me for days or even weeks after a particularly bad fight. My dad did the same thing when he fought with his second wife. Occasionally, both my mom and dad would arrive at my house at the same time. I was confidant to each of them. They'd tell me all about their problems and their fights. Though I didn't know it then, I had no business being drawn into their lives that way.— Melissa W.*

Most of us, and certainly the ACOAs we interviewed in our research, have difficulty identifying, protecting, and respecting our own and others' personal "boundaries"–those emotional barriers that define, separate, and protect us from the world. Often we're unable to recognize when our personal boundaries are violated by others. For example, in the quote above, Melissa's personal boundaries and those of her husband were repeatedly violated by her parents invading her home without invitation and triangling her in their marital disputes. It was years before Melissa could recognize that her parents had taken advantage of her and violated her boundaries.

Even when we recognize our boundaries have been violated, we're often unable and/or unwilling to defend those boundaries. In intimate relationships, we often violate the boundaries of our partners without knowing it. Much of the pain and unhappiness in our sexual relationships is due to boundary violations. How is it that we find ourselves so

ted and vulnerable? What contributes to our allowing others to
dly violate our personal boundaries?

## he Function of Boundaries

To understand the boundary problems we face, it's important to
understand how boundaries work in family systems. Boundaries, as
defined in family therapy, are the emotional places which define where
the individual or family begins and ends. Boundaries delineate parts of
the family system, organizing the ways in which family members interact. Boundaries establish how, when, and to whom members of families
relate. Through boundaries, the family system carries out its functions
through what family therapists call "subsystems" such as the individual
subsystem, the spousal subsystem, the parental subsystem, and the sibling subsystem. Additionally, each family member belongs to subsystems
formed by generation, by gender, by special interest, or by function.

The *individual subsystem* includes the personal self—who I am—and is
that part of you which interacts with the boundaries of others. It is the
"real self." It functions to surround and protect you from invasions of
your body, your possessions, your feelings, your beliefs, your opinions,
your decisions, your money, your time, and your privacy.

The *spousal subsystem*, whether heterosexual, bisexual, or homosexual,
consists of two persons who join together for the purpose of forming an
intimate relationship. The primary task of the spousal subsystem is to
develop boundaries which protect the spouses, providing them the space
in which their intimacy needs can be met. Boundaries protect the couple's
relationship from intrusion by friends, in-laws, children, and activities.

The *parental subsystem* involves childrearing and socializing functions.
This system can include grandparents, aunts, uncles, and even children
brought up from the sibling subsystem to carry out parental tasks. Adults
in the parental subsystem are to care for, protect, and socialize the children.
They are to make decisions related to the survival of the whole family
system.

The *sibling subsystem* establishes patterns for sisters and brothers to
negotiate, cooperate, make decisions, compete, and relate with one another.

The subsystems in our families interact with one another, greatly
affecting each other. *Dysfunction in any subsystem affects the functioning of
every other subsystem.* If, for example, your parents' spousal subsystem
was afflicted with alcoholism, it profoundly affected how they performed
as parents, how you and your sisters and brothers interacted as siblings,
and how you interact with your self and the world.

Subsystems, which organize the family into units, also contain boundaries. Those boundaries are the rules which define who participates in the subsystem and in what manner. In healthy families, the boundaries of each subsystem are clear enough for members to carry out their functions without undue interference. Functional parents attempt to understand and respect children's rights, such as honoring their choice of friends to invite to their birthday party. Siblings in healthy families are clear about the rights and responsibilities each have within the family.

Clear boundaries in healthy families also allow and encourage appropriate contact between members of the family and others outside the family. In contrast, in dysfunctional families such as alcoholic families, family members are not permitted to interact much outside the family, which limits constructive feedback to family members and tends to isolate them.

## Boundaries in Dysfunctional Families

In alcoholic family systems, social and psychological boundaries are often overly rigid or enmeshed. If your family had overly rigid boundaries, family members' roles were so strictly defined that there was probably little communication between family members or others outside your family. An example might be a parent who constantly tells her children, "It's this way because I'm the mother and I say so. I don't want your opinion." This kind of rigidity leaves little room for negotiation between family members. It also functions to insulate family members from one another and leaves them feeling isolated and lonely.

Overly rigid boundaries can be found in what family therapists often call "disengaged" families—in which members are psychologically distant from one another. If your family was disengaged, you and your family shared little emotionally with one another. The focus in your family discussions was probably intellectual, objective, and impersonal. It's likely you almost never discussed important feelings or problems with each other or with people outside your family. Your parents may have been so distant from you and your sisters and brothers they may have been unaware of what school subjects you were studying. Asking for help from one another was probably discouraged and seen as a sign of weakness. As adults, your disengaged family may have moved away from one another, living in distant cities, states, or even different countries and rarely phoning, writing, or visiting one another.

At the other end of the dysfunctional family spectrum are families with diffuse boundaries, the "enmeshed" family. If you come from an enmeshed family, boundaries were blurred and unclear. You may have weak personal boundaries and find yourself allowing others to do any-thing they want to you regardless of how painful it may be. You are likely to have tremendous difficulty protecting your boundaries by saying no to others.

Enmeshment is an extreme, unhealthy form of closeness and intensity of feeling between family members. Being a member of "the family" takes precedence over developing a healthy sense of self. Members of your family may have freely discussed every private detail of other members' lives. When one family member is in crisis, the news spreads rapidly to other family members, most often not initiated by the member with the problem.

In an enmeshed family, everyone has partial information, feelings run high, and advice-giving is rampant. If, for example, a daughter becomes premaritally pregnant and tells her mother, the mother tells the youngest sister who confides in the father that she is worried about "how Mom is taking it." Dad, never talking openly or directly to the pregnant daughter, goes to the oldest son in the family and instructs him to secretly check out the financial background of the young man responsible for the preg-nancy. The son gathers this information, but tells his uncle not his father because the "bad news" may distract Dad from important business trans-actions he's involved in at work. In the enmeshed family, everyone's busi-ness becomes everyone else's and all function to protect one another, while avoiding confronting each other.

If you come from an enmeshed family, the emotional climate was probably continually tense as the family cycled from one member's catas-trophe to the next. If it wasn't sister Sue's premarital pregnancy, it was Johnny's being kicked off the basketball team, or Aunt Martha's herpes diagnosis, or Mom's feud with the next-door neighbor, or Dad's income tax audit. Under the guise of love and concern, in enmeshed families each member's life becomes everyone else's and everyone violates each other's weak, poorly differentiated personal boundaries.

Enmeshed families generally lack privacy. You may recall breakfast table conversations involving intimate details of other member's lives. In the name of "helping," your enmeshed family probably committed numerous boundary violations daily—perhaps they screened or listened to others' phone calls, read letters and diaries without permission, or unmercifully interrogated you and other family members about private matters. You, like everyone in your enmeshed family, learned to nonver-bally "read" each other for trouble cues and learned to anticipate others' responses. Sometimes it seems that the only way to breathe in such a suffocating atmosphere and to discover yourself is to flee the family entirely, to cut off all emotional and physical contact, for months, years, sometimes for entire lifetimes.

All families can be found along the continuum between these two extremes of boundary functioning. Alcoholic families usually exist at the extremes—disengaged or enmeshed—sometimes incorporating both types of dysfunctional behavior. If you grew up in a disengaged family with rigid boundaries, you may have difficulty getting close to others. If you grew up in an enmeshed family, you run the risk of becoming overly involved with your partner, losing your autonomy. Coming from either an enmeshed or disengaged family system, you probably lack relationship problem-solving skills.

Our alcoholic families, full of rigid and blurred boundaries, provide us with inadequate definitions of power, dependency, and responsibility. Patterns of underresponsibility and overresponsibility in our dysfunctional families can be traced to ineffective patterns established by our grandparents and their grandparents before them. Our parents pass on the behavior to us, and we pass it on to our children. Without intervention, the unhealthy ways of relating can continue indefinitely.

Examining your own family's generational behaviors within each subsystem can teach you much about how your family interacts. Who's intimate with whom? Who helps whom during family conflicts? How does your family react to a crisis? Who worries the most? Who underreacts or overreacts to feelings? Who is the most likely to be unemotional? Who is the most controlling? Who abuses whom? Who takes primary responsibility for parenting? Who violates what boundaries? Who acts distant?

## Damage to the Family

When families have either unclear or too-rigid boundaries between the subsystems, the overall family system—especially the children—suffers damage. This damage, which continues to affect us as adults, may take several forms:

- Triangulation.
- Emotional cut-off.
- Revictimization of abuse survivors.
- Sexual-affectional affairs.
- Inability to set and maintain limits with others.

*Triangulation.* If you or your partner has suffered damage by ineffective childhood family boundary maintenance, as an adult, you may resort to "triangulation," involving a third person to intervene in a crisis or problem. When tension builds between you and your relationship partner, you or your partner may try to engage a third member to help resolve the issue. If, for example, you and your husband are sleeping separately because he came home drunk, your husband may confide in one of your children. "Mom made me sleep on the couch because I had a little fun last night. Go in and ask Mom if she's going to stay mad at me all day." Your child approaches you and asks her or his father's question. Feeling angry at your husband, you yell at the child, "I want you to clean all the dishes in the sink and then take an early nap." The child is left confused. In carrying out the directives of one parent, playing the go-between, the child is punished for it by the other.

Such situations are common in alcoholic households. The child was inappropriately brought into the spousal subsystem by the father's request, then told by the mother to get out of that subsystem immediately. Of course, no one ever explained to the confused child—just as no one probably ever explained to you as a child—that she or he was "triangulated" by the drinking parent. In a healthier family system, the couple would have shared their feelings with one another and intentionally protected the child from participating in their conflict.

In functional families with clear boundaries, a healthy coalition exists between parents, an alliance of power which affects the entire power distribution in the family. In such families, the parental power is clear and parent-child coalitions do not exist. In alcoholic families, however, marital partners are often not in coalition with one another. As one spouse struggles to control the substance abuse of the partner, the caring and mutuality between the couple decreases. Frequent arguments and conflicts further weaken the bonds between the couple and set the stage for unhealthy parent-child coalitions.

In many alcoholic families—and perhaps in your own childhood family—the parent-child coalition becomes so intimate that it comes to resemble the marriage relationship. This coupling unhealthfully blurs generational boundaries, leaving the child in the position of "parenting" the parent or of having to meet the intimacy needs of the parent.

ACOA research participant Jennifer Y. tells how as a young child she "parented" both of her parents. *I was the mother in the household*, she says. *I was my alcoholic dad's prime enabler. I always forgave him, covered for him. From the time I was fourteen it was my job to drive to the four bars in town, then later find him and bring him home so he wouldn't get a ticket for drunk driving. Before I'd leave to pick him up, Mom would be angry and hysterical. When Dad and I would arrive home, she'd yell at him and then march off to bed. I'd fix dinner for him and he'd ramble on about some beautiful woman he'd met in the bar that night. I'd listen, but I'd try not to show too much interest because I knew Mom was listening from the bedroom.*

We pay a heavy price for such triangulation. Many of us, like Jennifer, were robbed of our own childhoods. In our attempts to meet our parents' needs, we were expected to join the spousal subsystem. Karen P.'s alcoholic parents forced her to become part of their spousal subsystem. *When I was eleven, both my parents were drunk and fighting,* she says. *My mother came into my bedroom and told me my father was in the garage committing suicide. She wanted me to go out into the dark driveway and stop him. I was afraid to go, but my mother kept insisting. I went and found my dad in the car, engine on with his head laying on the steering wheel. I pulled him out of the car, dragged him into the house, and got him into bed. No one in my family ever discussed that night again.*

Your alcoholic parents may have "let off steam" or "confided in" you and your sisters and brothers in ways that violated your emotional boundaries. Ginger O. tells about her midnight conversations with her unhappy, codependent mother. *After hearing my mother's stories,* she says, *I knew I'd never get married or even have a relationship. My mother taught me that men meant pain. They lie and can't be trusted. She'd cry and tell me that she felt trapped in her relationship with my dad. She constantly talked about divorce. I wanted to make up for her pain, to give her a new life. From the time I was fifteen, I worked thirty hours a week while going to school and turned over my paycheck to her in hopes that it would help.*

Inappropriate parental self-disclosures to the child violate her or his emotional boundaries. The triangulating by one parent interferes with the relationship the child tries to develop with the other parent.

Like many children of alcoholics, you may have been asked to cross boundaries to meet your parents' unmet need for affection. Harriet D.'s father felt alone and lonely when his wife would enter the mental hospital. *When my mother went into the psych hospital for her periodic depression,* says Harriet, *Dad always made me come into his bed to talk and to sleep with him. There wasn't any sexual touching, but he'd tell me how he felt about Mom. From the time I was ten until I was fifteen, this happened at least six times a year.* Each time when Harriet's mother returned from the hospital, the father with no explanation told Harriet to remain in her own bed—to become part of the child subsystem again. This kind of generational boundary-crossing causes children intense confusion and anxiety.

Perhaps your family involved you in sexual triangulation. In subtle ways, the alcoholic family system ignores and disrespects the boundaries which exist to protect the child from sexual violation. Deanna W. says her father crossed the sexual boundary whenever he drank. *The more my dad had to drink,* she says, *the more often he'd sneak up behind me like he was going to give me a hug from behind and then he'd grab my breasts. He'd feel up my girlfriends in the same way. He'd grab their tits as we walked by into my bedroom. I'd smolder with rage and embarrassment.*

Many women in our study said sexual violations involved extended family members or their parents' friends and acquaintances. They tried to get protection against such violations from their parents and other adults, but they were often ignored or punished instead. ACOA Barbara Y. recalls, *In seventh grade, my father's drinking friends would touch my breasts. They'd laugh and brag about how long they could hold on before I could wiggle away. I felt humiliated and alone. Once I told my mother about it and my father yelled at me for telling on his friends.*

Your childhood sexual boundary violations may not have involved actual sexual touching, but your parents or other adults may have had inappropriate discussions about sex, made sexual innuendos, or criticized each other about sex in front of you. Violet S. says, *My dad used to criticize my mother's sexuality in front of me. He'd tell her she was frigid. He'd yell about how much she hated sex. She'd just look down at the floor, fists clenched, and never say a word.*

***Emotional Cut-Off.*** Emotional cut-off is another consequence of growing up with unhealthy boundaries in alcoholic families. You may have tried to escape from unresolved emotional conflicts with your family by moving geographically away. You may refuse to attend family functions, send no gifts or cards, never phone or see other family members. You may think that because you've eliminated physical contact with your family, you're free from the influence of their unhealthy dynamics. Your unresolved family conflicts, however, are only masked by this geographical and emotional cut-off. On some level, you remain involved and preoccupied with your family's pain and hurt. You invest much psychic energy in "being separate from" your alcoholic family.

Emotional cut-offs reflect underlying boundary confusion between generations. While cutting off your family may reduce some of your immediate anxiety, it doesn't involve a healthy working through of the pain you experienced growing up in an alcoholic household. On the surface, running away may look like a solution. However, it cannot provide true healing. Healthy separation from our childhood families—often only accomplished with professional help—comes through being able to differentiate ourselves from our families and becoming separate individuals.

## Consequences as Adults

As adults, the consequences of growing up in families with blurred boundaries and repeated boundary violations can be profound and far-reaching. For those of us who were sexually violated as children, one consequence is *sexual revictimization*. When our sexual boundaries aren't protected and are violated within our families, we are often sexually victimized again and again as adolescents and as adults. Unable to define and protect our sexual boundaries, we become natural targets for those looking for sexual victims. With each new sexual assault, we feel more ashamed and experience a deeper sense of inadequacy. Without intervention, our revictimization becomes an endless spiral of lower and lower self-esteem.

Faced with repeated sexual violations, we often use the same protective skills we developed during our childhood sexual abuse. Sally L. says, *When I date, I don't know how to say no and stop the guy when I don't want sex. Most of the time I'm drunk. I feel sick inside. Instead of saying no, I try to get into the sex because I think I'm supposed to. Inside I'm saying to myself "I hate this. I can't wait to get out of here." I've learned to detach from the situation by magically stepping away from my body.*

**Sexual Affairs.** Those of us who grew up in boundary-dysfunctional families are more likely to triangulate our own adult intimate relationships, often with extra-relationship affairs. By having affairs, we involve a third person in our relationship crisis. Repeating boundary-violating patterns learned from our alcoholic parents, we may inappropriately violate the boundaries of our intimate relationship with a secret lover.

Another consequence of childhood boundary violation is our inability to identify our own boundaries or the boundaries of others. As adults, most of us can't protect our boundaries. We do learn, however, how to violate the boundaries of others. Madeline V. couldn't understand why her lover was angry with her when she violated his boundaries. He couldn't understand why she was angry when he violated the relationship's sexual boundaries. While they can readily identify the boundary violations committed against themselves, neither can acknowledge the boundary violation they committed against the other. *The man I was involved with had sex with someone else while we were together,* she says. *I found out about it by reading his journal. He was really angry with me for invading his privacy, but it was the only way I could find out what was going on.*

**The Internal Zipper.** In their book, *Facing Shame: Families in Recovery*,

Merle Fossum and Marilyn Mason use the metaphor of the "internal zip-per" to describe the consequence of growing up in a family with unclear boundaries. They contend that healthy individuals have boundaries which encase the intellectual self, the emotional self, and the physical self. In each of those areas, we have an "internal zipper" which we can open or close to others. The internal zipper regulates our boundaries. When a healthy adult experiences fear or feels unsafe, she zips up access to her intellectual, emotional, and/or physical self. Using the zipper gives one a sense of control, especially within intimate relationships.

Our alcoholic families, however, gave us unclear boundaries and "external zippers." These outside zippers allow others unlimited access to our inner selves. It allows others to abuse us whenever they please. Such abuse might include someone telling us how we feel, translating what we "really" think to others, and/or interpreting our behavior for us and oth-ers. With our external zippers, we are at the mercy of others. When others violate our boundaries, we're left feeling frightened, ashamed, and con-fused. Unable to set realistic limits about how others treat us and unable to defend our "selves," we're ever-vulnerable to attack and disrespect from others.

It is only with an internal zipper, say Fossum and Mason, that we can develop true intimacy with others. With the internal zipper, we can moni-tor closeness with others. Using the internal zipper—making choices for ourselves—is the most effective protection of our sense of self. We can take a giant step in internalizing our zippers by developing the ability to say no. To tell others to stop invading our sense of self is an important step in developing intimacy with ourselves and with others.

Another consequence of growing up with unclear and frequently vio-lated boundaries, is that we select partners who most *closely match our own level of separation and individuation—partners with similar boundary limits and development of self.* Usually our partners' and our own childhood families have similar boundary patterns. Without conscious awareness, we repeat-edly select partners whose ability to separate self from others and whose ability to initiate and maintain intimacy is similar to our own. We're often surprised by this concept. Although our partners' external behaviors may differ, their ability—and their inability—to attend to the needs of their own selves and to our needs are remarkably similar to our own.

In Chapter Two, we talked about how we tend to repeatedly select unavailable partners to avoid being intimate. By selecting partners who match our own limited capacity for intimacy, we ensure that we won't have to give or receive levels of intimacy which feel uncomfortable or unfamiliar to us.

## Determining Your Intimacy Levels

If you're like most ACOAs, you often feel confused and anxious when you think about autonomy and intimacy in your relationships. You may wonder: "Why is it hard for me to maintain my sense of self when I'm in a relationship?" and "Why am I able to pursue my own goals and interests only when I'm living alone and not when I'm involved in a committed relationship?"

Growing up in alcoholic households, we didn't have parents who were able to develop themselves and simultaneously be truly intimate in their relationships. Instead, we saw adults who were unable to establish, maintain, and defend their personal and relationship boundaries. Our parents repeatedly violated others' boundaries and allowed their own boundaries to be violated. As a result of growing up with such role models, most of us did not gain the necessary skills to negotiate boundaries and to respect the boundaries of others.

One problem is that we often don't know which aspects of our relationships we can determine and which we cannot. We have responsibility for determining only two areas in developing intimacy with others: the level of emotional and physical intimacy we desire from others and the level of emotional and physical intimacy we're willing to give to others.

The degree of emotional and physical intimacy you desire from others belongs to *you* — no one else can tell you what level of intimacy you desire. Wanting a particular level of intimacy doesn't guarantee that you'll receive it. That choice belongs to the other person. Likewise, *you* are the only one who can decide what level of intimacy you're willing to give. While your partner may want a particular level of intimacy from you, *you* are the only one to decide how much and when you will give intimacy. Your partner can choose to accept or refuse your offered intimacy.

While this may seem like an easy concept, it's difficult for most ACOAs to accept and to practice. Many of us believe that if someone wants a particular level of intimacy from us, then we must give it. For example, if someone wants to have sex with you, you may feel compelled to say yes whether or not you want to. This is an incorrect perception. You alone determine the level of intimacy you give and receive.

You have no ability or right to determine, however, the level of emotional and physical intimacy your partner or others want from you. Likewise, you have no right to determine the level of intimacy others are willing to give to you. In other words: You get to choose the level of intimacy you want and what you're willing to give and receive from another. Others get to decide the level of intimacy they want from you and what they're willing to receive and give to you.

*Levels of Emotional Intimacy.* Ten years ago while conducting groups in assertive interpersonal skills, I discovered and adapted a chart originally designed by Therapist Pamela Butler to help clients to determine the level of physical and emotional intimacy they want from others and the level of intimacy they want to offer another. This tool is designed to help you identify and negotiate the level of intimacy you desire with your partner and others in your life.

---

*Emotional Intimacy*

**A.** Superficial interaction.
**B.** Small talk.
**C.** Honest expression of ideas, values, and opinions.
**D.** Honest expression of feelings.
**E.** Full intimate disclosure of ideas, values, opinions, and feelings (includes a combination of levels C and D, as well as an honest sense of past, present, and future expectations, a willingness to work through difficult issues without avoidance or running away, and a commitment to assertively problem-solve areas of difficulty).

*Physical Intimacy*

**A.** Little or no physical contact.
**B.** Friendly contact.
**C.** Affectionate contact.
**D.** Passionate contact.
**E.** Full sexual expression.

---

If you seek level A emotional intimacy with someone, you limit your exchange to greetings of recognition: "Hello. How are you?" The expected response is brief and non-disclosing. At level B, you may discuss the weather, the traffic, the latest fashions—a few sentences of casual conversation. Think about the people you know that you relate to on levels A or B. Maintaining superficial exchanges with certain people can be appropriate. At the same time, there are people who want only to maintain level A or B intimacy levels with you, too. It is normal to want limited or superficial interactions consisting of no more than small talk with some people. Likewise, you needn't feel inferior, inadequate, or defensive when others want superficial relationships with you.

At level C emotional intimacy, you honestly exchange personal thoughts and opinions with another. You state your position even when you know the other person differs or disagrees with you. This level requires more risk and vulnerability than A or B.

Level D emotional intimacy increases the vulnerability even further as you begin to disclose your feelings to another. If you know someone on level D, you express a whole range of feelings. Some of us believe we have level D emotional intimacy in our partner relationships when we don't. We may express feelings of joy, happiness, and excitement, yet rarely express anger, sadness, confusion, guilt, or resentment. Some of us can express anger and impatience easily, yet are unable to express feelings of empathy, tenderness, or compassion.

Ideally in level D emotional intimacy, you and your partner mutually share the full range of your emotions. Many of us, in fact, feel threatened when we express how we feel. We often fear rejection, ridicule, and abandonment. Instead, we protect ourselves by staying in levels A, B, or C.

The length of a relationship does not indicate the level of emotional intimacy. Some ACOA couples have been together for decades and maintain B or C intimacy levels. Others might meet someone at a party and talk about themselves on level D with that person for hours. Risking such an immediate level of deep intimacy on a first date often creates tremendous vulnerability after the two people separate for the evening, especially if the other person has disclosed little about themselves.

To maintain a level E emotional intimacy with another requires skills—negotiation, conflict-resolution, honest communication—and the willingness to allow your partner to fully experience you emotionally. Level E relating involves the commitment of time, energy, patience, humor, and continuous work. Not everyone wants level E intimacy. Many ACOAs opt for less intense levels of intimacy rather than risk the vulnerability of level E.

*Levels of Physical Intimacy.* We can also choose our level of physical intimacy. In many ways, physical intimacy can be more ambiguous than emotional intimacy. The perceived levels of physical intimacy often depend on ethnic, cultural, and/or gender norms. For example, a kiss may be considered level A intimacy by two Europeans and level C between two Americans. As a result, people are often confused by what a particular touch means.

Because there is so much confusion about physical contact and the level of intimacy it implies, the *intent* of the touch is important. Since definitions of the level of physical intimacy differ widely between people, it's important to continually clarify your intention and ask others to clarify theirs.

Level A physical intimacy might include a handshake, a brief hug, a kiss on the cheek, or a pat on the back. It is primarily a physical greeting. Think about the people in your life with whom you want no deeper physical intimacy than level A. You have the right to determine the level of physical intimacy you feel comfortable giving and receiving.

Since there is so much confusion between "friendly" (level B) and "affectionate" (level C) physical contact, as mentioned before, it's best defined by your intention.

Level D, "passionate" contact, is physical contact that generates sexual arousal. We often wonder if we're experiencing affectionate level C contact or passionate level D contact. Level D includes genital arousal. If you kiss or touch someone and begin to feel turned on sexually, you are experiencing level D physical intimacy. If you are aware of your own arousal pattern, you usually know whether you are feeling affectionate or sexual.

Many of us find ourselves in situations where we sense that a particular behavior is sexual. We may feel unsure and not know what to do. Unfortunately, for many of us, it's easier to touch than to *talk about* the intent and meaning of touching. If you have a question about the intent of someone's touch, ask the person. Instead of spending time and energy trying to interpret or second-guess someone's intention, we can inquire and request that their reply be honest.

Level E involves sexual behaviors intended to elicit sexual pleasure. It may be oral sex, intercourse, the use of a vibrator, manual stimulation, or mutual masturbation, but the intention is *mutual sexual satisfaction*. A level E physical relationship may involve teaching your partner about the type of sexual touch that is most arousing, comfortable, and pleasurable.

*Combining Intimacies.* The five levels of emotional and physical intimacy can be combined in a variety of relationship options. For example, you might want a relationship with deep emotional intimacy (level E), but with little or no physical intimacy (level A). You may want a relationship with moderate petting (level D) and the expression of feelings (level D). The combinations are almost endless. It's important that you ask for the level of emotional and physical intimacy you desire and let your partner know the level of intimacy you're willing to give. You cannot force someone to give you a particular level of intimacy nor can you make them want or accept the level of intimacy you give.

When two people desire the same level of intimacy, there's a "match." Most of us accept matches with little difficulty. Problems arise, however, when the level of intimacy we want differs from our partner's. For example, our partner may want more or less emotional or sexual intimacy than we want. We may feel fear, sadness, rejection, confusion, or sometimes even relief. Neither you nor your partner is wrong when there's a difference in desired levels of intimacy. However, the differences may cause conflict in your relationship.

In our culture, most men are more comfortable engaging in physical intimacy than emotional intimacy. Women commonly complain about their male partners: "He never talks to me or tells me how he feels." Men are taught that emotional intimacy can damage their sense of self. As a result, they tend to be more cautious about allowing themselves to be emotionally vulnerable. Heeding this caution, some men totally avoid emotional intimacy and never share their deep emotional feelings.

In contrast, our society generally teaches women to be more skilled at and more comfortable with emotional intimacy than with physical intimacy. Women are traditionally taught that their greatest vulnerability, the greatest danger to their sense of self, is sex. It is no wonder that heterosexual couples often have problems with the woman wanting emotional intimacy and avoiding sexual intimacy and the man wanting sexual intimacy while avoiding emotional intimacy.

In lesbian relationships, two women often develop such rapid and deep emotional intimacy that they become "fused," unable to see one another as separate beings. Their boundaries become quickly blurred. Until very recently, most gay men tended to develop sexually intimate relationships rapidly with little emotional intimacy. Since the AIDS epidemic, gay men are experimenting much more with postponing overt sexual contact in favor of developing deeper levels of emotional intimacy.

If we desire different levels of intimacy, how can we resolve those differences with our partners? The intimacy chart on page 48 can help you and your partner negotiate your desired levels of physical and emotional intimacy.

1. Using the intimacy chart, decide the levels of intimacy you desire.
2. Ask your partner to use the chart to determine his or her desired levels of intimacy.
3. Honestly tell your partner your desired levels of intimacy. Have them tell you what they want and what they will give to you. Practice listening to what each of you has to say.
4. If discrepancies exist, negotiate levels of intimacy and discuss compromises.

A negotiation might go like this: Lisa wants level D emotional intimacy (expressing feelings) and level C physical intimacy (affectional contact) with John. John wants level C emotional intimacy (ideas, values, opinions) and level D physical intimacy (passionate contact).

**Lisa:** John, I want you to share your feelings with me. I'd like to know what's going on inside you—your hopes, even your fears. I know you want me to have sex with you, but I'm not really ready.

**John:** It's hard for me to talk about my feelings, Lisa.

**Lisa:** I let you know what I'm feeling, even if it's hard for me. I need someone who's willing to share their feelings.

**John:** I want to, but I got pretty burned in my last relationship and it may take me some time to be able to trust you enough to really open up. I'm better at expressing myself sexually and you know I want to make love with you.

**Lisa:** I'm not ready for sex with you, John. I take that quite seriously. How long do you think it'll take until you can trust enough to talk more about how you feel?

**John:** I'm not sure, maybe several months. I'll agree to stop pressuring you to have sex if you'll give me six months or so to develop more trust. After that, we can talk and see where we want our relationship to go.

It's important to respect your own and your partner's sense of timing around physical and emotional self-disclosure. To pressure someone for emotional or physical intimacy before they're ready violates their personal boundaries. To surrender to such pressure against your wishes, violates your boundaries.

Because new levels of intimacy require greater risk and more vulnerability, it feels safer for most of us to progress *slowly* to more intimate levels. Take time to gradually explore and assess if it feels safe for you to move to the next level of intimacy. You are likely to increase your sense of self and your self-esteem by resisting efforts of others to push you deeper or faster than you want to go. If you do not allow yourself the opportunity to move at your own pace while developing intimacy with your partner, you risk losing your sense of self in the process.

We all surround ourselves with levels of physical and emotional space. When you make decisions about who you permit to enter that space and how and when you permit them to enter, you establish your boundaries. Once you've established your boundaries, you can tell others what those boundaries are, listen when your partner tells you about her or his boundaries, and develop skills to negotiate altering those boundaries. Understanding the options and assertive rights you have in negotiating the levels of intimacy with others is your best defense in maintaining your personal boundaries.

# CHAPTER 5

# If It's Painful, It Must Be Sex

*My alcoholic grandfather used to have me sit on his lap when I was small. He would rub me up and down his leg. I always hated my grandfather. My grandfather would sleep downstairs and my grandma slept upstairs. I think this only happened once. What I do know for sure is that I never allowed my grandfather to have access to my children.—Bridget S.*

*When I was in the eighth grade, my dad would come up from behind and run his finger all the way up my butt. I'd get mad at him and he would laugh.—Jane P.*

*My parents divorced when I was nine. My mother remarried when I was eleven. For about a year, I didn't even give my stepfather a chance to know me because I felt angry that my mother had remarried when my father hadn't. When I was 12, I decided to give my stepfather a try and I approached him one afternoon for a hug. All I wanted was a hug, but he misread my advances. He gave me a kiss on the cheek and then he started french kissing me. I pushed him away and said, "No!" I felt real hurt and then I felt angry. I felt he'd rejected me. We never said a word about it and I never told anyone.—Dorothy T.*

*My alcoholic uncle touched my breasts from behind me and would pat my buttocks. When I told my mother she said to me, "Don't say anything to your uncle Mel, it would hurt his feelings. He would never forgive you and besides that, he doesn't mean anything by it anyway."—Marsha L.*

*My brother and I got left alone alot while both our parents stayed in downtown bars until closing time. He used to crawl in bed with me saying he'd protect me from all the bad ghosts. But soon he started touching me all over. It felt good to my body. I was so alone in my family. Eventually, I gave him head and let him put his fingers in me. Then in junior high school he got a girl friend and he stopped getting into bed with me. Now everyone was gone. Sometimes his girl-friend came over and I could hear them fucking in his room. I never knew what I'd done to make him not like me anymore.—Christy E.*

*When I was seven and a little older my mother touched me in the bathtub in ways that made me feel uncomfortable. She would touch my genitals saying they "needed a good washing."—Geri R.*

For many of us, sexual abuse was a particularly painful part of growing up in alcoholic families. Our study participants repeatedly told us about incidents of incest, child molestation, first intercourse abuse, and rape. The women we talked with had experienced abuse that spanned the whole continuum of sexual behaviors first described by sexual abuse Author Suzanne Sgroi, M.D. in 1982—nudity, disrobing, genital exposure, kissing, fondling, masturbation, oral sex, and finger and penile penetration of the anus and vagina.

Growing up in an alcoholic family increases the likelihood that you were the victim of incest or child molestation. Family researchers have known for many years that a correlation exists between chemical dependency and sexual abuse. People who commit child sexual abuse often abuse alcohol. Many women in treatment for their own chemical addiction were victims of incest or childhood sexual molestation. Comparisons of alcoholic and incestuous families reveal similar family rules, roles, and myths. The alcoholic family system creates an environment that *encourages* incest and child molestation.

If you're a victim of sexual assault you might wonder: What good will it do me to go through the pain of remembering my past sexual abuse? Our primary answer to you is that past sexual abuse impacts our ability to have satisfying adult sexual relationships. Only by working through these early experiences can we begin sexual healing.

One known effect of early sexual trauma is revictimization, the tendency to be repeatedly sexually victimized as an adolescent and adult. If you've been a victim of incest or child sexual molestation, you're more likely to be a victim of other sexual exploitation such as rape and first intercourse abuse. Mental health professionals believe this revictimization is produced by several factors:

- Our early sexualization.
- Our tendency to overevaluate and overidealize potential sex partners.
- Our inability to identify people who are trustworthy.
- Our learned sense of helplessness.

ACOAs who are sexual victims often unknowingly reenact unresolved sexual assault dynamics in their adult sexual relationships. Although you may have no conscious memory of your childhood sexual abuse, you may unconsciously repeat patterns you learned as a child such as sexual betrayal and keeping sexual secrets. You may be suspicious and unable to trust others.

Those of us who were sexually abused developed defenses to help us emotionally and physically survive our traumatic childhoods. Although these defenses and coping strategies were necessary during the abuse, what protected us as children now interferes with our ability to form close, intimate sexual relationships as adults. Unless we identify the abuse, feel the painful memories, and are able to place the responsibility for the abuse with the abuser where it belongs, it's likely we'll be unable to establish satisfying sexually intimate relationships with those we love.

Although reading through this material may feel painful, especially if you've experienced sexual abuse, it's important to examine how early childhood sexual abuse continues to affect us long after the invasive touches have ended. Healing begins with looking back.

### Childhood Sexual Abuse

One out of two women we studied said they'd been touched inappropriately by a family member. More than 60 percent said they'd been sexually touched by a non-family member during their childhood.

Incest abusers are usually, though not always, men in our families. Our ACOA study participants said they were sexually touched most often by their fathers, step-fathers, brothers, grandfathers, brothers-in-law, uncles, and male cousins.

Tara W. says the incest with her father began when she was four. *It lasted until I was nine,* she says. *My dad would stick his fingers in my vagina and rub my genitals hard. I cooperated because it was my only interaction with him. It was the only affection I got, even if it hurt.*

Of the thirty-seven women in our study who said they were incest survivors, all but one said her abuser was male. The women reported they were as young as two years old and as old as sixteen when the incest occurred. Their average age when the incest began was seven. Their abusers ranged in age from fourteen to sixty with the average age being thirty-five. The abuse continued from one to eleven years with the average timespan being five years. Our ACOA incest survivors aren't unusual. Their experiences correspond with the information collected about incest survivors by Researcher Diana Russell in her large-scale study of incestuous abuse of females published in *The Secret Trauma: Incest in the Lives of Girls and Women*. It's quite possible that you have had similar experiences.

If you were sexually abused, you probably knew and trusted your assailant. Most often non-family abusers are friends of the family, friends of older brothers and sisters, or people in positions of authority such as priests, ministers, teachers, parents' friends, neighbors, and babysitters. Less than 10 percent of the women we interviewed said their attacker was a stranger. Many of the men molesting ACOAs had been drinking at the time. Your abuser may have gained your confidence through gifts, favors, and attention before the molestation. By virtue of the chaos in our alcoholic families, we were more vulnerable to the attention and "affection" of these sexual offenders.

Study participant Dorthea R. was molested when she was twelve. *During the summer between eighth and ninth grade, my friend's father unexpectedly picked me up at summer school and drove me home. Over several days, he gained my confidence. I trusted him. One day when he picked me up, he parked the car in a deserted spot. He told me he wanted to "show me the ropes." In a fatherly way he said, "I won't hurt you." I got into the back seat with him. He pulled down his pants. I'd never seen a penis before. He tried to enter me, but it was too painful. I never saw him again after that. Later I told my mom, but she never acted mad or even talked with him about it.*

### Phases of Child Sexual Abuse

Sexual activities between adults and children often fall into a predictable pattern. Suzanne Sgroi, author of the *Handbook of Clinical Intervention in Child Sexual Abuse*, says there are five phases in child sexual abuse: *engagement phase, sexual interaction phase, secrecy phase, disclosure phase,* and *suppression phase.* Researcher Roland Summit, describing what he calls the "child sexual abuse accommodation syndrome," which views abuse from the child's point of view, says children display five typical responses to sexual abuse: secrecy; helplessness; entrapment and accommodation; delayed, conflicted disclosure; and retraction. What follows blends the insights of these two experts.

If you've been abused, you can probably readily identify each of the phases and responses. Although it may be painful to remember, it's important to understand how child sexual abuse typically unfolds and how your responses helped you cope with the abuse.

*Engagement Phase.* Sgroi says for child sexual abuse to occur two things must be present: *access* to the child and the *opportunity* to commit the abuse. Most often sexual abuse of children is a planned event by the abuser who knows the child and holds some legitimate power over her. Since children are generally talked into sexual activity under the guise of a game or with offers of rewards, the assailant rarely has to use physical force. In Vickie F.'s case, her assailant was an old family friend. *I was eleven and he was fifty,* she says. *I was at a birthday party for his step-daughter. He gave everyone else except me money for the carnival. Instead, he took me into his car and french-kissed me. He talked about how much he loved me. I felt scared and dirty. I felt bad. He touched me in places I'd never been touched before. I'd been taught to mind and respect him. I didn't know what to do.*

*Sexual Interaction Phase.* Sexual activity with the child usually begins gradually with partial undressing by the adult and/or the child and showing one another their genitals. The abuser may masturbate and encourage the child to imitate him.

Next, fondling with kissing usually occurs and progresses to penetration of the child's body first with fingers and later leading to the penis and/or other object. Penetration most often begins with the child's mouth, then her anus, and finally her vagina. At this stage, the perpetrator may ejaculate in or on the child's body. During this predictable progression from exposure to penetration, the abuser often talks with the child in a friendly and supportive way. Carolyn H. recalls, *My father would give me a bath and let me pick out a book for him to read to me. One night when I asked him to read a second book, he told me he would if I would do something nice for him. He pulled out his penis and asked me to pet it like I'd pet my kitten. He stopped then, read the second book, and seemed happy. During the next months, he'd ask me to do more and more sexually with him. He was always soft-spoken and let me know how special I was to him.*

If you were sexually assaulted in your family, you probably felt tremendously helpless. As a child, you occupied a dependent position in the family. You needed the protection and security from your parents or other caregivers. You were taught to expect this protection from your family, but they did not protect you. Like many sexually abused children, you may have learned to separate from your body to protect yourself from painful emotional and physical feelings. Many ACOA sexual assault survivors report that distancing during the abuse, "numbing out," felt safer than feeling that what they wanted, what they said, and what they did made no difference to their family abuser. This perceived sense of helplessness, of being unable to fix, stop, manage, or control the sexual abuse contributes to many ACOAs' self-hatred.

*Secrecy Phase.* Secrecy enables the abuser to continue the sexual abuse and makes the child become an active participant in the abuse. Following sexual behavior, the abuser typically imposes secrecy on the child with bribes or through pressure to keep "their secret." The abuser may use threats to maintain the child's silence. You may recall your abuser telling you, "If you tell, I'll be taken to jail." "If you tell, I'll hurt you." "If you tell, I'll take your puppy to the pound where they'll put her to sleep." "If you tell, I'll say it never happened and Mommy will think you're a bad girl for lying."

Guilt often keeps children in alcoholic families from telling. Our study participants said their abusers told them if they cooperated with the abuser, they would "spare" other siblings from assault, or they would protect their mother from injury, and/or they would keep the family together. Randi W. was four years old when her father started sexually abusing her. *My father severely beat my mother and put her in the hospital. During her hospitalization, he sexually abused me. He promised me if I let him do what he did, he'd allow my mother to come back home to us. He promised he wouldn't beat my mother again. He was drinking when he asked me to touch his penis and watch porno movies with him. When my mother came home, I thought I'd saved her life. I never told anyone.*

These guilt-inducing messages yield cooperation from children, but force them to sacrifice themselves emotionally, physically, and sexually to protect, take care of, and serve those they love. This type of compromising behavior fuels the development of codependent identities in which children come to believe they must protect and take care of anyone they care for. These guilt-inducing messages also create for the children a feeling of omnipotence, another codependent characteristic. They come to believe they possess an exaggerated degree of control and power over others' lives. Paradoxically, this omnipotence develops alongside the sense of powerlessness they develop when they're unable to prevent further abuse.

As the children keep their painful secrets, they feel trapped. They begin to see their options as "die" or "comply." If they resist, refuse, or tell, they believe, on an emotional or physical level, they will die. To comply becomes a safer option.

As the sexual abuse continues and no one intervenes, children recognize that their "protectors" are also their abusers. Their protectors betray rather than protect them. They may deal with this agonizing contradiction by accommodating to the reality and making the abusers "good." Although they spare themselves the disillusionment of viewing their assailants as bad, they begin to see themselves as the cause of the hurt, the one full of "badness."

Adult survivors may have survived their own sexual abuse with this type of psychological "splitting," or by perfectionistically "being good." Those of you who were sexually abused may have learned to take expert care of others, to excel at athletics, or get the highest grades in school. Sexual abuse survivors often overfunction in the family, preparing meals, doing the wash, watching younger sisters and brothers. On the outside, you may have appeared to have everything in control, to be quite normal. In fact, your internal world probably became filled with self-hatred, self-destructive behaviors, and an inability to trust or confide in others.

*Disclosure Phase.* Child sexual abuse may be revealed accidentally or purposefully. Sometimes an adult or another child witnesses the abuse, or discovers the child's pregnancy, physical injuries, or sexually transmitted disease. Other times, the child abuse is reported when the child begins to act sexually precocious and displays sexual knowledge inappropriate for her or his age.

When sexual abuse is accidently discovered and the abuser is unknown to the family, the child usually receives more support and protection than when the abuser is a relative or family friend. When the family knows the abuser, often conflicting loyalty issues rob the child of the support and help she or he needs.

When the disclosure is purposeful, it's usually the child who tells. For example, an abused girl most often tells during adolescence when her abuser becomes jealous and possessive and tries to rigidly control her normal social life. The telling often comes during a family fight with the girl blurting out her long-held secret. Because telling comes with her anger and rebellion, she's often not believed and she may even be punished for telling. When the secret is finally revealed, most alcoholic parents are unable to give the child the continuing support she needs to heal her sexual wounds.

*Suppression Phase.* After the child tells or someone accidently discovers the sexual abuse, the child's extended family then begins to talk her or him out of telling anyone else. Survivors may recall telling and being ignored, mocked, disbelieved, punished, and/or blamed. The cries for help break the alcoholic family's "no talk" rule and are rarely reinforced or affirmed. Anna W. was sexually molested by a friend of her stepmother and illustrates this family denial. *He used to watch me bathe. Once he tried to pull my legs apart. When I told my stepmother, she said she couldn't do anything about it and that it was my responsibility to stay away from him. She valued his friendship more than she valued me.*

Most often the family doesn't support the child because they want to protect the abuser, they feel guilty for not protecting their child more effectively, or they fear unwanted publicity or court or agency intervention. They may undermine the girl's credibility by calling her "crazy," "disturbed," "trouble-maker," or even a "pathological liar." When Deborah T.'s mother discovered her son was sexually abusing Deborah, she protected the boy and punished her daughter. *My brother and several of his friends would touch me in front of one another,* she says. *My brother had intercourse with me in front of his friends. Once he entered my anus. It was painful and I bled. I never told anyone about it, but one day my mother found us down by the railroad tracks. She said I was "playing doctor" and needed to be punished. She told me I was dirty, a trouble-maker, and that I'd shamed her. She beat me all the way home and locked me on a screened porch for a week.*

Not only are the parents unsupportive, but the community—the police, the courts, the child protective system, friends and other relatives—often also punish the child. Sometimes sensing her family's hostility and signals of disapproval, the child reverses her statement to the authorities and adamantly denies that the abuse occurred. Connie H. says her mother reported her father's molestation of her and her siblings in a fit of drunken rage. *Mom had known for a long time, but she'd never done anything about it,* she says. *After she called the police, they came and questioned us. It was so demeaning. I was telling a total stranger about my dad. The shame came back on me. They took my dad away that night. We were left with a drunk mother. Two days later, they came and took all of us to a group home for abused kids. Later at the police station, we all agreed not to tell the truth to the police. The police got really angry at us for our silence. I remember being in the court-room and hearing, "Lock him up, child molester." The court sent my dad to prison for several years. I began living with his parents who blamed me for telling. My grandparents said, "It's your fault that he's in prison. You shouldn't have told. It's very common, you know." My grandparents blamed the incest on my mother and her drinking.*

If you told and were betrayed by your parents or other adults who left you unprotected and/or punished you for telling, you learned that you were on your own. Early on, you discovered that you could not predictably rely on anyone to protect you. You had to figure out then how to keep yourself safe.

Often sexually abused children, especially children who've grown up in alcoholic families, simply don't tell. They know or believe they won't be taken seriously. They've been conditioned to "keep the secret" by the dynamics of the alcoholic family. The abused child is placed in a familiar double-bind: if she keeps the secret to herself, she's likely to feel fear, anxiety, and loneliness. If she tells, she may be blamed and punished.

In our study, more than 90 percent of the women who were sexually abused said their childhood sexual abuse made them feel frightened, anxious, guilty, ashamed, humiliated, and dirty and said they had no safe place to express those feelings. If you were sexually abused, you probably "contained" your feelings inside. You may have felt alienated from your peers. Since you had no "safe" way to directly tell others what was going on, you may have "told the secret" in creative nonverbal, disguised messages. Unfortunately, all too often those messages went unheard.

Hilary U., a forty-five-year-old ACOA, was sexually abused by her alcoholic father. *My mother was institutionalized in the state hospital for a brief period. During that time, my father held me captive with locked doors and pulled shades,* she says. *He'd tie me down and have intercourse with me. He'd make me suck him. He told me if I told anybody, he'd kill my cat Fluffy or he'd take away my bike. I loved my little bike. He also said he'd send me away like he did my mother. One day in fifth grade, I sucked the skin on my arms and made lots of hickies so someone would think I was physically abused and take me away. I intentionally wore a short-sleeved shirt to school. My teacher saw the marks and sent me to the school nurse. She said I'd put those marks on myself, told me to stop doing it, and sent me back to class. I felt depressed and disappointed. To me it was an obvious cry for help. After that I never tried to tell again, but I started carving my forearms with razor blades. No one ever asked me about the cuts. How could they have not noticed?*

The self-damaging behavior Hilary used is another example of abuse survivor revictimization. Often the sexually abused ACOA has been so conditioned to the victim role and her self-esteem so eroded that she continues the abuse process even after the initial victimizing has stopped. She becomes both victim and perpetrator. Self-damaging behavior may reflect self-directed rage and hate. It may represent attempts to feel, to gain control over her body, or to distract herself from emotional pain.

If you've been sexually abused, you can break the secrecy and self-destructive behavior surrounding your childhood abuse and get some much-needed support and relief. With help, you can learn to use limit-setting tools around self-damaging behavior and find self-affirming and self-respectful methods of relieving your anxiety and of expressing your long-held rage.

## The After-Effects of Childhood Sexual Abuse

How deeply the experience of childhood sexual abuse impacts us depends on a variety of factors:

- *Duration and Frequency of Abuse.* The longer and more frequently the sexual abuse occurs, the more serious the later emotional and sexual consequences.
- *Type of Sexual Activity.* Sexual abuse which involves penetration is the most damaging.
- *Use of Force and Aggression.* The greater the use of physical force or violence, the greater the subsequent consequences.
- *Age at Onset.* Some sexual abuse professionals believe the younger the child is when the sexual abuse occurs, the more damaging it is. Others believe that younger children are more emotionally insulated and that the most damage takes place in older abused children.
- *Age, Gender, and Relationship to the Abuser.* The closer the relationship of the victim and the abuser and the greater the span of years that separate them, the more harm.
- *Passive Submission or Willing Participation By the Child.* The child who willingly submits to the abuse and who actively participates in it suffers more negative effects.
- *Direct or Indirect Telling with No Support.* When a child tells and isn't helped, the consequences are more severe and long-lasting than when the child keeps the abuse secret.
- *Parental Reaction.* Children suffer further trauma by parents who react negatively to the truth by blaming the child or denying or minimizing the abuse.
- *Institutional Response.* Negative or ineffective responses by social service agencies to the child's sexual abuse serve to compound the negative effects of the abuse.

We know a great deal about the devastating effects of child sexual abuse from numerous researchers including Eliana Gil, Christine Courtois, Diana Russell, Ellen Bass and Laura Davis, and Wendy Maltz and Beverly Holman. Their excellent books, among others, are listed in the Resources section at the end of the book. Each contributes to our overall understanding of how childhood sexual abuse can affect our later sexual functioning.

Here is a summary of their findings, which clearly demonstrate the extent to which every aspect of the survivor's life has been affected by the abuse. These symptoms of sexual abuse may exist in varying combinations and varying degrees. Some survivors experience only a few of these symptoms, while others may experience many.

*Emotionally,* sexual abuse survivors may experience:

- Guilt.
- Fear.
- Self-blame.
- Powerlessness.
- Problems saying no to others in relationships.
- Inability to trust own perceptions and feelings.
- Inability to see the positive aspects of oneself.
- "Splitting" mind from body.
- Feeling invisible.
- Difficulty relying on others.
- Shame.
- Anxiety.
- Dissatisfaction.
- Helplessness.
- Difficulty nurturing self.
- Mistrust of others.
- Emotional shut down or "numbing."
- Perfectionism.
- Need to seek and maintain control at all costs.
- Problems giving and/or receiving affection.

*Physical* symptoms of child sexual abuse may include:

- Physical symptoms with no medical cause.
- Withdrawing or flinching from touch.
- Not being "present" in own body.
- High pain tolerance.
- Drug/alcohol addiction.
- Self-mutilation.
- Feeling betrayed and repulsed by own body.
- Sleep disturbances.
- Inability to rest or relax.
- Denial of bodily needs.
- Addiction to crises and conflict.
- Eating disorders.
- Suicidal thoughts/behavior.
- Self-imposed isolation.

*Relationship* problems might include:

- Idealizing, overvaluing, or devaluing relationships.
- Fear of commitment.
- Self-imposed isolation or excessive neediness.
- Triangulating others.
- Involvement in abusive, criticizing relationships.
- Humiliating interactions.
- Difficulty trusting self/others with intimacy.
- Toleration of abusive patterns.
- Emotional and physical caretaking of others at own expense.
- Giving or receiving abuse.

*Sexual* symptoms can include:

- Inability to differentiate/combine sex, affection, intimacy.
- Sexual orientation confusion
- Violent or sadomasochistic fantasies/behaviors.
- Unwanted pregnancy/abortion.

- Loss of sexual desire.
- Genital numbness.
- Sexualizing all relationships.
- Sexual guilt about sexual pleasure.
- Belief that one's only worth is sexual.
- Alternating between sexual abstinence and compulsive sexuality.
- Sexually transmitted disease.

- Sexual exploitation through prostitution.
- Pain during intercourse.
- Inability to orgasm alone or with partner.
- Intrusive flashbacks of forced sex.
- Deep hatred of body and its sexual responses.
- Sexual revictimization.

*Behavioral* effects of child sexual abuse may include:

- Hyperactive, hypervigilant behaviors.
- Compulsive spending, stealing, lying, gambling, or working.

- Impulsively entering/leaving relationships.
- Dangerous risk-taking behaviors.

*Loss of Self.* Perhaps most importantly, childhood sexual abuse results in a serious loss of children's sense of self. Alcoholic childhood caregivers disregard the developmental needs of children, are unable to provide empathy, cannot offer them a secure base, soothing care, or consistent attachment. Those who are supposed to provide protection for children, periodically neglect or abuse them. They neither encourage nor facilitate the expression of children's feelings or needs. For many children growing up in alcoholic families, inappropriate sexual touching becomes merged with love and hurt.

A child's true self cannot survive the disregard and lack of care from her parents or other caregivers. Out of necessity, the child makes her abusers "good" and herself "bad" and deserving of abuse. Her false self begins to dominate her interaction with herself and others. She develops a deep sense of her isolation, of her separation from her true self, of who she really is as a person. The unique "heart of the child" cannot develop. All of the emotional, physical, relationship, sexual, and behavioral problems discussed in this chapter are the result of the loss of self.

In a fundamental way, child sexual abuse undermines the sacredness of the child's individual being. When she is sexually invaded, she develops an inability to distinguish between her own psychic and physical energy and that of others. Without intervention, her confusion about where her self begins and ends predisposes her to a lifetime of codependency and revictimization. Healing the injured child within the adult and helping to discover, reclaim, and activate that child's true self is the challenge of all people who've survived sexual abuse.

### First Intercourse Abuse

Often the sexual abuse we face does not stop in childhood. In many cases, our first intercourse experience is abusive—we consent when we don't want sex, we have sex with partners we don't like, or we have been physically forced to have sex. Often our first intercourse experience has been with partners who were uncaring and disrespectful to us. Our first experience with intercourse may have included rape, impulsive sexual decision-making, drug and alcohol use, and unprotected sex.

Jennifer K. describes her first intercourse experience at sixteen. *Even though I loved petting,* she says, *I didn't want to go further. He said, "If you don't have intercourse with me, how will I know you haven't had intercourse with someone else?" He manipulated me. I did it to prove myself to him. But afterward he told all of the guys at school that he'd made it with me. When I heard he'd told other people, I wrote him a letter telling him that it was a terrible thing to share with others what had been private for us. Later I discovered that when he first told the guys about it, they didn't believe him. Then he showed them my letter and they believed it. We never had sex again.*

In order to get a clearer picture of ACOA first intercourse experiences, we asked the women in our study several questions: Who did you select for your partner for your first fully sexual exploration? How old were you and your partner? What sexual behaviors did you engage in? How sexually and emotionally satisfied were you? What happened to the relationship after your first intercourse?

The ACOAs in our study first experienced sexual intercourse from ages six to thirty-three. The average age for first intercourse was seventeen. First intercourse partners included family members, casual acquaintances, steady dates, and people they'd just met. More than thirty percent said their first intercourse was *involuntary*—they were physically forced, psychologically pressured, drugged, or under the influence of alcohol.

We often experience violations of trust and privacy in our first intercourse experience. Fran E. was fourteen when she engaged in intercourse with her boyfriend and was "caught" by his mother. *I had a real crush on this boy,* she says. *We were in his bedroom alone in his house. I made a spontaneous decision to have sex with him. We'd just begun to have intercourse when his mother burst into the room and screamed, "I knew you'd do this to my son." She pushed me out of the house while I was still putting on my clothes. She told him never to speak to me again and he never did.*

You, like many ACOAs we talked with, may have been "talked into" your first sexual experience with threats of rejection, guilt induction, promises of love or a relationship that never materialized. You may have submitted because you wanted to caretake or please another, even to the point of denying your own feelings and preferences.

Many of us choose first intercourse partners who are married or in committed relationships. Sometimes they are people we casually meet on vacations or people who our parents would never approve of. In such cases, there is a built-in safety valve lessening the chance that real intimacy can develop.

Some of us intentionally select a first intercourse partner with whom we have no emotional connection. One lesbian in our study picked a homosexual man so she could "try" intercourse. After meeting the man at a political rally, she told him she'd like to have intercourse with him to find out what it was like. She told him she didn't want to become friends and that she'd only have sex with him once. He agreed. Afterward she never saw him again.

More than half the women we talked with said they or their partner used drugs and/or alcohol before or during their first intercourse experience. Some of us use alcohol to reduce our inhibitions. Darla V. describes her first genital experience at thirteen. *We'd both been drinking. Although I was scared, I wanted to know what it was like and he was persistent. It hurt when he went inside me. I was unprotected. I told him it hurt too much and to stop, but he kept pushing his penis into me. I felt scared and bled. I felt nothing during it or afterwards, just afraid. Our relationship ended immediately.*

While alcohol can reduce our inhibitions around sex, we often make poor sexual judgements under its influence. Often sex while under the influence leaves us feeling regretful with a sense of personal loss. *My best friend's boyfriend was drunk,* says Sherri W. *I was staying there are had been drinking too. In the middle of the night he came into where I was sleeping. He pinned me down and I couldn't get away. He tried to penetrate me. Things were spinning, a blur. The next morning my girlfriend just said, "I think you should go." My friendship with her was over.*

## Rape

Rape is a painful and common experience for one in four women in our culture, but it's even more common among those of us raised in alcoholic families. Of the one hundred ACOAs we interviewed, thirty-nine said that they'd been raped. Their experiences included being sexually assaulted as children, as adolescents, and as adults in date and acquaintance rapes, stranger rapes, and marital rapes. Six women said they'd been raped three times by different assailants. More than half of all the rapes were committed by a friend or acquaintance.

Several women told us how they felt emotionally susceptible and vulnerable to "someone being nice to me" or to "someone showing an interest in me." When assailants use that approach, many ACOAs are unable to protect themselves, to establish and maintain their personal boundaries, or to ask for help from others. Often such rapes involve men with whom the ACOA has previously been sexual. Even though she says no, her assailant refuses to hear or respect her wishes and rapes her.

Paula C. is an ACOA rape victim who knew her attacker. *I'd been dating him, but I didn't even like him,* she says. *I told him I didn't want to have sex with him even though I'd had sex with him before. He went into a rage and grabbed a gun he had in the car. I was scared so I agreed to have sex with him. It was the most hateful feeling I've ever had. During the rape, I looked out the window and thought about being home. Afterward, he acted satisfied and content like he was happy, like nothing had happened. He wanted to take me out to breakfast.*

## Healing Sexual Assault Wounds

The more often our sexual boundaries have been violated in childhood, the greater difficulty we have differentiating ourselves from others and the more likely we'll become victims of continued sexual abuses. Blurred family boundaries in our alcoholic families cause us to feel stressed and confused when we try to identify our own limits and goals in relationships. Plagued with an inability to identify a solid sense of ourselves, we doubt our own rights in relationships. We feel unsure. That uncertainty and lack of self often leaves us even more vulnerable to sexual, physical, and emotional attack from others.

All of us who have suffered multiple sexual assaults can be helped by directly confronting our sexual abuse. Fortunately, recovery doesn't have to take place alone. Sexual assault healing can include participating in self-help groups, Twelve-Step programs, and individual and/or group therapy. The kind of treatment we need and how long the healing takes depends largely on how much damage the abuse caused us.

Sue Saperstein, M.A., a therapist in private practice in San Francisco, California, says that to achieve sexual healing we need to learn to respect the child within us as "innocent, powerless, and good." She says, "Acknowledging our good, innocent, powerless child begins to help us shift our perspective from shame, guilt, and self-blame."

Saperstein says that it's the child in us who was hurt. It is the adult who remembers. We must begin to separate from identifying with our abusive parents and gradually develop a nurturing internal adult/child relationship. In other words, we must learn to be our own parent. "This allows our self-hate," Saperstein says, "to become self-love and allows us to nurture our bodies. It allows us to experience being loved. Sexuality then becomes a *choice* of being touched. Arousal becomes an experience of *choice*, rather than a response to aggression or internal betrayal. Arousal becomes centered in our own place of control rather than outside ourselves. Sexuality, arousal, and choice then become empowering for us."

In her comprehensive book, *Healing the Incest Wound: Adult Survivors in Therapy*, Christine Courtois suggests treatment goals for healing. Although these goals were originally intended for incest survivors, we've adapted them to apply to all forms of sexual abuse. We've also added treatment goals recommended by Sexual Abuse Experts Eliana Gil, Ellen Bass, and Laura Davis. While some of the goals may not appear to relate directly to sexual healing, each of them can positively affect the development and maintenance of healthy, sexual-affectional relationships. For those of you abused sexually as children, sexual abuse therapy can:

1. Assist you to commit to the treatment process by offering you hope and by encouraging you to envision a picture in which your actions can lead to realistic life changes.
2. Help you develop a supportive, therapeutic relationship with your therapist.
3. Guide you in making contact with the vulnerable child within.
4. Help you acknowledge and believe your sexual abuse memories and experience(s).
5. Challenge minimizing and denial of past and present abusive behaviors.
6. Assist you in disclosing the sexual abuse in therapy while helping you to avoid running away from therapy or punishing yourself.
7. Begin the process of breaking your isolation and low self-esteem.
8. Help you recognize, label, and begin to express the full range of your feelings.
9. Confront your tendency to blame yourself and/or protect your abuser.

10. Assist you in transferring responsibility for the abuse from your-self to the abuser and to other non-protecting family members.

11. Guide you in identifying your coping and survival efforts and help you view those coping skills and behaviors with self-empathy.

12. Assist you in learning to trust, confide in, feel safe, and reach out to others for assistance by forming healthy interactions and broadening your base of support.

13. Help you see the rewards of relationships in which you are really seen, heard, believed, understood, and validated.

14. Allow you to redefine your sexual abuse history as an "influence" rather than an "obstacle."

15. Support your grieving process with compassion. This process involves expressing your feelings of loss, anger, and sadness.

16. Challenge the internalized negative beliefs about yourself and begin to replace them with more positive, less distorted beliefs about yourself and what you deserve and are entitled to want for yourself.

17. Provide you with information about alcoholic family system rules, roles, and dynamics and help you identify generational interactional patterns, especially shame, within your family.

18. Help you examine the role that chemical addiction, eating disorders, codependency and other compulsive behaviors may play in your childhood family and in your own life and find appropriate treatment options.

19. Increase your ability to make changes in your life based on what you want and feel, to learn new roles and methods of relating to others, and to accept and nurture your body and your sexuality.

20. Encourage the development and expression of your spirituality and of your inherent creativity.

21. Teach you basic life skills in parenting, communication, decision-making, conflict resolution, boundary-setting, and initiating and maintaining friendships and intimate relationships.

These goals take time, support, and patience to achieve. You can work on them in steps and stages at your own pace. Changes in one area of your life can indicate and support changes in other areas. The journey, while long, results in the development of a life to which you are entitled.

# CHAPTER 6

# If I'm in Control, I'm Safe

*I'd meet men in bars. We'd dance, talk, then go to their place or a motel and have sex. It wasn't just the sex—I was aching to be loved. I'd rarely have sex with the same person more than once, so there were lots of one-night stands. Although I'd have sex with these men, they didn't fulfill my need to be loved. I pursued men who didn't desire me. If anyone wanted to continue having sex, I'd say no and cut it off. I wanted someone to be strong, to take care of me. Although I was very sexually active, I never had an orgasm with any of them. I had to be the best sex partner they ever had—then they'd love me and want to be with me. The men always went back to their homes sexually satisfied, but I'd be left feeling empty and cold toward them. I felt loved, secure, and important before the man's orgasm, but afterward it would be all downhill. I'd feel hurt, angry. They'd reject me by failing to ask for my phone number. So I'd reject them. I'd think, who cares about this person? I still felt an overwhelming need, a horrible loneliness, an aching to be loved. That intense need sent me back out to the bars in search again and again.—Peggy R.*

All of the one hundred ACOAs we interviewed indicated a strong need to be in control of their sexuality. Like them, you too may try to put some stability into your life by controlling your sexual fantasies, your pattern of masturbation, and your own and your partner's sexual feelings and behaviors. You may also control who you select for a sex partner, what sexual behaviors you'll permit or refuse, where sex takes place, and whether or not to allow yourself to orgasm in the presence of your partner.

These carefully orchestrated sexual decisions may give you a sense of personal safety and protection and keep you from feeling emotions that are overwhelming. Most of us *unconsciously* engage in these protective behaviors. Our need for control, which developed in childhood, runs so deeply that our controlling behaviors become automatic. Without recovery, we cannot recognize that these repetitive behaviors have become compulsive and we don't understand why we use them. We continue to try to control because it seems to be what works best for us, even though we aren't sure why.

Unfortunately, our attempts to "manage" sexuality give us only an *illusion* of control. Instead of finding the emotional and sexual intimacy and fulfillment we seek, many of us find ourselves repeatedly disappointed by our carefully controlled intimate lives. Gayle W., a twenty-seven-year-old executive, describes her use of sexual control: *I was always in control. I'd plan it. I'd go into a bar by myself and pick up a guy. I wouldn't allow oral sex. I only had sex with people I didn't care about. I'd fall in love with guys I couldn't have—guys who were married or ones I just couldn't attract. With the hundreds of men I've had sex with, I've never orgasmed. But I was always in charge.*

## Addictive Control

Addictive and compulsive behaviors—behaviors that are uncontrollable—are common among ACOAs. All of these behaviors are attempts to control the world, to somehow protect us from hurt and pain. John and Linda Friel, coauthors of *Adult Children: The Secrets of Dysfunctional Families,* list the following as common ACOA compulsive activities:

| | |
|---|---|
| · Prescription drugs. | · Illegal drugs. |
| · Non-prescription drugs. | · Television. |
| · Food. | · Reading. |
| · Sex. | · Nicotine. |
| · Speed/dangerous activities. | · Relationships. |
| · Caffeine. | · Work. |
| · Power. | · Stress. |
| · Spending money. | · Gambling. |
| · Sleep. | · Shopping. |
| · Alcohol. | |

By growing up in an alcoholic family, you're at risk for developing one or more of these compulsions. Often eliminating one compulsion such as alcohol soon leads to developing another compulsion. If, for example, you give up drugs or alcohol, you may replace your addiction with overwork, exercise, compulsive over- or undereating, or compulsive sex. It's rare to find ACOAs with only a single compulsion. What accounts for this compulsive behavior? *Compulsions are symptoms of dis-*

*comfort with self.* Underneath the surface of any compulsive behavior, we can find a deeper, underlying dependency problem that has its origin in our childhood alcoholic families. The compulsive behaviors protect us—at least temporarily—from having to confront our underlying unhealthy dependencies.

As infants, we are born totally dependent on our parents for survival. If our biological and safety needs are not met by others, we cannot thrive. Later in childhood and adolescence, our need for care and nurturance is more subtle, but still exists. When such early needs are ignored in dysfunctional alcoholic families, we become adults with a collection of unmet needs.

In functional families, the child receives healthy support for developing into her own person, for being able to maintain a clear and separate identity from others, and for recognizing when she needs help and support from others. Through this process, we learn to become "interdependent"—both dependent and independent—with others.

Growing up in alcoholic families, most of us were not encouraged to achieve a healthy balance between self and needing others. We grew up believing the only way to get our emotional and sexual needs met is to be entirely self-sufficient. We learn to rarely rely on others and we avoid trusting that intimate others will give us support and guidance. We believe we must solve our own painful problems alone and so we share little of ourselves with others. As a result, many of us feel a deep sense of isolation and loneliness. We become susceptible to unhealthy relationships, which give us an *illusion* of "belonging" in the world. As our sense of alienation grows, our dependence on these unhealthy relationships can grow into chronic addictions. Clearly, our capacity to be sexually intimate with another depends on our ability to develop interdependence with others.

According to John and Linda Friel, as we grow up in alcoholic families, we often develop a "paradoxical dependency." While we appear independent and self-reliant, we are filled with insecurities and self-doubt. This outer illusion and inner conflict pave the way for coping with normal stress with addictive behaviors. The addiction or unhealthy dependency on jobs, persons, or substances acts to mask our inability to be interdependent with others and conceals our painful unmet dependency needs from childhood.

Compulsive behaviors or addictions can temporarily reduce anxiety and stress. For a while, addictions bring us feelings of power and well-being while allowing us to avoid identifying and expressing our true feelings. Nina R. used her addictive behavior in relationships to feel powerful. *I'd date for a month or so, have sex with the man, and then he'd dump me. Then I realized I could dump them. The realization gave me a wonderful feeling of power. We'd have sex and I'd dump them with no explanation or apology.*

Compulsions allow us to avoid life's problems, but perhaps even more importantly, they allow us to *avoid intimacy with ourselves and others.* To be intimate, you need to trust, to be open, and to feel safe and accepted. Stephanie Covington, author of *Leaving the Enchanted Forest*, says that truly intimate relationships include:

- Sharing decisions.
- Emotional self-disclosure.
- A balance of power.
- Mutuality in which both people decide they want to be together.
- Reciprocal empathy in which each partner willingly enters the other's world and attempts to understand it from their perspective.

Unfortunately, such qualities aren't a part of alcoholic families. It makes sense that since we didn't see intimacy between our parents and were not able to develop intimacy skills, that we may try to avoid situations or people that expect or want to us to be intimate.

Jana S. uses a series of relationships to avoid intimacy. *I have a sexual restlessness. I can't seem to settle down. I've been in a series of relationships, each lasting less than a year. I go from relationship to relationship. I never leave a relationship until I'm in the midst of a new affair.*

Like many of us, Jana leaves relationships *before* any serious intimacy can develop. Once the "high" that accompanies her compulsive sexual behavior in a new relationship wears off, she feels vulnerable to feelings of guilt, loneliness, conflict, and low self-esteem. Unable to bear these feelings, she immediately becomes involved with another lover, which enables her to avoid developing any self-intimacy.

Geri H., a fifty-four-year-old housewife uses secretive extra-marital affairs to avoid intimacy. *I've been married nineteen years. After the first eight, I started seeking outside friendships with men because I felt bored and lonely in my marriage. I began having sex with my men friends in order to maintain their friendship. Most of my affairs are brief and my husband doesn't know anything about them. I get mad at myself when a new affair starts and promise myself it will be the last one. The truth is that these affairs are happening with increasing frequency.*

Although Geri attempts to control feeling bored and lonely in her marriage with her secretive affairs, she never addresses the roots of conflict and dissatisfaction within her marriage. Her dishonesty keeps her from developing any intimacy with her husband and leaves her feeling badly about herself. Becoming more honest about what she is feeling in her relationship is the first step toward giving up her need to control through multiple affairs.

### Codependency and Compulsivity

Psychiatrist Timmen Cermak, author of *A Time to Heal,* has devoted many years examining the alcoholic family system and the codependency it produces in children raised in them. He and others have found that ACOA codependents engage in a wide variety of compulsive behaviors, all which serve to add "drama" and "excitement" to their lives. Codependents often say they feel more fully energized and more intensely alive when they engage in their compulsive behavior. Cermak notes that compulsive behaviors like the chronic sexual affairs which Nina, Jana, and Geri engage in require large amounts of time and energy which effectively keep them away from deep, disturbing feelings about their own lives. Sexual compulsions, like other compulsive behaviors, keep us from acknowledging and feeling the pain inside ourselves.

ACOA research participant Vivian S.'s efforts to protect herself from pain lead to her sexual compulsivity. *With the fifty men I've had sex with — most of them one-night stands — I felt like I had to have them. I always spent hours getting ready — deciding what to wear and how to fix my hair and make-up so I'd attract a lot of attention. I'd go into bars, see some man, and say to myself, "I have to have that man." I'd do whatever I needed to do to leave with him and have sex. It was an ego thing that I had to have sex with him right away. The thought of going home without someone felt devastating. I had to make them pay attention to me. I'd take anybody. Once I'd get the man alone, I'd always make him shower, then I'd rub his body with lotion, give him oral sex, and then have intercourse."*

### Sexual Compulsions

As we mentioned in an earlier chapter, Therapists Merle Fossum and Marilyn Mason say that alcoholic families are "shame-based" systems that inhibit the development of authentic intimate relationships, promote secret-keeping, instill shame in family members, and produce only a vague sense of personal boundaries among members. In their work with ACOAs, they've found that members of alcoholic families frequently

compulsively abuse themselves and/or abuse others. They list the following sexual compulsions common among shame-based families:

- Incest.
- Voyeurism.
- Exhibitionism.
- Casual sexual encounters with strangers.
- Making obscene phone calls.

- Frequent use of prostitutes.
- Rape.
- Compulsive masturbation.
- Extramarital affairs.
- Compulsive use of pornography.
- Compulsive intercourse.

Many of us may participate in sexual addiction, sexual behaviors
which leave us feeling badly about ourselves, fearful of detection by loved
ones, and unable to stop the behavior through our willpower alone.
Understanding more about how these addictions manifest can help us
break their hold on us.

**Stages of Sexual Addiction.** Patrick Carnes, author of *Out of the Shadows:
Understanding Sexual Addiction*, describes four stages of sexual addiction:
*preoccupation, ritualization, compulsive sexual behavior,* and *despair*. In the
preoccupation stage, persons become obsessed with the search for exciting sexual stimulation. Thoughts of sex rarely leave their minds. In Vivian's
case, she goes relentlessly bar to bar searching for sexual partners.

During ritualization, the second step, the sexual addict performs special routines which lead to sexual behavior such as Vivian's elaborate
application of make-up and provocative clothing before going into bars.
Vivian also has strict rules about what sexual behaviors she'll allow and
in what order they'll occur. Ritualization serves to intensify the arousal
and excitement.

The third stage, compulsive sexual behavior, involves participating in
the sexual act. ACOA Wendy F. says *Out of the several hundred sex partners
I've had, I've experienced emotional relationships with only seven of them. I was
in love with only one. It was hard on me to tell him I loved him. Both of us were
drinking, smoking pot, and freebasing cocaine together. It felt horrible when
I realized I was in love with him. I was completely terrified. I was especially
afraid to be around him when I was sober. I could hardly look him in the face
when I wasn't on drugs. It felt too intimate. The only way I could talk to him and
express myself was with anger. When our sex became less frequent, I freaked out.
I thought he was pulling away so I started having sex with other men. I played
games with him, pretending I didn't need him. I never wanted him to know the
clinging need I felt for him.*

All of this preparation and finally engaging in sex leads the sexual
addict to the final stage, despair. After sex the addict feels powerless,
hopeless, worthless. The addict feels she or he has failed. She or he has

been unable to live up to previous resolutions to stop sexually compulsive behavior. Again, the sex didn't provide her or him with the desired love and fulfillment. This failure plunges the addict's already low self-esteem even lower. Peggy, whose story introduced this chapter and whose words inspired the title for this book, speaks eloquently about her feelings after the men she had sex with left: "I still felt an overwhelming need, a horrible loneliness, an aching to be loved." In an effort to relieve these negative feelings, she again escapes into compulsive sex.

Sexual addiction protects us from experiencing deep feelings of pain, fear, self-doubt, and grief. At times we may allow in some of the despair and sadness we feel, but as long as we continue to participate in addictive behavior, we avoid feeling the deeper and more intense pain we carry inside. Commenting on this process, Paul Curtin, author of *Tumbleweeds*, says that ACOAs prefer to feel the dull, chronic pain of ignored, ongoing problems than face the short-term, intense pain of addressing and resolving those issues. The dull, chronic pain, unfortunately, brings no resolution of the deeper, often buried sense of loss and inadequacy.

The sexual addict sees sex partners as conquests. Most often, sex is shrouded in secrecy. ACOA Katie D. describes her sexual addiction: *My first year out of high school I started using birth control and fucked a lot of men. I considered the men I met in bars potential conquests. I was the initiator. If I wanted somebody, I made sure I got him. I'd have sex with him, then get rid of him. I'd never stay over night.*

JoAnn Loulan, author of *Lesbian Sex*, says among the lesbian couples she sees, sexual compulsivity often surfaces during extremely stressful periods and prevents any working-through of the relationship's stresses. Much like drugs and alcohol, sex offers a comforting, relaxing retreat. One common sexually addictive pattern she sees among long-term couples involves one partner having extra-relationship affairs while blaming the other for all the problems within the relationship. The sexual addict shifts the blame for her infidelity to her partner. She rationalizes that she's having an affair because her primary lover "neglected" her. This enables her to minimize the responsibility for her sexual addiction, not unlike alcoholics blaming others for their drinking.

Loulan compares the "sexual coaddict" to codependents in alcoholic relationships. The sexual coaddict, she says, focuses all of her attention and emotional and physical energy on trying to get the sexual addict's behavior "under control." She excuses, minimizes, and "manages" the sexual behavior of her addicted partner and portrays herself as the martyr in the relationship.

## Common Sexual Compulsivities

In our research, more than 60 percent of the ACOAs said they'd engaged in compulsive sexuality. Two out of three of the women we interviewed said they'd engaged in sexual behaviors with "casual acquaintances" or with people "they'd just met." They said they'd experienced from one to one thousand male sex partners. The median number of partners was eleven. More than one-third of them had intercourse with more than twenty men. Ten percent reported more than one hundred sex partners.

We asked, "How many women have you experienced genital contact with?" Their answers ranged from one to one hundred with the median being six. Five percent of the women reported being sexual with twenty or more female partners. One percent said they'd had sex with one hundred partners.

Several women who said they were heterosexual reported having experienced genital sex with female partners just as several women who identified themselves as homosexual reported having experienced intercourse with men.

Although the numbers of female and male sexual partners in our ACOA study were higher than the norm, such figures need to be interpreted with caution. Previous research studies from which comparative figures are drawn use the general public as a sample. We don't know the number of ACOAs in these surveys. Norms for random samples of ACOAs have yet to be established.

*Compulsive Fantasies.* One common way we express our sexual compulsivity and sexual control is through our sexual fantasies. Some of us need to be in sexual control in order to orgasm. Many of us compulsively fantasize about being sexually "out of control." Rita D. says her compulsive fantasies simultaneously make her feel betrayed and sexually stimulated. *I regularly fantasize about things that I later feel guilty about. I'm always the victim in my fantasies. In one fantasy, I see my husband having sex with another woman. Sometimes they're engaging in oral sex. The other woman is aware I'm watching them. I feel betrayed and turned on at the same time.*

Some of us compulsively fantasize about force and violence. *A recurring fantasy for me is being raped,* says ACOA Patti T. *The rape involves a man kidnapping me or breaking into my home. He forcefully strips off my clothes and makes me engage in oral sex. Although he threatens violence, he never hurts me. At the end of the fantasy, I submit to anal intercourse. When the fantasy involves several men, I'm simultaneously raped vaginally and anally. I've always had to* use this rape fantasy in order to orgasm with my husband during intercourse. Once I told him about it because I felt so troubled and guilty. He said he thought the fantasy was exciting and wanted to try it. I couldn't believe that he missed my intense feelings of shame and confusion about the fantasy.

Physical, emotional, and sexual abuse can be recurring fantasy themes. My fantasies are of being attacked by several men who hate me, but who have to have sex, says Nanci B. They have to get off. They hold me down and I hate them touching me. There is abusive oral sex or intercourse. For me to orgasm, I have to imagine extreme force and degradation. I don't want this fantasy, but I've tried to come without it and I can't.

Sexuality research has largely neglected the study of female fantasies in favor of male fantasies and as a result we still have much to learn about the purpose, content, and meaning of women's fantasies. It's important to understand why some of us fantasize about our own or other's abuse. Ellen Bass and Laura Davis, coauthors of The Courage to Heal: A Guide for Women Survivors of Child Sexual Abuse, say that women who can only become sexually aroused or orgasm when their fantasies involve abuse, powerlessness, and being out of control are often survivors of sexual abuse.

Such fantasies often have their basis in real life experiences. The circumstances under which we first experienced sexual touching affects our sexual fantasies. What occured during sexual abuse and the fears, anxiety, and confusion we felt sometimes become linked with our sexual arousal as adults. For some of us, our abusive sexual histories cause us to pair pleasure with pain and love with fear and/or humiliation. In fantasies, we often replay old feelings of shame, danger, secrecy, and the forbidden.

Our fantasies often contribute to guilt. Gail H. says her lesbian fantasies have made her feel guilty for years. From about ten years old, I've always fantasized about having sex with women, she says. My husband doesn't know. Sometimes I don't think it's fair to him that I can only have an orgasm by fantasizing about sex with a woman. I think I deserve to be punished for my fantasy. Often we fight after having sex. I wonder if my fantasy has anything to do with that?

It's important to keep in mind that we use fantasies to become sexually aroused. We choose specific fantasies and use them over and over because they help us become aroused and can often hasten our orgasms. Fantasies which leave you feeling frightened, humiliated, or ashamed are worth examining more closely. Fantasies which create such feelings can interfere with your self-worth and interrupt your ability to orgasm.

Some of us never have sexual fantasies. One reason may be that we live in a culture which does not encourage or support women's sexual fantasies. You may intentionally avoid sexual fantasies because you fear the message that might emerge from them. Like dreams, our fantasies are rich sources of information about our inner lives and deserve to be developed and explored.

*Compulsive Masturbation.* Compulsive masturbation is another way we try to control our sexuality. Ninety-one percent of our study participants said they'd masturbated to the point of orgasm at least once in their lives. Most said they masturbate once every five or six days. Nearly 80 percent reported they always or almost always orgasm with masturbation. Lonnie D. expresses how a number of ACOAs feel about masturbation. *I don't enjoy casual sex,* she says. *It's more trouble than it's worth. I have a hard time with relationships and masturbation is easier. I've done without partner sex for more than four years. When I think about it, masturbation isn't an adequate sex life, but it alleviates some needs. It can't take care of the whole person.*

Many of us enjoy masturbation, as much as or more than, sex with our partners. Twenty percent of the women we interviewed said they found masturbation as physiologically and psychologically satisfying as partner sex. One out of three said she "sometimes" or "always" preferred masturbation to partner sex. Cora W. is one of these. *I've never been married and I began masturbating at nineteen. For the last ten years, I've masturbated six to ten times a week. But I feel ashamed and guilty every time. Once when my stepmother was drunk she found me touching myself. She told me that masturbation is dirty. I use masturbation as a tension reliever. It's easier to please myself than to risk a partner leaving me.*

A few of us become preoccupied and obsessed with masturbation. When masturbation becomes compulsive, like any other addiction, it takes on its own urgency. Helen G. traded her addiction to alcohol for an addiction to masturbation. *I rely on masturbation to help me through the day the same way that booze used to,* she admits. *I masturbate around the same stress situations that I used to drink over. I'm always in search of a safe place to get off. I might do it in a store restroom while shopping, in my office at work, in the shower at the gym, or even in my car while driving. Finding a place to get off outside my home takes on a power of its own. I worry excessively about getting caught. Masturbation removes me from contact with others. Sometimes I wonder, would a hug from a friend or lover meet my needs better?*

*Performance.* For many of us, it's important to perform well sexually for our partners, even to the exclusion of our own pleasure. Many women who engage in compulsive partner sex speak with pride about focusing almost exclusively on pleasing their sexual partners. ACOA Kit A. says,

*With the men I decided to go home with, I'd allow no fondling, kissing, or touching, just really fast intercourse. I'd give them oral sex and then have intercourse. I wouldn't let them have oral sex with me. With nine out of ten men, I wouldn't orgasm. I'd try, but it wouldn't happen. It was more important to me that I satisfied them. My performance was important to me. There was no limit to what I'd do to please them. But receiving sexually was hard for me. I didn't want them to touch me.*

**Controlling Orgasms.** One of the most frequent ways we use to stay in sexual control and feel safe is to control our orgasms. Some ACOAs intentionally plan ways to avoid experiencing orgasm with their partners. For many, experiencing orgasm with a partner means surrendering power, feeling exposed and vulnerable, and having to trust and depend on another—feelings too overwhelming and frightening to allow. Several ACOAs told us that sexual "success" was *not* having an orgasm, while sexual "failure" was accidently allowing an orgasm to happen. Meredith G. says, *I've had more than seventy-five partners, but I've never in my life had orgasm through oral sex or intercourse. I need to control men and I can do that with sex. To have an orgasm with them would feel like I was giving my power to them. It would feel too vulnerable. So I fake orgasm regularly.*

ACOA Monica E. says she doesn't have orgasms with her partner either. *I don't want to be hurt. I don't want to depend on the other person too much. Having orgasms means I'm depending on someone other than me to please me. I don't trust people who want to please me. My mother and father were never there for me. Why should anyone else be?*

Janice R. controlled the sexuality in her marriage by withholding her sexual responsiveness. *In sexual situations, I'm in utter control. I give but I don't receive. In my first marriage, it got to the point where he could have been fucking a corpse. I never said "Don't touch me."*

Many of us fake orgasms regularly with our partners. Six out of ten ACOAs we interviewed said they periodically pretend to have orgasms with their partners. Anita W. says she's been faking orgasms with her husband for thirteen years. *I've gotten myself into a terrible trap. All of these years, I've faked orgasms because I wanted to please him. If I told him I'd faked it all this time, he'd look so hurt.*

**Love or Sex, Never Both.** Some of us actively seek orgasms, but we have difficulty "relaxing into it." Sometimes it seems, the more deeply we care for our partners, the less able we are to experience orgasm with him or her. Therapists Wendy Maltz and Beverly Holman, coauthors of *Incest and Sexuality,* found that incest survivors often have problems attaining orgasm with partners they love. These same women, they say, often easily reach orgasm with strangers. ACOA and incest survivor Veronica F.

says, *I've purposely stayed out of relationships. It's rare for me to last longer than three months with someone. As soon as I notice the other person wants more from me, especially more of my feelings, I end the relationship. Sex is fine, but I don't want a relationship.*

"Splitting" in which we're either sexual or affectionate, but not both, is a common adaptation for many of us who have experienced some type of abuse or serious neglect in childhood. Unable to combine sex with affection because it stirs painful incest memories, we may opt for one or the other. In our study, the women said they either had nonsexual relationships with men or women they genuinely valued or loved or engaged in frequent sex with strangers, which allowed them to avoid partner intimacy.

Cynthia Cooley, therapist and professor at California Family Study Center says she frequently sees such splitting among her ACOA clients. "ACOAs control emotionally," she says. "If they have emotional closeness, they can't have sexual closeness and vice versa. It becomes too overwhelming. It's the whole issue of having a sense of self. They worry, 'if I let you in too much, I'm going to get in touch with feelings that terrify me. So I need to control you and keep you at a distance.' It might mean that she needs to be in charge sexually or she needs her partner to control her sexually."

Another solution for those of us unable to combine sex and emotional closeness is to completely avoid sex or affection. This choice requires extreme control over yourself and over your partner. If you've chosen this option, you probably have a well-developed rationale for your decision. Laura B. says, *I've been married for thirty-one years. I don't ever masturbate. I have no need or desire for it. I have intercourse two or three times a year, if that. I'm involved with parenting, caretaking, and holding down my job. I've been living in the fast lane for years and sex doesn't occupy much of my consideration.*

Francis A., who's also married, says, *I withhold sex from my husband. I feel that if I get too close to him or allow him to get too close to me, I'll get hurt. He'll hurt me by emotionally withdrawing from me. It's safer and more fulfilling for me to simply work on the garden, the house, and on investment projects. I can't remember the last time we had sex. We've slept in separate rooms for the past four years. I don't even miss sex anymore.*

Francis may unconsciously believe that if she resumes sex with her partner she'll lose the life she's developed for herself in the absence of sex. Like many ACOAs, she believes that autonomy and intimacy cannot coexist, that they are mutually exclusive. But as we said in chapter 4, it is possible for mutually motivated couples to work on maintaining both autonomy and intimacy in their relationships. To settle for one or the other exclusively is to suffer a serious loss.

## Sexual Rules

One of our most interesting findings in interviewing ACOAs was the variety of "rules" many of us have developed around sex in order to maintain sexual control. We apparently establish these rules to protect ourselves from feelings of powerlessness and vulnerability. Rules can provide us with a sense of power and help us create the *illusion* of sexual boundaries. Rules for ACOAs around compulsive sex vary widely. What is a rule for one ACOA may not be a rule for you. Some ACOAs create a few general rules while others create many elaborate ones. The most common sexual rules include:

1. *Experience orgasm with strangers, but never with a lover.* "Having sex with strangers was better than sex with someone I knew. I could experience orgasm with strangers. After I had sex with someone, I'd never want to see them again."
2. *Seek emotional closeness and involvement through compulsive sexuality.* "I'd usually have sex on the first or second date. Most of the sex was lousy. I rarely had an orgasm. Most of my dates were more focused on their own satisfaction than on pleasing me sexually. I really wanted to be nurtured and held by them. I wanted to feel desired and loved by them. But in reality, I felt like an unpaid whore."
3. *Never seek emotional involvement through compulsive sex: seek only orgasmic release.* "Most of the guys I went with I knew would be only short-term. I'd agree to have sex with them because orgasms reduced a lot of my tension and I knew things wouldn't develop into a serious relationship."
4. *Give oral sex to partners and refuse oral sex for self.* "I'd give the man oral sex, but I'd never let him give it to me. It seemed too personal."
5. *Never give oral sex and never receive it.* "I'd perform virtually every other sexual behavior without question, but I'd never give oral sex to anyone. I'd either distract them or tell them, 'I don't know you well enough.'"
6. *Never bring a one-night stand into own living space. Only go to his or her place, to motels, or to a car.* "Usually we'd go to the car and be

sexual. Sometimes I'd go to a motel, but I'd never let them come to my house. I wouldn't have known how to get rid of them."

7. *Always bring partner to own apartment or home.* "I never go to his place or to motels. In my own territory, I feel I'm safer and have more control."

8. *Group sex or three-ways are acceptable when high on drugs or alcohol, but never when sober.* Our research clearly demonstrated a connection between compulsive sexual behavior and the addictive use of alcohol and other drugs. ACOAs' use of mood- and mind-altering drugs manifests in sexual compulsivity in a variety of ways. Some ACOAs engage in compulsive sexual behaviors to get money for their drug addiction. In our study, eleven out of the seventeen who engaged in prostitution said they'd worked as prostitutes primarily to support their drug addiction.

Others use drugs to bribe or entice potential compulsive sex partners. One study participant said, *I slept with men I met through friends, in bars, and at peace marches and rallies. I'd spot the intellectual type and act seductively because he'd be a challenge for me. I'd make eye contact, use body language. I'd entice him with good pot.*

Often a woman's sex partner is addicted to a drug and insists on performing certain sexual acts under the influence, never discussing it afterward.

After being clean and sober for several months, some ACOAs suddenly begin to have affairs, switching one compulsion for another. *I've used compulsive affairs and sex as another addiction to keep me away from myself.* Another woman told us, *When I first got sober, I had a lot of sex. Sex replaced the drugs and alcohol. It kept my mind off me and my feelings.*

## Giving Up Compulsive Control

Stephanie Brown, author of *Treating Adult Children of Alcoholics*, says that of all the defenses available to us we most frequently use control in our intimate relationships. However, maintaining control prevents sexual spontaneity. As long as we need to control, we can never have true negotiation or interdependence in our sexual relationships. When we control compulsively, we can rarely share our true selves and may often feel desperately lonely.

Relinquishing the *illusion* of sexual control isn't easy. Sexual recovery requires a *gradual* letting go of control. Here are a few suggestions to help you begin the process of giving up sexual control in your relationships:

- Talk with your partner about the fears you have about relinquishing sexual control.
- Begin to allow others to give to you sexually.
- Begin to let go of the belief that you must be sexually self-sufficient at all times. Controlling everything may allow you to cover up many sexual insecurities, but it creates distance between you and your partner.
- Avoid sexual perfectionism and begin to form more realistic sexual expectations for yourself and your lover.
- Be willing to make some mistakes by risking more of yourself with your lover. Admit when you make mistakes.
- Don't try to solve your partner's sexual problems. Give your partner the chance to figure out what's happening for him or her and let him or her approach you for assistance if it is wanted.
- Give up trying to win your partner's constant approval. Be who you are.
- Introduce fun, laughter, and playfulness into your sexual interactions.
- Read *Hope and Recovery: A Twelve Step Guide for Healing from Compulsive Sexual Behavior.* Written by members of the Twelve-Step organization, Sex Addicts Anonymous (SAA), this book can offer direction and encouragement for those of you who suffer from sexual compulsiveness.

It's not enough to focus on healing the sexual control you exert in your relationship. It's important for you to develop an awareness about how your sexual control affects your sense of self. Therapist Sue Saperstein describes a process she uses to assist a woman in developing this kind of awareness: "I help her track how she feels when she thinks about going out to find a partner, when she meets a partner, when her partner touches her, during sex, and afterward. I help her track the whole experience, then I ask her to use her *own observations* to see whether the experience felt hurtful, whether she can see any self-abuse in it. How was it hurtful? I begin to help her identify what she does that helps and hurts her— what feels good, what feels bad, what feels hurtful. I also help her identify her true needs and how she can better meet those needs. This begins to seed ideas about her self-abuse and about self-nurturance."

# CHAPTER 7

# I Have Too Many Tears to Cry

*My mother and father were divorced when I was two. I lived with my maternal grandmother, who became my mainstay. I'd always end up returning to her. At different times, I lived with my grandmother, my mother, my mother and her boyfriend, and my father and my stepmother. In twelve years, I attended twenty-four schools. My caregivers changed twenty-eight times. Now I have a hard time pinning down time. If I can remember a teacher's face, I can track back to who I was living with at the time. They moved me around a lot because my mom was dating lots of different men. I did terribly in school because I was always the new girl. I never knew when I'd be leaving next. I gave up forming friendships.*

*When I was three, my mom married an alcoholic bartender who constantly beat her up. When I was twelve my stepfather was shot and killed in a bar. A few years later, my mother started living with another alcoholic.*

*My real father is still alive and drinking. He married a woman who hated me because I look just like my mother. She always accused my dad of still loving my mother. My stepmother would be cruel to me, but she'd let me live with them for awhile. Then suddenly she'd send me back to my mom. She never let me play with my friends. She even tried to control my food—she was obsessed with how much I ate, how much I left uneaten. She'd accuse me of throwing up right after eating. Sometimes she was right—Jeanne W.*

Those of us who grew up in alcoholic families often feel overwhelmed by the pain of the accumulated losses in our lives. In addition to the daily losses we suffer in the chaos and unpredictability of alcoholic homes, many of us also suffer:

- Losses resulting from multiple caregiver changes—being shuffled from one uncaring adult to the next.
- Losses from family deaths, often suicide or other drug/alcohol-related deaths.

· Losses from abortions and adoptions.
· Losses from sexual revictimization.
· Accumulated lifetime losses.
· Loss of the real self.

Most of us never fully grieve our accumulated losses. Our pent-up grief interferes with our ability to trust others and to form loving, intimate relationships.

## Multiple Caregiver Changes

Because of the chronic instability in our alcoholic families, many of us were passed from relative to relative or other adult, or to institutions for caretaking. In our research, we wanted to know how multiple caregiver changes affect the lives of young children of alcoholics—how do such changes affect our developing sense of self? How do we as children cope with the physical and emotional loss of our primary caregivers, the persons who are expected to comfort and protect us from the world? And how do these early caregiver changes affect our subsequent adult intimate relationships?

In order to measure the loss of caregivers, we assigned a score of one for each caregiver change our research participants experienced from birth to age eighteen. If a child was born to and lived with a mother and father who never divorced and who lived together, her caregiver score would be zero. However, if, for example, a woman lived with her parents until they were divorced when she was nine, then she lived with her mother, later with her father and his new wife, her score would be three caregiver changes.

Among the one hundred women in our study, fifty-five said they experienced between one and twenty-eight caregiver changes, with the median number of changes being four. Women with alcoholic fathers had the fewest number of caregiver changes. Women who had alcoholic mothers had twice as many caregiver changes as those with alcoholic fathers. One reason for this difference may be that nonalcoholic men frequently divorce their alcoholic wives, leaving the children with their mothers. These divorced alcoholic mothers, often forced to support their children alone, find themselves economically disadvantaged and must rely heavily on relatives, neighbors, and friends for childcare. Nonalcoholic wives typically stay married to their alcoholic husbands.

*Abrupt Changes.* Most alcoholic families compound the trauma of loss of caregivers by failing to prepare the child for the change. Many of us weren't told about impending moves or changes in caregivers – they just happened. We woke to find a strange man living in our house; or our clothes were packed, we were removed from school, and abruptly shipped off to another relative; or children's protective services hustled us off to a strange foster home or care facility.

These abrupt, impulsive decisions to change our primary caregivers reflect the problems and internal struggles of alcoholic families – violent fights in the middle of the night, problems with job changes and financial struggles, divorce of spouses or leaving lovers, and arrests by police authorities for alcohol-related crimes. Unable to cope with their own lives and their addiction, our alcoholic parents may have left us with people who were equally unable to physically, emotionally, and sexually protect us. The relatives, neighbors, or friends we were left with may have themselves been addicted to drugs and/or alcohol and may have been more neglectful and abusive to us than our alcoholic parents.

Janet G. says being with her stepmother was worse than being with her alcoholic mother. *My mom and dad separated when I was very young,* she says. *When I was twelve, my father, a physically and verbally abusive alcoholic, married a woman I didn't get along with at all. She'd drink in the mornings and become very mean. I just tried to stay out of her way. After seven months of living with her, I ran away.*

As children, with every caregiver change, we felt hopeful that the new situation might at last give us the safety and comfort we so desperately needed. However, frequently, the situation was not better and we were left feeling bitterly disappointed, disillusioned, and hopeless. No one seemed able to relieve our fear and pain. ACOA research participant Nyla D. says in her many painful caregiver changes even her foster home became a source of confusion and degradation. *Since I was born, my mother and father never lived together,* she says. *My mother remarried seven times. During my first five years, I lived with my mother, my dad, my grandmother, and my aunt and uncle. When I was eight, I lived in a foster home for a year. At age twelve, I went to my second foster home and lived there until I was eighteen. All during this time, my parents, who were both alcoholics and prescription drug addicts, fought for custody. If I lived at my dad's I had to take care of his house, the pool, and the lawn, and go to bars with him all the time. I felt safer at my foster home, but not very safe because my foster mother turned out to be a drug addict too. When she was drunk or high, she'd become violent or really playful with me – always inconsistent. She'd come into my bedroom really wasted and want to kiss and hold me. She'd touch me like a lover. I'd just lie there. I didn't know what to do. Everyone else was in bed. I'd never had any kind of touching from my mother. What was I supposed to do?*

*Sense of Powerlessness/Lack of Control.* It's likely that these multiple caregiver changes contributed to our sense of powerlessness and lack of control as children and later on, as adults. No matter what we did, we were passed from caregiver to caregiver. Nothing in our world stayed the same. There was little or no stability or security onto which we could hold. As adults, this sense of powerlessness and lack of control may manifest in staying in unhealthy relationships no matter how dissatisfying they become. Many of us, trapped in unhappy relationships vow: "I'll never subject my kids to the horror I felt getting shuffled from person to person, house to house. They'll have the same two parents and the same roof over their heads . . . no matter what."

Although you may not have experienced as many changes as some ACOAs, *each* caregiver change was important and has powerfully impacted your life. With each change, you learned something about yourself and came to conclusions—often erroneous and self-deprecating—about your worth and importance. Take a moment to reflect upon the caregiver changes in your life. For each caregiver change consider:

- Your age when each caregiver change occurred.
- The circumstances surrounding the changes.
- A description of each caregiver and your feelings toward them.
- The specific losses you incurred in each caregiver change.
- The conclusions you drew about yourself as a result of the changes.
- How your relationship history as an adult may reflect what you might have learned from caregiver changes.

Even those of us who experienced zero caregiver changes learned about relationships and ourselves from the absence of change. Some of us experienced loss from parents who remained together and unhappy. For others of us, the loss involved our parents refusing to recognize and seek outside help for the pain in our alcoholic families.

*Coping.* For those of us who experienced caregiver changes, the assortment of dysfunctional and often drug and/or alcohol dependent adults moved in and out of our young lives with little or no notice or explanation. We learned to stop expecting people to take care of us and meet our needs. In self-defense, many of us became self-sufficient. There was little predictability, little we could really count on. We adapted by ceasing to invest any of our "selves" in others. We watched the parade of people through our lives and wondered, "Who are these people? Why are they here in my home? How long will they stay?" For most of us, there were no goodbyes, only the mysterious disappearance and reappearence of people, or violent endings with screaming scenes, slamming doors, and screeching tires. No one acknowledged the pain we felt around missing absent loved ones. Some of us were forbidden from even mentioning the name of the departed lover or spouse. Instead of feeling the loss, we felt panic. Who will be next? Who will leave me now? Unable to feel the painful loss, some of us blocked all feeling and began a life-long process of numbing ourselves to attachment.

## Family Deaths

Among many of the ACOAs we interviewed, and perhaps in your own life, death is a common loss. Alcohol-related deaths of parents, siblings, grandparents, and stepparents often include illnesses such as liver disease, auto or other accidents, and suicides of the alcoholics or codependents. In alcoholic families, the childrens' feelings of guilt or responsibility for death are rarely discussed or worked through. ACOA Carrie F. talks about the violence and death in her alcoholic family. *When I was nineteen my father took me out to dinner and gave me a beautiful necklace. When we returned home, my alcoholic mother tried to hit me and choke me with the necklace. I moved out that night and my dad helped me move my stuff to a friend's. After I left, he'd visit me often. He'd beg me to come back. He told me that his life alone with mom was cold and empty. But my mother had hated me for years and I was afraid to move back in. So I refused. Four months later, my father committed suicide. He was a doctor and intentionally overdosed on pills. I heard about his death from friends after they'd heard about it on the radio. I felt very guilty for refusing to move back in with them. I also felt angry with him for leaving me behind stuck with my mother. She blamed me for his death. I can't believe he didn't even leave me a note.*

Deaths of family members often stimulate a variety of conflicting feelings in children of alcoholics. One ACOA said she was "delighted" when her abusive, alcoholic stepfather died. For more than ten years, she'd been afraid he'd kill innocent bystanders when he drove drunk. She says, *It feels good to see him dead, not able to criticize me or brag about his sexual conquests. But I think it's wrong to feel this way.*

For many of us, guilt keeps us from recognizing feelings of relief when an abusive parent dies. Alcoholic parents often die violent alcohol-related deaths. One alcoholic father stumbled drunk onto a freeway and was killed by a passing truck. Another fell asleep while smoking and drinking and burned to death. A drunken mother died of massive head injuries when she fell down a flight of stairs outside a bar. The children of these parents suffer shame, embarrassment, and sometimes rage over their parents' violent, premature deaths. The child thinks, "Why did she have to die? If I'd mattered to her more than the booze, she'd be alive today." We often translate the deaths into a devaluation of ourselves and assume blame and responsibility for the deaths.

## Adoptions and Abortions

Among the ACOAs we talked with who had been pregnant, they aborted 45 out of 190 pregnancies—nearly one out of every four. Several women experienced multiple abortions. For many of us, an unplanned pregnancy only serves to underscore our isolation and lack of support. Due to multiple sex partners, we may be unsure about the identity of the baby's father. We may be alone without emotional or financial support from lovers or family in our difficult decision to abort or to have the baby and keep it or give it up for adoption.

For some of us, abortion loss becomes complicated by the identity of the child's father. One such tragic case is Joan U., whose mother died of cancer when she was seven. After her mother's death, Joan lived off-and-on with her father, her married sister and brother-in-law, and with her grandfather and aunt. When Joan was eight, her brother-in-law began sexually molesting her. She began having intercourse with him when she was thirteen. He was thirty-two. *I was drugged and high,* she says. *I felt guilty because of my sister, but he was so sensual and gentle with me. He told me my sister wouldn't mind.*

Joan became pregnant twice by her brother-in-law. When her sister found out, she told Joan she must be psychotic. The brother-in-law wanted Joan to have an abortion, but refused to accompany her to the clinic. For both abortions, Joan went by herself. *I felt so ashamed,* she says. *After I stopped having sex with him, my sister and brother-in-law divorced. He remarried immediately. I've often thought that if I'd just kept having sex with him, maybe my sister wouldn't be alone today.*

In Andrea Z.'s case, the father of her child may have been her stepbrother or a casual date. *My stepbrother started sexually touching me when I was eight and he was fourteen,* she says. *We started having intercourse when I was fifteen. I went on a date with this guy from school who kept pushing me to have sex. I didn't want to, but I was afraid he'd stop liking me if I refused. I felt the same way about my stepbrother—if I didn't do what he wanted, he'd hate me. I thought all I had to give them was my body. I had sex with both of them the same month and became pregnant. I never told either of them.*

Any unplanned pregnancy is stressful. An unplanned pregnancy in a dysfunctional alcoholic family almost always guarantees little family support. When Susan D. went to an out-of-town aunt to confide in her about her pregnancy, the aunt immediately violated her trust and called Susan's parents telling them about the pregnancy and demanding money for an abortion. Instead of sending money, Susan's parents threw all of Susan's belongings out into the street. The message was clear to Susan. She was on her own. She'd receive no support or help from her family. She confided in no one else and aborted the pregnancy.

Those of us from alcoholic families often receive little space or encouragement to grieve over unplanned pregnancies. Some of us are punished if we show our grief. The familiar alcoholic family message rings out clearly: "Tell no one. Keep your feelings to yourself. Feelings are immature and unnecessary. Be stoic." Most of us accept this message without question. We tell no one. We keep our grief, anxiety, and our increasing sense of isolation deep inside. We assume all the responsibility for the pregnancy. The false self convinces us that it's our fault, we're bad. Those of us whose religious beliefs condemn our sexual behavior and prohibit us from having abortions particularly suffer from overwhelming guilt, often to the point of physically hurting ourselves as "punishment for our offense."

## Sexual Revictimization

In addition to the losses from caregiver changes, family deaths, adoptions, and abortions, we're also often victims of sexual losses. Those of us who've experienced sexual assault as children are more likely as adults to be either socially and sexually withdrawn or indiscriminately sexual. Some of us switch back and forth between the two extremes. Each may give us some feeling of control over our body and our sexuality. By socially and sexually withdrawing, we can avoid any sexual feelings. By being sexually compulsive, we can feel power over our partners.

More often than not, we continue to experience loss in our lives through revictimization. Those of us who were victims of incest and child molestation are much more likely than nonvictims to repeatedly become sexual victims within and outside our families. Our history of early traumatic sexual experiences, our inability to protect our emotional and sexual boundaries, and our sexualized behavior make those of us who are incest/molestation survivors especially vulnerable to adolescent and adult sexual assault.

## Accumulated Lifetime Losses

Many of us feel we cannot cry or grieve. In my practice, many ACOA clients tell me they're fearful that if they ever started crying, they'd never stop—they have too many tears to cry. It is this heavy load of not one or two losses, but a lifetime of accumulated losses that most of us carry. Not only have we experienced major losses of abortions and adoptions, deaths of family members, sexual assaults, and multiple caregiver changes, we've experienced a thousand other daily losses—the loss of carefree childhood days, the loss from having trust and boundaries violated, and the loss from embarrassing alcoholic and codependent episodes. These daily losses are just as hurtful and equally damaging to our spirit and self-esteem. The accumulation of losses may lead us to conclude that the potential pain in caring for another is simply not worth the risk and may cause us to avoid intimate relationships altogether.

The real tragedy is that our losses are rarely acknowledged by our families. We usually receive minimal or no support for our feelings about our losses. Instead, we suffer in silence and isolation, often believing that the recurrent losses are mounting evidence of our own inherent "badness" and of the shame we carry inside.

Denial and the tendency to minimize our pain interfere with our ability to recognize all the losses we may have experienced as a child growing up in our alcoholic family. Often it's easier to look at others' lives and identify their losses than to focus on our own. It's also difficult to gain a sense of the enormity of the ungrieved losses many of us accumulate. To that end, we present the complete case history of research participant Patricia, a thirty-seven-year-old ACOA whose father was alcoholic and her mother codependent. By studying Patricia's painful, albeit not uncommon story, you may be able to see how as a child you encountered and coped with your own accumulated losses.

*When I was thirteen and returning from my friend's house, I saw an ambulance in front of my house. They said it was my dad, but they wouldn't let me go inside. I felt scared and couldn't understand why they were keeping me from someone I loved. I knew the neighbors were lying to me when they said my father was going to be okay because they'd whisper to one another. When they finally let me go home, my minister and my mother told me dad had died from a heart attack. He was only thirty-nine. I couldn't believe he was gone, that he'd never come back. I felt angry that it was my father and not my mother who'd died. I still feel that way.*

*Now my mother was all I had. I believed she was the only family I could count on. Yet I had to take care of her. I'd help her pick out clothes for dates and tell her how good she looked. I helped her with the cooking and cleaning, making financial and household decisions, and emotionally validated her. If we hugged, I had to initiate it because she was the needy one. When I needed a hug, she never hugged me.*

*When I was fifteen, my mother remarried and my stepfather's two children came to live with us. For the next couple of years, my mother was suicidal. One night I heard her crying. I went into the kitchen and saw her standing at the kitchen sink all bloody with a knife in her hand. I can still see that knife. There was blood all over the stove and the sink. I took the knife away from her and yelled for my stepfather. He came and bandaged her up and acted like nothing happened. I cleaned up the kitchen and felt angry that he acted like nothing had happened.*

*The next morning, my mother went to work at the high school where she was a teacher. I called the high school guidance counselor and told her what had happened. She talked with Mom and told her to see a doctor which she did. The doctor committed her that day to a psych unit. It was a dreary place and I felt responsible for her being there. She had to stay the mandatory three days even though she didn't want to.*

*After that, she tried to kill herself several more times with pills. It would always be late in the evening, so at night I became very sensitive to the slightest noise. I'd wake up anytime she cried.*

*When I was nineteen my stepfather was in a near-fatal car accident and suffered permanent brain damage. He was in a coma for three months. It took him four more months to relearn to walk and talk. It left him despondent and seriously suicidal. Once while we were visiting him and my mother was drunk, he became angry and physically attacked her. The next year, she divorced him. I never saw him or my stepbrother or stepsister again after that.*

*When I was twenty-four I met a man, became pregnant, and married him. He was addicted to pot and hash and dealt drugs a lot. Much later, I discovered he was also a compulsive gambler and pathological liar. Periodically, when he ran out of money and drugs, he'd beat me.*

*Within the first six months of our marriage, my husband spent my entire ten-thousand-dollar savings account. After my daughter was born, I'd often sit in the closet in the dark and cry. I felt like my baby daughter had become an unending dependency on me—just like my mother had been.*

*My husband and I fought a lot during our marriage. He'd put pressure on me to have orgasms because he needed to prove something to himself. If I didn't have an orgasm, he'd complain. I wanted to meet his needs, so I faked it. I was afraid to have anything wrong with me. I divorced my husband at twenty-eight. His relationship had been more with chemicals than with me anyway.*

*Five years later, my mother was diagnosed with liver cancer. The doctor told me she was terminal. After spending a week in the hospital, she came home. Every night after work, I'd go there and bathe her and put her on the potty. I even wiped her after bowel movements. It reminded me of taking care of my baby. My mom died in my arms only twenty-eight days after her diagnosis.*

*The last intercourse I had was more than three years ago with a one-night stand. I hardly ever masturbate. I'm not willing to complicate my life with a relationship because I'm too needy right now. I could not give to anyone—there's so little left inside me to give. I feel so depleted. I would only bring need to a new relationship.*

Like in so many of our lives, there are significant losses reflected in Patricia's life history. She suffered loss from multiple caregiver changes, the death of her father, numerous suicide attempts by her mother and stepfather, the betrayal of trust and physical and emotional abuse in her marriage, loss of contact with her stepsiblings, loss of financial security and resources, and loss of sexual self-esteem. Each of these losses seriously affected Patricia's sense of "self." The most significant loss suffered by Patricia is the loss of her real self.

Some of you may compare your own losses to Patricia's and decide that yours aren't as extreme or as important as hers. As ACOAs, it's common to compare ourselves with others and minimize our pain. However, your losses belong to you. They are important. Each loss caused you hurt, pain, and confusion. To move through your losses, begin to fully acknowledge them and feel the feelings that emerge. Examine the decisions you made with each of your losses and explore how these early decisions surrounding loss have impacted your adult intimate relationships.

## Loss of Our Separate Self

Growing up in alcoholic families has caused many of us to lose our development of a separate self, a sense of who we are. A primary goal of family systems therapy is to help ACOAs separate or "individuate" from parents, stepparents, and other primary caregivers. Family therapists can help us learn to say "goodbye" to our former caregivers. The act of saying goodbye occurs when we can relinquish our childlike, emotional dependence on our parents and begin to assume full responsibility for meeting our own emotional, social, and physical needs. If, as adults, we don't individuate from our caregivers, we may remain in a dependent child role with them, forever unable to form a healthy adult relationship with a lover and always suffering from conflicting loyalties between our partners and our caregivers.

Family Systems Researcher and Therapist, Donald Williamson, Ph.D., says the final goal of individuation from one's childhood family includes renegotiating the relationship between parents and child so that it becomes more equal, more of a peer relationship. In such a healthy relationship, the child and parent give and receive mutual support and develop a new, mature intimacy.

It's probably unwise and unrealistic for most of us to expect to reach Williamson's final individuation goal with our dysfunctional parents. Although we may be recovering through therapy and/or through a Twelve-Step program, often our parents remain untreated codependents and/or remain actively chemically dependent. If we attempt Williamson's individuation with chemically addicted family members, we're likely to encounter suspicion, hostility, ridicule, and criticism. Attempts at individuation with family members can teach us much about our family's structure, its rules, roles, and rituals. In order to reach Williamson's final individuation goal, both we and our parents must be motivated and emotionally "present." Parents and ACOAs who still abuse substances are emotionally unavailable for this work.

Those of us in our thirties, forties, fifties, and sixties who have not been able to make the emotional separation from our caregivers, often continue to act in a childlike role with our parents. We may talk daily to them through visits and check-in calls. Our parents may continue to control our important career, relationship, and financial decisions. We may be unable to take independent action without our parents' knowledge and permission. As a result, we may doubt our own ability to care for ourselves.

In some alcoholic families, the reverse is true. The adult child is drawn into nurturing, protecting, defending, and enabling the alcoholic and/or codependent parent. As young as age five, some of us were expected to assume major caretaking roles. As the parent-child boundaries blurred, we became confused, resentful, and unable to develop the emotional and social skills we need as adults.

When we look at Patricia's detailed history, we can see how from an early age she "parented" her mother. She took care of her mother emotionally and physically through her suicide attempts, her dating and marital strife, and finally through her terminal illness. Patricia's well-defined "caretaker script" in the alcoholic family prevented her from separating from her mother. In family therapy, Patricia would receive much-needed support in clarifying her relationship with her mother, father, and stepfather. She'd be encouraged to examine the unachieved goals, fears, and problems of her three parental caregivers. If her parents were living, the therapist might invite them to a family session to gather insights into their interaction with Patricia and Patricia's interaction with them. However, in Patricia's case, both her biological mother and father are dead. Fortunately, there are still ways to say goodbye to deceased parents and complete the individuation process.

Williamson developed a method of separating from parents who are dead, but who continue to "live on" in others, negating the selfhood and autonomy of their children. His method involves group therapy in which a daughter, like Patricia, shares family memories and photographs with the group. Later she makes a tape-recorded letter to the dead parent and shares it with the group. The therapist and group members help clarify the daughter's perceptions, concealed issues, and unanswered questions about her own parent-child relationship. She then talks with friends and other family members about the parent, comparing this outside information with her own perceptions. Finally, she selects a private place to go and "talk" with her dead parent and say goodbye.

The encouragement and support of the therapist and group members are vital to the success of Williamson's technique. They can help us untangle the relationship and provide the validation for our feelings and permission to express feelings that we've previously felt unsafe to feel. Watching other group members progress through their own individuation process can provide comfort for us as we realize we are not alone in our thoughts or feelings about our deceased parent(s).

*Idealized Images of Childhood.* Many of the one hundred ACOAs we interviewed described emotional, physical, and sexual abuse, but without acknowledging the abuse as losses. Often they told their painful stories with little or no emotion. Eliana Gil, author of *Treatment of Adult Survivors of Childhood Abuse,* says that confronting our early childhood losses forces us to give up our often idealized images of childhood. Many of us, in an effort to protect and comfort ourselves from the abusive reality of our childhoods, create an idealized image, a fantasy of our parents and our childhoods.

Mary K. says her idealized fantasy "worked" for her for years. *When I left home at eighteen and moved out of the area, I developed a story I'd use whenever anyone asked about my family. I came to believe it myself. It went something like this: "My parents married, had four children, and never argued with each other. My father worked two jobs to put all of us through Catholic school. My dad and I were great friends, went to mass together, and placed his real estate signs on vacant lots together. We were buddies." Using alcohol daily for twelve years helped me tell my story the way I wished it had been. When I became sober, painful memories from my childhood began to surface and longterm physical and emotional abuse from my mother and sexual abuse that continued for ten years from my father and two of his friends. I fought those emerging memories because they did not coincide with my idealized version of childhood. The process of accepting the reality of that abuse brought tears, anger, and disillusionment. I had to feel the grief of not having the childhood I'd created in my mind, the childhood I'd hoped for. Recovering the memories and feeling the feelings, though painful, was the beginning of my healing.*

**Confronting Trauma with Silence.** Children living in alcoholic families deal with trauma differently than children living in non-alcoholic families. Therapist Wayne Kritsberg, author of *The Adult Children of Alcoholics Syndrome,* finds that alcoholic families tend to confront trauma and pain with silence. No one ever talks to the child or explains to her or him what is happening. Interpretation of the trauma is left to the child. Predictably, such children assume responsibility for the trauma and pain in their families. With the alcoholic "don't talk, don't feel" family prohibition, children rarely seek support outside the family, and instead, bottle up their feelings. Since no one speaks directly about the trauma—and, in fact, usually denies the trauma exists—children do not learn to even recognize trauma and abuse in their lives.

Barbara M.'s case illustrates this silent ACOA response to pain and trauma. When she was fifteen, Barbara was pressured by her twenty-six-year-old boyfriend, Ron, into having sex. Although she'd been previously sexual with other boys, she decided she wouldn't engage in sex again until after she was married. When she told Ron she wanted to wait, he suggested they move in together. Since Barbara felt she was a burden to her family, she agreed and ran off without her parents knowledge and began living with Ron. Soon afterward, she became pregnant. Four months later, Ron dropped her off at her parents home. She never saw him again. Her parents kept her home throughout her pregnancy and hired a teacher to come in to tutor her.

*Since both of my parents worked full-time, the only contact I had was with my tutor,* she says. *I took care of my parents' house and my five younger sisters and brothers. It was a year of isolation for me. I felt sad, but I didn't talk to anyone about anything. My parents decided I should adopt out the baby. When labor began, my mom dropped me off at the hospital at six in the morning and picked me up three days later. The doctor never explained to me what labor was. Even the nurses left me alone. I thought it was because I was bad. I felt so alone. I never saw the baby. I wonder now if he's a drug addict or an alcoholic. It was such a traumatic experience, but no one ever talked about it.*

In Barbara's family, like in most other alcoholic families, the "no talk" rule holds firm. No one talks about Barbara's elopement or her pregnancy. Because she's prevented from talking to others about her feelings, she shuts down emotionally. She becomes numb. Her parents criticize and condemn her and feel perfectly justified in withholding support from her. Her parents never wonder why their fifteen-year-old has already had numerous sexual partners and what that might say about them and their family system. It's easier for them to simply blame the child.

Alcoholic families create environments that aren't conducive to working through and resolving losses. Barbara's parents are probably as emotionally shut down and unable to grieve as she is. Their inability to effectively deal with her loss has undoubtedly been modeled for generations in the family. It's likely that her grandparents and their parents before them would have dealt just as poorly with the situation. Without effective intervention, each generation passes down its dysfunctional ways of coping with trauma. Without help, Barbara learns to deal with trauma by emotionally shutting down, refusing to feel her feelings, not asking for help, and blaming herself.

In contrast, in a healthy, nonalcoholic family system, Barbara's pregnancy would have been discussed fully by her family. She would have been allowed to talk about the trauma of the four months spent with Ron. Her parents would not have condemned her, judged her harshly, or found fault. Even though her parents may have felt confused and disappointed in Barbara's decisions, she'd still have received her family's love and support. They would look at what they might have contributed to their daughter's early sexuality. She and other members of her family would be encouraged to express their emotions freely. The end result of the healthy handling of a difficult situation is that the child learns that trauma is a part of life, not something to be repressed or unnecessarily dwelt on, and that traumatic events can be resolved.

*High Tolerance for Pain.* Another reason we don't mourn our losses is that most of us have developed an unusually high tolerance for physical and emotional pain. From the earliest age, we are taught to deny our feelings, to discount and abuse ourselves. By watching our parents, we learned how not to take care of ourselves. Many of us come to believe that hiding pain is admirable. Some of us even learn to tolerate physical pain without complaint. It's not uncommon for ACOAs to postpone necessary medical treatment for weeks or even months out of denial of the physical pain, believing that to acknowledge pain connotes weakness.

Many of us are unable to identify our emotional pain. For us, it's easier to simply deny pain than to sit still long enough to feel it and work through it. Working compulsively, keeping chronically "on the run," we can temporarily prevent questions and painful feelings from surfacing.

When we slow down or spend quiet time alone with no projects, we may feel overwhelmed with fear and anxiety. Some of us avoid thinking about our lifetime losses because we know we lack the necessary skills or support to work through our painful memories.

It's true that most ACOAs have "buckets of tears" to cry from all the major and minor losses accumulated over a lifetime. These tears deserve to be respected and released. With a supportive network of professionals and friends, ACOAs find that their tears can be released slowly and safely.

### Healing Losses

Grief is a natural, albeit painful process, that contributes to our healing. Christine Courtois, author of *Healing the Incest Wound*, says that accepting our losses means recognizing our inability to control all things. Our attempts to control losses only contribute to more loss. When we allow ourselves to accept the lack of control we have over losses, we stop blaming ourselves, free ourselves to feel our pain and grief, and ultimately allow ourselves the time and energy needed to heal.

Confronting and resolving past losses is difficult. For many of us, reading books devoted to addressing loss can help our process. Two excellent resources are *After the Tears* by Jane Middelton-Moz and Lorie Dwinell and *Necessary Losses* by Judith Viorst.

Healing losses involves three steps: *recognizing* the losses, *feeling* the feelings the losses bring, and *grieving* the losses. Step one, recognizing and naming the losses, means acknowledging the reality of your past and present and no longer denying or minimizing your pain. Recognition of the losses may mean having to shift from the *illusion* of how you'd have liked things to have been to the reality of how it really was.

The second step in healing losses is to give yourself permission to *feel* the losses you uncover. Many ACOAs say, "Why do I have to go back and feel the pain? Can't I just recognize the loss and move on from there?" Unfortunately, it's critical to your healing that you feel your losses. *If you recognize losses without feeling them, the losses continue to be reenacted in your life.* Subconsciously we try to resolve our losses by re-creating them over and over. Our choice is to feel the feelings within a safe environment with supportive help and work through the losses or to repeatedly act out buried losses and feel helpless and out of control. Feeling losses may hurt, but it can empower you by giving you more knowledge about your present life and help you stop repeating self-destructive patterns generated by old unresolved losses.

Most of us don't know how to grieve our losses. In *After the Tears,* the authors encourage ACOAs to:

- Accept rather than deny the loss.
- Experience the feelings associated with the loss.
- Acknowledge that the loss—whether it's material, physical, psychological, or the loss of a person—is gone and is not retrievable.
- Finally, withdraw emotional investment in that which is lost and move on.

This final step—withdrawing emotional investment and moving on—involves recognizing that only you can create healing experiences for yourself and move beyond your past losses. It means reparenting yourself, providing self-nurturing and self-soothing which contribute to increased self-esteem. The increased self-esteem, in turn, can help you relate sexually with yourself and others in ways that protect and nurture you.

# CHAPTER 8

# Sex Is Dirty, and Other Sexual Messages

*My parents divorced when I was ten and my father moved out of state. In the summer, I'd travel to visit him. My grandmother encouraged me to sleep in the same bed with my dad. One morning, I woke up and found him touching me. One of his hands was on my breast, the other between my legs. I thought, "Oh no. Not him too." My mother's boyfriend, John, had previously come on to me sexually. I think my mother knew about it, but she ignored it. When I told my mom about John she said, "If he gets a little help, do you think it would be okay if he stayed with our family?" I couldn't believe it. I figured she must want John more than she wanted me. I told her I wasn't comfortable with him staying. She made him leave, but she kept seeing him.*

*With Dad, I just pretended nothing had happened. But something shattered inside me when he sexually touched me—I closed off, put up a wall. I developed a keen awareness of everything that was going on around me. Since then, I've never been able to relax around men and I make sure I'm never alone with a man. I never let them get too close. Whenever I'm with men, I stay alert, vigilant.—Jan T.*

Like Jan and other ACOAs, you probably received many erroneous messages from your alcoholic family about sex and relationships that continue to influence your adult life. In Jan's case, when she was sexually touched by her father and by her mother's boyfriend, she learned that her body was not her own. Her privacy could be invaded at any moment. Those who violated her weren't punished. No one, not even her family protected her. Jan received the common ACOA message: "You can only count on yourself."

The behavior and attitudes of Jan's mother, the boyfriend, her father, and her grandmother delivered messages to Jan about her body, her sexuality, and about relationships—"No one, especially men, can be trusted"; "You're in charge of making adult decisions"; "You're not important"; "You're powerless." Unchallenged, these sexual and relationship messages continue to permeate Jan's adult life and interfere with her ability to develop satisfying intimate relationships with others.

### Family Messages

We learn about sex from our families. Sex researchers say that in most families, children stop asking their parents questions about sex by the time they're nine or ten. As children, we usually learn basic values and information from our parents about love, birth, pregnancy, anatomy, and the dangers of sexual molestation. It's rare, however, that we receive accurate information about other important sexual topics such as intercourse, premarital sex, birth control, sexually transmitted diseases, and homosexuality and bisexuality. In most families, children don't receive the kinds of information they need to make the crucial sexual decisions they face as adolescents. In alcoholic families, the situation is even worse.

Governed by rigid rules which limit question-asking and the expression of feelings, those of us who grew up in alcoholic families are even less likely to have received the guidance and support we needed to make our own sexual decisions and develop healthy sexual identities. Even more damaging were the distorted messages we received about sex and relationships that negatively affect our ability to achieve satisfying sexual relationships as adults.

Within all families, children explore and learn about sexuality, usually from observing and listening to those closest to them: parents, stepparents, siblings, grandparents, and other caregivers they might live with throughout childhood and adolescence. Sexual messages children receive may be overt or covert, verbal or nonverbal. Messages may be sent only once or many times. The messages usually contain both fact and myths and often contradict one another.

Children also receive sex and relationship messages from *absent* family members—those who have left or those who have always been absent. The absence of a family member communicates many things to a child. The absence itself is always a message. For some children, the message may be "You're not important enough for me to live with you or to visit you often," or "Parents can't live in the same house together" or "When two people disagree, rejection or abandonment are the only alternatives."

Whether the absent parent is male or female affects the child developmentally. If a girl's parents divorce and she and her sister are raised by her mother, she may learn about females interacting and expressing feelings, but miss out on learning about female/male relating. If she's very young when her parents divorce and her mother doesn't remarry, she may not learn about masculinity and social relating to men. The absence of such "gender learning" can later affect her close relationships.

If the child periodically visits an absent parent, she absorbs sexual-relationship messages not only from her parent, but also from anyone the parent lives with. Too often, mental health professionals ignore or minimize the important messages children learn from these step- or absent family members.

Before we can fully understand how growing up in alcoholic families affects the "truths" we learn about sex and relationships, we need to understand the process of healthy sex education. Effective sex education within the family ideally includes:

- Biological facts about anatomy, sexual development, and sexual functioning.
- Expressions of feelings around sexual issues and behaviors.
- An open atmosphere in which children may freely ask questions and receive respectful, informed responses.
- Discussions about sexual values.
- Disclosures about how parents and children feel about sexual development and sexual behaviors.
- Appropriate, non boundary-violating, sharing of the parents' sexual history and experiences.
- Modeling of assertive skills that contribute to relationship intimacy.

Probably none of you—regardless of whether you grew up in an alcoholic or nonalcoholic family—experienced the kind of ideal sex education just described. In America, sexuality remains a taboo subject. Most parents flounder when trying to communicate sexual facts and values to their children. In alcoholic families, the problem is simply compounded. The alcoholic family's turmoil and crises create dysfunctional rules and roles which add to an already existing cultural awkwardness about sex.

### Alcoholic Sexual Messages

It's apparent from the sexual chaos in most ACOAs' lives, that alcoholic families do a poor job of educating children about sex and relationships. In some families, alcoholic parents don't convey basic sex education such as accurate information about menstruation. ACOA research participant Lynne G. describes the trauma of her first menstrual period in her alcoholic family. *When I started my period, I had no idea what was going on. No one had ever bothered to tell me. My gym teacher explained it to me and I went home to look for something to use in my panties. I found my stepmother's dust rags in a closet and used those. Two days later, my stepmother found the bloody rags in the garbage and screamed at me. She was enraged—her eyes bulged, her hands shook. She accused me of stealing her things and she tried to hit me with a coat hanger. I pulled the coat hanger away from her and she hurt her hand.*

*The following afternoon I came home and found my father, stepmother, and her brother and her sister waiting for me in the living room. My stepmother brought the bloody rags into the room and showed them to everyone. They all yelled at me and said I stole them. I was shocked, and felt afraid and embarrassed. I felt angry, but I had no way of expressing it. There were all of them against just me. Right then, I decided that I was virtually alone in this world. I couldn't count on anyone except myself. I wanted my father to defend me, but he just couldn't. He didn't ask those people to leave that awful day; he never told his wife to stop. No one ever protected me.*

Lynne received powerful sexual messages from her family. Uninformed and ill-prepared for her first menstrual period, she learned no one would explain or help her with the important events in her life. She discovered she could not expect empathy or support from her family. Her stepmother's abusive reaction to the discovery of the bloody rags gave her the sexual message: "Your body's changes are bad and dirty. Your body gets you in trouble." Publicly shamed, her physical and emotional privacy deeply invaded, she learns that if she is at all vulnerable she will be humiliated.

Lynne's case is not unusual. In reviewing the stories from the ACOAs we interviewed, we found that few of them received healthy sexual or relationship messages from their families. These unhealthy sexual and relationship messages tend to cluster around several themes:

- Invasions of sexual privacy.
- Being forced to become a parent's sexual confidant.
- Sexual triangling.
- Sexual betrayal.
- Sexual shame and negative body images.
- Abusive spousal relationships.
- Sexual avoidance.

***Invasions of Sexual Privacy.*** Since alcohol reduces inhibitions, alcoholic parents frequently make remarks or engage in inappropriate behavior that violates the sexual privacy of their children. The sex/relationship message to the child becomes: "You have nothing that is your own. You don't deserve privacy." In some alcoholic families, these violations occur so frequently and by so many family members that the children never learn what constitutes normal sexual privacy.

Those of us who grew up in alcoholic families and had our sexual privacy violated as children, often have difficulty as adults protecting our boundaries, establishing our sexual limits, and saying no to others. We may frequently violate the sexual privacy of our mates and our children.

Sometimes the invasions of sexual privacy are subtle as when Mary F.'s mother invaded her privacy by reading her diary. *When I was twelve, I kept a diary in which I'd described the sex play that I was having with my cousin. I hid it behind my chest of drawers. My mother found it and read it. After that, she kept my diary stored in the hall closet. Years later, my brother found it and teased me about it.*

Other times, the invasion is more blatant. Darla W. tells about her alcoholic stepfather's invasion of her sexual privacy: *He never allowed us to close the bathroom door when we needed to go,* she says. *In the evenings when my mother would fall asleep, he'd come strolling out, nude and drunk. He'd sit naked in the living room and pretend to be reading.*

Another form of sexual privacy invasion involves sexual accusations and interrogation—what did you do, who did you do it with, what did you feel? You, like many children in alcoholic families, may have been mercilessly grilled by your parents about your sexual thoughts, feelings, and behaviors. You may have been asked to describe in detail your own sexual feelings and activities or the sexual behavior of one of your parents. Fran W. says she hated seeing movies with sexual scenes with her alcoholic mother. *She'd make all of us tell her what it made us feel like to watch the sex scenes,* she says. *We were so embarrassed. Then when my brother got his girlfriend pregnant, she made him tell her in front of all of us exactly how he'd done it. It was painful. He was so humiliated and my mother enjoyed every minute of it.*

ACOA Nancy T. says, *My dad had multiple affairs and would take me to his lovers' homes. Mom knew about the affairs and she'd pump us for information about the other women. She'd ask "How much does she weigh? What's she look like? What kind of house does she have? What was your father doing with her? Did they touch, kiss, shower together?" It made me feel embarrassed and really uncomfortable.*

**Sexual Confidant.** As the alcoholism progresses in the family, often a parent selects one child to confide in. If you were your parent's sexual confidant, you were probably told intimate details about your parents' sex life. You were expected to provide support, advice, and sympathy. It's likely that this role caused you to feel great anxiety and confusion. While you were given secret information, you couldn't tell anyone else. Keeping the secret probably made you feel disloyal to your other parent.

Sheri T. was her alcoholic mother's confidant. *From the time I was thirteen, my mother told me my father was a homosexual, that he preferred men to women, that he couldn't perform in bed. She said he wasn't a sexual partner to her.*

Gina R. was her father's confidant. *When I was in high school, my stepmother would go to bed by nine and my dad would get drunk and come in and tell me how neither my mom nor my stepmother liked sex. He'd look really sad and say they just didn't enjoy sex with him. I never knew what I was expected to do about it.*

Sharing sexual confidences with a child confuses the child about her role—is she the child or an adult? Should she try to problem-solve for her parent? Is she responsible for how her parents feel and behave?

***Sexual Triangling.*** Daughters of alcoholics who are selected as sexual confidants are often later "triangled"—expected to *do* something to make the parent feel emotionally better. Often this triangled child is held more accountable than the spouse for what occurs in the marital relationship.

Vicki P.'s mother laid the responsibility for her husband's infidelity on her daughter. *When I was fifteen, my dad had an affair. My mother talked to me constantly about it. It obsessed her. She wanted me to do something about it. She'd say, "It's killing me. I'm going to die from this. You're my oldest, strongest, most intelligent daughter, you must make his cheating stop." The affair went on for eleven years and she never stopped talking about it. She did the same thing about my dad's drinking. From the time I was three or four years old, my mother would send me inside bars to sit with my father so he wouldn't drink so much or stay too long.*

Triangling often drives a wedge between children and their parents, forcing the child to choose between one parent or the other. Kathi W. says her mother was jealous of her relationship with her dad. *When he was drunk, my father would get angry with my mom and tell her she should try to be more like me, even look more like me. He set it up so we'd fight over him.*

Janet D. says her mother blamed her for not saving her parents' marriage. *Mom tried to commit suicide when I was fifteen because Dad wanted a divorce,* she says. *She told me the divorce was my fault because I didn't tell Dad that his affair was wrong. She didn't know that I did tell my dad I thought it was wrong. He still wanted the divorce.*

Janet learned common ACOA sexual/relationship messages from being triangled into her parents' marriage:

- *You are expendable.* Others, especially those close to you, can use you for their needs at your expense and you are not supposed to object or complain about it.
- *You can manipulate anyone and anything.* You have power and control over the feelings and behaviors of others and should use it.
- *If others don't change their feelings and behavior, it's completely your fault and you're a failure.* You will be blamed and held accountable for the behavior and feelings of others.

*Sexual Betrayal.* Alcoholic parents' behavior often convey sexual betrayal messages: "It's okay to cheat on your partner." "It's okay to lie." "You can't trust anyone, not even your lover." "Commitment means nothing." "Trusting someone and opening yourself to them means you'll be hurt." Parents in alcoholic families often lack the assertive skills to confront their partners with the hurt and frustration they feel. Instead, they act out their hurt by having numerous affairs, often with lovers known to the spouse.

Claudia P.'s alcoholic father had numerous affairs. *When I turned eight, my father started having multiple affairs with women he knew in my parents' social circle. She'd accuse him and he'd lie about it. When I started dating, he'd bring my dates into the house and tell them that I didn't like to be hugged or French-kissed. He'd get jealous of every date I had.*

Claudia's father's affairs gave her the messages that no one can be trusted and that lying is okay. His boundary invasions of her dates told her that she wasn't equipped to develop her own sexual desires, values, or decisions, that she was not a separate person from her father or her boyfriend, and that nothing in her life was private.

Sometimes alcoholic parents actually compete with their children for sexual partners. This type of sexual betrayal occurs especially in families with blurred or nonexistent boundaries, violating the lines that distinguish the child role from the parent role. Janet E.'s mother was always in competition with Janet for her boyfriends. *My mother was young looking and very beautiful,* she recalls. *She'd have a few drinks and openly flirt with my boyfriends in front of me. When I'd confront her about it later, she'd say I was being paranoid or that the guy was too old for me anyway. One afternoon I came home and found her in bed with a guy I'd been dating.*

If you grew up with sexual betrayal messages, you probably find it especially hard to trust yourself or your partners in your own intimate relationships. The model you learned from said no one can be trusted. Like your parents, if you received this message, you may frequently engage in multiple extra-relationship affairs.

*Sexual Shame.* The often bizarre sexual behaviors and attitudes common in our alcoholic families made many of us feel ashamed not only about sex, but about ourselves. We were robbed of our dignity. We may have concluded that we are "bad" and "unworthy." We may have personalized the numerous violations—the inappropriate, often vulgar sexual comments and behavior—and blamed ourselves for the things that happened to us.

This kind of sexual shame becomes generational, passed from one dysfunctional generation to another. Each family member carries the shame of past and current family members' rapes, elopements, abortions, incest, prostitution, premarital pregnancies, compulsive sexual extra-marital affairs, sexual dysfunction, avoidance of marriage, or too early or too late age at marriage.

Rita F.'s alcoholic mother's casual sexual liaisons became a deep source of shame for Rita. *Before I went into high school, my mom would bring home men to have sex while dad was at work,* she says. *I'd come home and find her lying on the living room floor or on the couch drunk without any clothes on. If she saw me, she'd just go into the bedroom with the man or leave the house with him. She never acknowledged she was screwing all these men. She probably didn't even know their names.*

Janet W. describes one of many shame-producing incidents with her alcoholic mother. *I was in eighth grade when I came home from school and found my mother drinking with some guy I'd never seen before. When my mom saw me she started gushing about how big I was now, so grown up. "Why it was only a few years ago that I held you on my lap and nursed you," she said. She started to talk "baby talk" to me. She insisted I sit on her lap. I said no, but she commanded me to. I thought if I did I could escape into my room. Instead, she unbuttoned her blouse and unsnapped her bra and urged me to "Come suck on my tits like you used to." The man was laughing. She pulled me down to her bare breasts. She reeked of Scotch. I felt mortified and scared. She held me there until I put my mouth on her breasts and sucked. I thought I was going to throw up. I didn't cry until I got into my bedroom by myself. I sobbed and sobbed and then I ripped up some special drawings I'd been working on.*

Janet's response to her mother's drunken behavior is typical. Instead of holding her mother accountable, she puts the blame on herself—she is bad—and she punishes herself by destroying her special pictures. For many of us, this self-blame manifests in a variety of self-destructive behaviors—alcoholism, suicide, self-mutilation, drug addiction, compulsive eating, compulsive sexuality, and selecting abusive partners.

*Negative Body Images/Sexual Attitudes.* Often alcoholic caregivers use degrading adjectives to describe genitals and natural sexual behaviors. As children, they give us the messages: "Your body is disgusting. Your new interest in sex is dirty." These messages imprint deeply, limiting our ability to accept and love ourselves fully as sexual human beings.

Puberty, which starts about age eight, begins a predictable cycle of emotional and bodily changes, many of which are confusing, frightening, and embarrassing to teenagers. Between eight and thirteen, a young girl's breasts develop; between eight and fourteen, she begins to grow pubic hair, with underarm hair developing about two years later. She grows rapidly between nine and fourteen and most often experiences her first menstrual period between ten and sixteen. ACOA Terri G. says her mother's comments made her feel ashamed about the sexual changes which took place in her during puberty. *I always got the feeling, especially as I entered my teenage years, that my sexuality wasn't okay,* she recalls. *She'd say, "The boys are coming around like flies." Like flies? It made me feel like I was a piece of garbage. She told me I constantly needed to wash myself "down there" and told me I should take showers twice a day. From the time I was in first grade, she implied I was having sex with everyone.*

It was Wanda G.'s alcoholic grandmother who gave her negative messages about her body and her sexuality. *When I was six, I went to live with my grandmother after my parents divorced,* she says. *Grandma had really negative ideas about sex. She'd slap my hands if I touched my genitals when I had to pee. She made me change my underwear twice a day because she said I smelled.*

Alcoholic fathers seem particularly uncomfortable with their daughters' emerging sexuality. *My dad hated that I was becoming a mature woman,* Tanya F. says. *Once when he was drunk, I was going out of the house braless and he yelled, "Hey get back here. Your nipples are showing." The whole family and my best friend heard him. I felt ashamed of my body, ashamed of my sexuality.*

Often alcoholic parents label normal sexual exploration as sick, sinful, selfish, or crazy. Yet children are born sexual beings. Newborn baby girls show vaginal lubrication and clitoral erection within the first twenty-four hours of life, often during nursing. Baby girls begin to touch themselves and rub their genitals as soon as they develop the motor coordination to do so. By age two, girls are curious about their body parts and discover their bodies are different from boys'. They're soon aware of the sensual feelings that come from genital stimulation and they often touch their own genitals. Although masturbation is both normal and healthy among children, alcoholic parents often react in ways that halt children's normal sensual exploration and pleasuring. Patti R. says, *When I was in kindergarten, my mom saw me playing with myself. I was just exploring. She just stared at me and never said a word. She looked angry and I knew she disapproved. I quit touching myself and didn't do it again until I was eighteen.* The messages Patti received include: "Your body is bad or dirty." "Touching yourself, although it feels good, is bad." "You can't trust your feelings." "Your body betrays you by wanting things that get you in trouble."

Around ages six through eight, girls sexually explore with other girls or with boys, with objects, and/or with animals. Children inspect their friends' genitals and sometimes engage in mutual masturbation with both sexes. This sex play is universal, harmless, and healthy, but parents' harsh, judgemental reactions to such explorations cause children shame and confusion. Harriet F. says she still remembers her mother's reaction to her same-sex sexual exploration when she was seven. *My mother babysat for a neighbor whose daughter was my age. During naps, we'd touch each other. Mom walked in on us one day and absolutely freaked out. She immediately called the mother of the girl and they had conferences behind closed doors. My mom yelled at me and told me how much I'd disappointed her. She punished me by ignoring me. The neighbor's girl was never allowed to come over again. I didn't know what was so awful, but I knew I was an awful person.*

ACOA Barbara I.'s experience with a boy in her neighborhood caused the child similar confusion and shame. *I was six and I let this neighbor boy lie on top of me,* she says. *He rubbed himself on me and it felt good. But a neighbor next door looked over the fence and caught us. Suddenly, there was all this yelling and screaming. The boy was a little older so he got in a lot of trouble. My mother kept asking me over and over what he did—did he "penetrate" me? "Go in" me? I didn't even know what she meant. I felt really embarrassed. I didn't understand what exactly we'd done wrong, but I knew it must be really bad.* Some of Barbara's messages included: "Good feelings from your body are bad." "Boys do bad things to you." "You are bad."

***Spousal Sexual Abuse.*** Many of us can remember one or both of our parents being physically, emotionally, or sexually abused by their partner. When a parent "tolerates" the abuse by staying in the relationship, the child receives powerful relationship messages: "Abusive relationships are normal." "Stay in the relationship no matter how bad it gets." "You're not worthy of anything better." "You can never change your mind about a relationship." "Taking care of yourself, protecting yourself, is unimportant because you are unimportant."

Often the abused partner in an alcoholic family can't talk to the other partner and can't leave the relationship. Instead, one or more of the abused partner's children is confided in, and is told about her or his pain and frustration. Like in sexual triangling, making the child the abusive relationship confidant violates the child's boundaries, makes the child feel disloyal to the other parent, and confuses the child about how relationships should be. The child feels sorry for the abused parent and feels responsible to "fix" the situation. Without intervention, the stage is set for her or him to develop a lifetime of codependence. Such was the case with Diana A.'s mother. *When I was seven, my mother rousted me out of bed one night because she'd just learned that my dad was having an affair. She said we were leaving him. I felt sorry for my mom because she was crying and I wanted to help her, but I felt sad because we had to leave my dad. Just before we were ready to leave, my dad came in and talked to my mom and got her laughing. Before I could stop crying and feeling scared, they were hugging and kissing. They told me to go back to bed. I just laid in the dark, confused and crying.*

Nancy W. says the abuse between her parents was both emotional and physical. *I never saw them hug,* she says. *Most of the time, they gave each other the silent treatment. They'd separate, get back together, then separate again. They'd hit and slug one another plenty, but they never kissed or held each other tenderly.*

When we witness years of extreme unhappiness and torment between our parents and see them stay together despite the unhappiness, we often feel ashamed and guilty about any joy or pleasure we find in our own intimate relationships. If we get into an abusive relationship, which is likely, we may feel powerless to leave, telling ourselves, "How can I possibly leave? After all, Mother's still with Dad." We may feel that we are somehow betraying our parents if we leave our unhappy, abusive relationship. "If Mother put up with everything that happened to her and she didn't leave, what makes me think I have the right to leave?" Instead, we "sentence" ourselves to remaining in dissatisfying and unfulfilling relationships.

*Absence of Sex.* In many alcoholic families, although there is no physical abuse, there is little or no sex or affection between the parents. In some alcoholic families, the parents sleep in separate bedrooms. In other families, the alcoholic or codependent simply uses the couch. Parents rarely explain such sleeping arrangement changes to the children and they are left feeling embarrassed trying to explain the arrangements to curious friends and neighbors. When parents do not mention the changed sleeping arrangements, they indirectly tell the child: "This topic is off-limits. Don't ask." The message to children growing up in such an asexual atmosphere is: "Sex and affection aren't necessary in relationships. Sexual and affectionate touching isn't comfortable or needed."

Connie S. describes her alcoholic parents: *I never saw my parents kiss or hug one another. They slept in separate rooms from the time I was five. They never kissed or touched me much either. Now I'm not much of a toucher at all.*

Despite the lack of sex in many alcoholic families, the atmosphere within the family is extremely emotionally charged with obsessive worry. Sexual energy is replaced by "trauma drama" energy. The family reels from one chaotic episode to the next, thriving on the "charge" the alcoholic and codependent incidents carry. Actual sex becomes incidental or nonexistent.

*Parenting Dysfunctional Parents.* If you're like many ACOAs, you may have been "put in charge" of the alcoholic parent in your family and indoctrinated in codependent behavior. Your other parent may have felt helpless and dependent and may have looked to you to resolve your family's pain. Invariably, you may have come to feel overwhelmed and exhausted. The relationship messages you received include: "Caring for another human being means controlling their feelings and behavior." "You can and should exert control over others." "It's your responsibility to make things better." You, like many other ACOAs, may have learned that your primary role is to caretake, to rage, to blame, to complain, to obsess over another, and to never expect sex or affection from a partner.

Debbie W. says she was the "mother" in her alcoholic family. *I mothered everyone,* she says. *I was my dad's prime enabler. I believed all of his lies. I always forgave him, covered for him. When I was a teenager, I'd drive him to bars and wait for him in dark parking lots so that he wouldn't get a driving-under-the-influence citation. The later it got, the more angry, frightened, and hysterical my mother would become. When we'd finally arrive home, I'd have to calm Mom down too and step between them when they'd begin to verbally throw punches at one another.*

Bonnie F. says her mother put her in charge of her alcoholic father when she was thirteen. *My mother was traveling in England,* she says. *Mom said I was supposed to stay and take care of Dad. I'd wait for him on the corner to come home from the bar. One night when he said he'd be home by 4:00 P.M., I waited and waited. He finally came around the corner at 8:00 P.M. and proceeded to smash the car right into our neighbor's house. The police came and took him to jail. When he came home the next morning, I fixed him breakfast. I felt really sorry for him. It was my job to emotionally take care of them both. They always complained to me about each other.*

## Untangling the Messages

One of the first steps in untangling the distorted and limiting sexual and relationship messages we received as a child growing up in an alcoholic family is to recognize what those messages were. The key is to begin to see beyond the childhood experiences and recognize the underlying messages. Consider for a moment your own history with your family.

What sexual messages did you receive about your body? About your developing sexuality? How did your parents' messages and behavior leave you feeling about sex? What incidents made you feel ashamed? What messages did those shame-producing incidents convey? Who became the sexual/relationship confidant in your family? Did your parents' sexual messages or behavior make you want to disappear or numb uncomfortable feelings? How do you think the messages you received as a child now affect your sexual/affectional relationships?

Many of us can identify the harmful messages, but most of us are unsure how to let go of those messages and develop healthier sexual and relationship attitudes and behaviors. One common response to dysfunctional messages for many of us who have children is to totally reverse the messages we received as children. If, for example, you were raised with the message that "nudity is bad," you might allow unlimited or inappropriate nudity in yourself and in your children. Women raised by parents who never discussed their own sexuality, often end up telling their children boundary-violating personal details of their sex life.

Diane S. says her mother was prudish about sex and made Diane and her sisters think that it was dirty. Her mother also withheld sex from her husband as punishment. Diane is determined to be different. *I go to dirty movies with my husband,* she says. *He's very horny so I read* Hustler *magazine with him and we call and listen to telephone sex tapes together. We make love even when I'm not in the mood. I'll never say no to him like my mother did with Dad. My husband will never be able to tell my kids that I wouldn't put out. We tell our four-year-old son everything about sex. I even point out sexy girls on the street to the two of them. We're very open and it's all very healthy. I'll never use sex as a punishment or hide it as something dirty like my mom did.*

By reversing unhealthy messages, we try to protect our children from the pain we experienced as children as a result of our childhood sexual messages. Unfortunately, these extreme reversals often deliver equally unhealthy messages.

A women's therapy group might help you untangle the sexual and relationship messages you received as a child growing up in an alcoholic family. One of the greatest benefits of a group is that you begin to realize that you aren't the only one. Other ACOAs experienced equally unpredictable family environments and received similar distorted messages about themselves and about relating intimately with others.

Another effective way to decrease the power of early sexual and relationship messages is to get accurate information through attending a human sexuality course. It's also a way to help ensure that you won't give your own children the same distorted messages you received. Perhaps you can take a course with one or two friends who, like you, want and need the information, but are unlikely to seek it out alone. Most community colleges and universities offer comprehensive sexuality courses through departments of health, psychology, or sociology. These classes offer curriculum on masturbation, sexual anatomy and hormones, gender roles, birth control, sexual orientation, sexual function and dysfunction, sexually transmitted diseases, sexual fantasies, the sexual response cycle, sexual assault, the development of sexual "scripts," and love and relationship skills.

*Passing On New Messages.* For those with children, as you recognize the inaccurate messages you received and gain accurate information about sexuality, you can begin to transmit that information to your own children. You can begin to reverse the generational pattern of passing on to children inaccurate and insensitive sexual messages. Along with factual information about sex, your children can benefit from the sharing of your own sexual values, your beliefs and feelings about sexual issues. It's helpful for you to listen to your children's concerns and feelings about sex and relationships—in many cases feelings which may differ from your own.

As a parent, we can work toward gradually creating an open environment in which our children feel encouraged to ask and discuss sexual questions. Children deserve to feel good about their bodies, their sexual exploring, and their first sexual encounters. It's important to withhold harsh judgements and criticism and allow children to explore sensitive sexual topics with you without ridicule or condemnation.

Children occasionally receive factual information about sex in a relatively impersonal manner. Deborah T. recalls finding a sex information book on her bed when she arrived home from school in the tenth grade. *The book provided factual, explicit information about sex, yet nothing about how you make sexual decisions. Neither of my parents ever acknowledged putting the book on my bed. I really would have liked hearing about what this sex stuff was like for my parents when they were in high school.*

Children learn from the process of modeling. They are keen observers and attentive listeners. They are often able to detect the verbal and non-verbal messages which pass back and forth between their primary caregivers. How you relate to your partner can teach them about intimacy, caring, trust, and mutual respect.

## Achieving Intimacy

All of us strive for intimacy, but the unhealthy sexual and relationship messages we received can interfere with our ability to be intimate with others. Identifying those messages and developing healthier ones can lead us to more intimate relationships. Striving for intimacy is a goal many of us share. But what exactly is intimacy? The word *intimacy* has its root in the latin word *intimus* meaning "deepest" or "innermost." Intimacy is a process in which two caring people mutually share their feelings, thoughts, and behaviors.

Intimacy has several components:

- Self-disclosure.
- Trust.
- Commitment.
- Honesty.
- Empathy.
- Tenderness.

*Self-Disclosure.* One of the most frequent problems we experience as ACOAs is rarely feeling safe enough to share our innermost thoughts and feelings. Developing a sense of self can assist you in beginning to trust yourself more deeply. As you trust yourself more, you'll be able to more accurately assess the trustworthiness of others. Over time, you'll likely find it easier to share, to self-disclose your thoughts and feelings. As you share the good times and the difficult times with others, you strengthen your capacity for intimacy.

*Trust.* Most of us who grew up in the unreliable, ever-changing world of alcoholics and codependents have difficulty trusting others. As children, when you shared your inner thoughts and feelings, they may have been used against you. Promises may have been continually broken. You probably learned not to trust those who claimed to love you. As an adult, you can begin to break down that lack of trust a little at a time. Over time, you can begin to develop trust when you notice your partner's behavior matches his or her words. Eventually, you can trust that what your partner says is most frequently accurate and honest.

*Commitment.* As we learn to disclose our feelings and attitudes with our partners and learn that they are primarily trustworthy, commitment can follow. Commitment means that both you and your partner agree to work to maintain the relationship's intimacy through periods of joy, crisis, anxiety, frustration, anger, boredom, success, and disappointment —"for better or worse." In a committed relationship, both partners are willing to confront themselves and each other about major and minor issues that affect the relationship. Commitment means being willing to confront any attitudes, feelings, or behaviors which may threaten the relationship.

*Honesty.* Commitment implies the expression of honesty within the relationship—honesty with ourselves and with our partners. Most ACOAs were raised in dishonest family environments. In your own adult life, you can begin to change that. You can create relationships in which you reduce or eliminate lying, deliberate deception, and intentional misrepresentation, all of which corrode intimacy and self-esteem. Dishonesty builds in an atmosphere of distrust and eventually creates deep hurt and resentment. Honesty thrives on trust and works to create feelings of love and safety.

*Empathy.* Another element of intimacy, empathy, is a tool for understanding one another and is achieved by open and receptive *listening*. By really listening to our partners, we can gain knowledge and understanding of their feelings, values, hopes, dreams, and ideas. Empathy encourages you to listen to the inner experience of another without blaming, judging, or condemning. Most of us grew up in families where no one really listened to one another. You can develop empathy in your relationship by learning to listen while suspending your problem-solving thinking. Instead of immediately thinking, "I must have done something wrong," or "How can I fix this?" you can provide time for your partner to speak without interruption. This will help you feel what they are saying. Empathy requires getting close enough to your partner to understand what he or she is saying to you. Empathy is a valuable skill that you can learn and develop through practice.

*Tenderness.* An element of intimacy that many of us did not experience as children, the ability to express tenderness, is one of the most neglected keys to developing intimacy. You can express your tenderness physically through affectionate hugs, glances, smiling, cuddling, kissing, and hand holding. You can verbally express your tender feelings for another through comforting words and empathic comments. Your actions toward your partner can also convey tenderness. If you are able to empathize with your partner—really understand them through nonjudgmental listening—tender feelings and the ability to express them can emerge naturally.

By modeling intimacy with your partner, you can teach your children—and yourself—healthy messages about sex and relationships. It may take you time to learn how to be intimate—how to care and share with another, freely exchange thoughts and feelings, reveal part of yourself, express empathy and tenderness, and gradually let go of interfering, self-protective defenses. The benefits to you and to those generations that follow you, can be well worth the effort.

# CHAPTER 9

# If I'm High, Sex Is Okay

*I first drank alcohol when I was fifteen. When I was seventeen and my boyfriend was out of town, I smoked some pot, began touching myself sexually and learned to masturbate. Two years later, I had intercourse for the first time after this guy and I got drunk in the back seat of his car at a drive-in.*

*Then I got together with a guy for two years. We used alcohol heavily and other drugs intermittently. Our sex together was never physically satisfying, but I was emotionally dependent on him. At one point, I got involved in an affair. When my boyfriend learned about it, he ended our relationship.*

*I stayed with this new lover for three years. It was sexually unfulfilling, but we drank together and the alcohol kept us together. When I met someone who introduced me to coke, amphetamines, and sleeping pills, I left and began a new relationship with this guy. He eventually got involved in illegal drug activity. I slept with a gun underneath my pillow.*

*By that time, my drug use had really escalated. I was drinking alone and heavily using methamphetamines. I became obsessed with my weight and started compulsively exercising, taking diet pills, and eventually became anorexic.*

*After I left this lover, I began to have multiple sex partners, but no committed relationships. I became involved with a married man who was much older than me. We did a lot of pot, alcohol, and other drugs together. I quit my job and moved to another state to be with him, but his jealousy and possessiveness became too much to handle and I left him. I immediately got involved with an alcoholic who was exciting, successful, and physically attractive. I became pregnant twice with him and had two abortions. He had sexual problems. The more he drank, the less able he was to screw. I left him and I became involved in numerous uncommitted affairs.*

*From age nineteen until now, I've probably had sex with at least a hundred men. But since I got sober last year, I've had sex with only three men. I can't seem to do it sober. I feel too controlled, confined, and distrusting to have sex easily. I can't ask for what I want sexually and have never been able to. Now that I'm sober,*

*I fear rejection more than ever. I just want the men I have sex with to like me. I can say yes to sex, but I say no to intimacy. I guess I'm a lot like my dad. I can't stay with one person for any length of time, drunk or sober. My mom and dad got divorced because of his constant infidelity. At least I never married. — Beth G.*

If you grew up in an alcoholic family, you're at risk for developing your own drug and alcohol abuse. Experts estimate that children from alcoholic families are at least *four times* more likely than children from nonalcoholic families to abuse drugs and alcohol. Among ACOAs who become drug dependent, many combine drugs with sex. Those who don't become addicted to alcohol or drugs often select partners who are addicted and experience sex with partners who are under the influence. Drugs and alcohol often serve to protect us from our fears around relating sexually to another.

### Chemical Dependency Denial

Many of the ACOAs we interviewed were addicted to chemicals or were involved with partners who used mind/mood altering chemicals. Like them, many of us feel confused, afraid, and anxious around our own and/or our partner's drug and alcohol use. We often are unable or refuse to recognize the extent of our partner's or our own chemical dependency. Like our alcoholic childhood families, we tend to minimize, rationalize, or blatantly deny our own or our partner's addiction.

*Alcohol Abuse.* In his classic book, *The Disease Concept of Alcoholism*, Dr. E. M. Jellinek first defined alcoholism as a chronic, progressive, and potentially fatal disease. For more than thirty years, the American Medical Association (AMA) has recognized alcoholism as a disease with identifiable and progressive symptoms. The AMA says that, if untreated, alcoholism progresses relentlessly and can lead to mental damage, physical incapacity, and early death.

Most of us from alcoholic backgrounds wonder, "If my parents were alcoholic, what are the chances I'll become an alcoholic?" Many alcoholism authorities suggest that without intervention ACOAs have an *80 percent* chance of:

- Marrying an alcoholic or drug-dependent partner.
- Becoming alcoholic or drug dependent.
- Becoming involved with partners who suffer some type of compulsive behavior such as gambling, overworking, overeating, or acting out sexually addictive behaviors.

An excellent review of research investigating the transmission of alcoholism across generations is *The Alcoholic Family,* by Steinglass, Bennett, Wolin, and Reiss. The authors conclude that the genetic predisposition to alcoholism is a "priming factor." This predisposition does not in and of itself lead to alcoholism. They say that alcoholism develops due to the complex interaction between the biological predisposition to the disease and what occurs in the family. They believe that the disease of alcoholism is generationally transmitted in families where the genetic predisposition is combined with daily routines and family rituals that revolve around alcohol. Much remains to be learned about how the psychosocial aspects of families and the genetic predisposition to alcoholism interact to transmit alcoholism to children in alcoholic families.

Among the ACOAs we studied, ninety-nine out of one hundred had used alcohol. Thirty-eight percent currently use alcohol, most in combination with other drugs such as marijuana, amphetamines, tranquilizers, and cocaine. While 61 percent said they presently abstain from alcohol, more than one-third of these alcohol-abstainers currently use other drugs.

While most of us are aware of our increased risk in abusing alcohol, few of us are aware of our risk potential for addiction to other drugs. *If you are alcoholic or have a genetic predisposition to alcoholism, you are at risk for becoming addicted to other mood- or mind-altering drugs.* Often we abstain from one drug, only to move onto the addictive use of another.

Jenny F., a thirty-four-year-old ACOA who works as an executive in a bank, hasn't had a drink of alcohol in the past seven years. Although Jenny is dry, she uses pot and tranquilizers daily for "the stress on her job" and snorts cocaine with her new lover, David, every few weeks. Jenny says she's not concerned about the frequency of her drug use and feels proud of her success in giving up alcohol.

More than *one-half* of the ACOA research participants we interviewed have a past or present problem with alcohol. Thirty-nine women identified themselves as alcoholics recovering through Alcoholics Anonymous. They were sober from one to twenty-three years, with the average being four years. *Nearly 100 percent of the ACOAs in our study had mixed drugs and/or alcohol with sex through their own or their partner's use.*

## Drugs, Alcohol, and Sex

Sexologists and alcohol researchers know that alcohol is a depressant. In small amounts, alcohol tranquilizes the mind and body. It releases inhibitions that may interfere with sexual enjoyment. In large amounts, however, alcohol impairs all the body's reflexes, including sexual responsiveness. Chronic alcohol use greatly impairs – or even halts – sexual response.

Researcher V. Malatesta studied women's orgasms while they drank alcohol and watched erotic films using an instrument which measures blood flow to the vagina (increased blood flow is an indication of sexual arousal). The study showed that as the women's blood alcohol level increased, they had more difficulty achieving orgasm, took longer to orgasm, and experienced less intense orgasms. Paradoxically, the women said when they drank large amounts of alcohol, they felt more aroused and claimed to enjoy their orgasms more.

How is it that alcohol impairs the physical sexual response, yet these women said they felt more sexually satisfied? Our expectations about alcohol's effects have a powerful influence on how we react to it. Most people, particularly ACOAs, believe that alcohol and sex go together. The mass media has spent billions of dollars on films, soap operas, and advertisements promoting the idea that sex is better with alcohol. The messages seem to say, "If you want sex with someone, especially with a woman, give her alcohol." And "If you want to be sexually attractive, sip alcohol seductively." In our culture, sex and alcohol have become synonymous and many of us are convinced you can't have one without the other.

Research on the physiological effects of alcohol on women's sexuality conducted by D. Powell concluded that in alcoholic women, alcohol acts as a gonadal toxin or poison that has devastating effects on sexuality including masculinization, premature menopause, menstrual irregularities, breast atrophy, cessation of ovulation, and a reduction in the production of natural vaginal lubrication.

*Fear of Sex/Intimacy.* W. Murphy evaluated the sexual functioning of eighty-seven alcoholic women at an alcohol rehabilitation center and half-way house. While he found that very few sexually active women reported physiological sexual arousal problems, he discovered the vast majority said they felt little or no sexual desire. Several other research studies have found that both practicing and recovering alcoholic women have reduced interest in sexual activity. Most sexologists believe this lack of sexual desire is a *psychological* rather than physiological problem. The lack of sexual desire, they say, stems from feelings of isolation, inadequacy, depression, low self-esteem, fear of intimacy and worry about being unable to perform sexually.

Recent research by Powell cautions us that sexual "dysfunction" among women alcoholics shouldn't be confused with sexual "dissatisfaction." He reports the most common sexual complaint of alcoholic women is disinterest in sex. He suggests that this disinterest may be the result of intimacy issues and relationship disharmony rather than any physiological change caused by alcohol consumption.

A fundamental belief in our culture and certainly a belief held by most alcoholics is that alcohol improves sex. In a 1984 study of women entering treatment for alcohol abuse, Researcher David Smith, M.D., found that 65 percent said alcohol improved their sexual functioning. Most of these women said they doubted their ability to engage in sex without alcohol. They acknowledged they use alcohol to self-medicate their fears and anxiety around sex. During one of our interviews a newly recovering alcoholic said, *When I was drinking and using drugs, I could have sex easily. Since I got sober, I feel sexually inhibited. Lately, I've shut down sexually. When I'm sober and having sex, I feel like I'm watching what's happening from a distance and my head takes off with a running negative commentary about what's going on.*

The link between alcohol, sexual functioning, and sexual fears was further underscored in research by Beckman which concluded that women alcoholics are more likely than nonalcoholics to believe that alcohol increases their desire, enjoyment, spontaneity, and frequency of sex. However, Sexologist Mickey Apter-Marsh showed in her 1983 study that while 80 percent of female alcoholics said they felt alcohol improved their sex life, as they became sober, they changed their perception about it. The longer they were sober, the less they clung to the "sex is better with alcohol" idea. Until newly recovering alcoholics discard the idea that alcohol enhances sex, they are at high risk for relapsing.

***Shame-Producing Sex.*** Alcohol and other drugs function to allow many of us to engage in sexual behaviors we might not ordinarily consider and have sex with partners we'd otherwise never choose. Linda S. says she tolerated intercourse with her husband only when she was drunk. *I could only have intercourse with him if I was too plastered to remember,* she says. *He'd tell me the next day we'd made love, but I'd have absolutely no memory of it.*

Maureen P. confided that during her heaviest drinking periods, she'd engage in sex simultaneously with two men. *One watched while I was sexual with the other,* she says. *Almost all of my sexuality has involved alcohol or other drugs. I can never imagine doing some of the things I've done sexually without being wasted.*

For many of us, drugs and alcohol let us engage in sex that would otherwise make us feel guilty, ashamed or embarrassed. Recovering alcoholic Lorna W. describes her drug- and alcohol-filled sexual experiences. *We used ties, whips, bondage, golden showers. Sex was a game for me like drugs.*

*We always had drugs and alcohol with this kind of sex. When I was drunk, I'd engage in group sex. I'd have to be wasted to do it. The next day, I'd have trouble facing myself.*

Carla R. used drugs to assert her sense of power sexually. *I'd tie up my partner. I was always in control. It gave me a sense of power. The more I drank, the more orders and commands I'd issue. I'd make love in a rough way that aroused me. But I only did S&M with drugs. I've never done it or wanted to do it when I was sober.*

Linda Beckman's study compared 120 women alcoholics with 118 nonalcoholics and showed that 55 percent of the alcoholics said if they drank they'd have sex with people they wouldn't normally become involved with. Only 24 percent of the nonalcoholics said they would. Three times as many alcoholics said they'd engage in sexual acts while drinking they would not engage in while sober. These women alcoholics were also more likely than nonalcoholics to have had at least one sexual encounter with someone of the same sex. They also said their alcohol-related sexual choices frequently left them feeling guilty.

Nan V., an ACOA and recovering alcoholic, says she still feels guilty about having a sexual relationship with her sister and brother-in-law. *My sexual relationship with my sister and brother-in-law was based on drugs,* she recalls. *They initiated it and I didn't know how to say no and be polite about it. It fed into my sexual fantasies and I was desperate to be cool, but I felt bad about it.*

Joanna K. describes the guilt she feels around her affair with a married co-worker and her subsequent pregnancy and abortion. *I met him in a bar and he told me that first night that he was married and that his wife was expecting a baby in a few months. I went against all the values I thought I held about avoiding married men. We drank together in the bar and then at my place. I kept coming on to him. Every time I thought about his pregnant wife, I'd tell myself she probably wouldn't want sex with him anyway. The next day after spending the evening with him, I'd want to quit work in shame.* Joanna believes that her pregnancy and abortion from this affair with a married man was her punishment for betraying her early moral values.

Researching differences between alcoholic and nonalcoholic women, Valerie Pinhas found that those of us who abuse drugs and alcohol often have more sexual guilt and feel less control over our sexual lives than nonabusers. We may feel guilty about participating in adultery, same-sex behavior, excessive masturbation, and "unusual" sexual practices. Pinhas indicates if we abuse chemicals we:

· Are less able to prevent pregnancy through birth control.
· Experience less success in achieving orgasm.

· Are less able to attract emotionally, physically, and sexually available sexual partners.
· Have difficulty expressing our own sexual needs with partners.

Thirty-two-year-old ACOA Sheila W. says because of her drug and alcohol use, she had difficulty protecting herself emotionally and sexually from a man who didn't care about her. She was unable to set effective boundaries to protect herself. *I was in love with him, but he wasn't in love with me,* she says. *He'd been drinking and we took some drugs and had sex. But the next time I saw him he acted really aloof. Then he just dropped out of my life without a word. Later when I saw him at a party, he was drunk and said he wanted to have sex with me again. I said no. He pushed me into the kitchen and pulled me onto the floor. He ended up rubbing against my stomach and ejaculating. On the one hand I felt gratified because he was showing me some affection. On the other, I felt sad because I'd been used. He'd fuck me, but he wouldn't call me. Today I look back at the humiliation and embarrassment and grief of that young girl. I wanted love and affection so much, but I kept myself from having it. Not loving myself, disregarding my own needs, I fooled myself into thinking that I could be loved by these means. I set myself up to get the opposite of love.*

**Sex for Drugs.** For some of us, sex becomes the avenue to get the drugs we crave. More than 17 percent of our ACOA study participants said they'd engaged in prostitution for drugs. Pat R. says she had numerous one-night stands before she decided to exchange sex for a reliable supply of coke and alcohol. *For two years during my heaviest drinking period, I was involved in prostitution. I became the mistress of a married police officer. He set me up in an expensive condo and made sure I got 'safe' drugs. In exchange, I had to be available to him on very short notice and agree to wear whatever he wanted me to. I wanted the drugs so bad that I'd do anything he wanted sexually. Most of the time when we had sex, I'd pretend to be somewhere else. I dreamed up elaborate fantasies during sex that took me away from him and the life I was living. For me, drugs and sex became synonymous and sex became my tool to get drugs. After I got sober, the prostitution stopped.*

## Assessing Your Own Addiction

Most of us who addictively use drugs and alcohol are unable to experience intimate sexuality within a relationship. We tend to feel less emotionally, are less "present" to our partner during sex, and lose much of the richness that clean and sober sex provides. Fortunately, there are effective resources available to help us become chemical-free.

In addition to many of the resources listed in the Resources section of this book, we particularly recommend Kathleen Whalen Fitzgerald's *Alcoholism, The Genetic Inheritance,* Jean Kirkpatrick's *Goodbye Hangovers, Hello Life,* Merlene Miller, Terence Gorski, and David Miller's *Guide for Recovery from Alcoholism,* James Milan and Katherine Ketcham's *Under the Influence,* and *Alcoholics Anonymous,* originally published in 1939 and now rereleased in paperback. Each of these books focuses on breaking the denial which may surround identifying our own or our partners' addictions.

One of the most paradoxical characteristics of the disease of alcoholism is that the alcoholic usually denies or doesn't recognize her or his own illness. Kathleen Whalen Fitzgerald's recent book, *Alcoholism, The Genetic Inheritance,* offers the following questions for self-assessment. These questions have been adapted to include the use and abuse of alcohol and other mind- or mood-altering chemicals.

1. Do you lose time from work due to drinking/using?
2. Is drinking/using making your home life unhappy?
3. Do you drink/use because you're shy with other people?
4. Is drinking/using affecting your reputation?
5. Have you ever felt remorse after drinking/using?
6. Have you gotten into financial difficulties because of your drinking/using?
7. Do you turn to lower companions and an inferior environment when drinking/using?
8. Does your drinking/using make you careless about your family's welfare?
9. Has your ambition decreased since drinking/using?
10. Do you crave a drink or a drug at a definite time every day?
11. Do you want a drink or a drug the next morning?
12. Does drinking/using cause you to have difficulty sleeping?
13. Has your efficiency decreased since drinking/using?
14. Is drinking/using jeopardizing your job or business?
15. Do you drink/use to escape from worries or trouble?
16. Do you drink/use alone?
17. Have you ever had a complete loss of memory as a result of drinking/using?
18. Has your physician ever treated you for drinking/using?
19. Do you drink/use to build up your self-confidence?
20. Have you ever been to a hospital or institution on account of your drinking/using?

If you answered yes to any *one* of these questions, you may be addicted to alcohol and/or drugs.

If you or your partner are addicted to drugs and/or alcohol, there are excellent self-help support groups such as Alcoholics Anonymous (AA) and Narcotics Anonymous (NA) which are available in every state. Phone numbers for these and other organizations are available in the white pages of your local phone book. Locations for Women for Sobriety meetings, another helpful resource, can be found by calling (215) 536-8026.

The most comforting news is that you don't have to take the first steps toward sobriety or abstinence alone. Although this journey requires continuing commitment and hard work, embarking on it can be the most significant decision of your life. It necessitates a personal journey toward your "self" and later toward others.

### Getting Clean and Sober: The Sexual Effects

As recovering ACOAs, we must confront and deal with the sexual guilt surrounding our past behaviors and partners or risk losing our newly found sobriety. Many of us suffer sexual guilt around our:

- Inability to experience orgasm.
- Loss of interest in sex.
- Sexual molestation.
- Same-sex relationships.
- Abortions and adoptions.
- Chronic pattern of selecting abusive partners.
- Prostituting ourselves for drugs, intimacy, affection, and/or emotional and financial security.
- Incest.

ACOA research participant Karen G. recounts her inability to deal with her sexual pain and guilt and her unsuccessful attempts to maintain her sobriety. *I was sober for six years and then I smoked pot for a year and I started drinking again,* she says. *I finally entered a treatment program and managed to stay sober for four more years. Then I binged on alcohol for about three months. I've always relapsed over the sex in my relationships. I'm addicted to people who don't want a relationship with me. I become obsessed with having them. It makes me feel crazy. They leave me and I feel abandoned. I don't think I'll be able to stay sober until I find out why I keep getting into relationships like this.*

*Emergence of Memories.* Without the buffer of chemicals, many of us who are newly recovering don't know how to feel about sex or our intimate relationships. Although we've promised ourselves not to use or

drink, we're usually unprepared for the feelings that
sobriety. During the early stages of recovery, many of us a
memories of humiliating or degrading sexual relationsh
made during our years of using and drinking. We may feel
by what we begin to learn about ourselves. This remember
especially true for those of us who've been sober only a sh

Many of us have unconsciously used chemicals for years to block
confusing and painful memories of sexual assault. Some of us have no
conscious sexual assault memories, others have hazy memories or vague
feelings, and still others vividly recall past assaults, yet use chemicals to
keep from confronting the helpless feelings surrounding these experiences. We stack sexual assault upon painful sexual assault during our
years of chemical abuse without ever telling anyone or sharing our pain.
Once sober, we may begin to experience flashbacks, nightmares, and
intense fear and anxiety about past incest, child molestation, and rape
experiences. Often we have little choice but to directly confront these
memories. As we recover, we need and deserve a safe place to explore
and reexperience our feelings of anger, guilt, confusion, and sadness.
Without appropriate support to confront our sexually abusive experiences, our relapse is almost certain.

*Sexual Abuse and Drug/Alcohol Abuse.* The link between alcoholism
and drug abuse and sexual abuse—both between victims and assailants
—has been well established. Numerous researchers have found that
incest survivors suffer a higher incidence of problem drinking, alcoholism, and other drug addiction. In 1982, Researcher Jody Yeary found
that men and women who sexually abuse children often drink alcoholically. She also found that many women in treatment for chemical
dependency were incest victims.

In an early study of incest in 1977 among 118 chemically dependent
women, J. Densen-Gerber found that 44 percent had been sexually
abused as children by one or more family members. E. Weber found that
70 percent of chemically dependent adolescents in his study had been
sexually abused. In a 1982 study of two hundred San Francisco prostitutes, 61 percent said they were victims of incest or molestation and
59 percent were active drug and/or alcohol users.

Therapist and Incest Researcher Wendy Maltz concludes that both
alcoholism and incest in families often pass from one generation to
the next. She says the families' behavioral patterns, which allow and
encourage alcoholism, if left untreated, may foster sexual abuse.

Many of us who are now or who have previously been addicted to
chemicals have been victims of some form of sexual assault. For many

of us, recognizing and identifying ourselves as drug and/or alcohol dependent is the first step in a long process of sexual healing.

Often those of us who are chemically dependent and survivors of incest or rape feel ashamed about our past sexual abuse and/or our drug and alcohol addiction. We may enter a treatment facility and hide the sexual abuse which contributes to our addictive behavior. Or we may begin group or individual treatment to deal with our past sexual abuse secrets and struggle to conceal our drug and/or alcohol abuse history. Accepting the label of "sexual assault survivor" or "alcoholic" or "drug addict" may create even more self-hate for us. Those of us in treatment for sexual abuse need assistance in revealing our chemical dependency history; as we recover from chemical dependency, we need assistance in exploring our sexual histories. Our long-term healing and recovery depends on our willingness to reveal and explore these secrets. With help, our internalized shame can be addressed and eventually replaced with self-compassion.

***Sexual Orientation Confusion.*** While some of us are confronted with memories and feelings about past sexual abuse as we recover, others of us find that we have questions and intense feelings about our own sexual orientation. Work conducted in 1980 by Psychotherapist S. Evans, showed that lesbians suffer from a disproportionately high incidence of chemical abuse and chemical dependency. ACOA lesbians appear to be at far greater risk for alcoholism and drug dependency than heterosexual ACOAs. Studies continue to reveal high risk for lesbians—*one in three lesbians is chemically dependent.*

In our sample of ACOAs, 57 percent said they felt confused about their sexual orientation. They felt unsure about whether they were heterosexual, bisexual, or homosexual. Some of the alcoholic ACOAs said that when they got sober, they were confronted by memories and feelings about being touched by or about touching another woman.

ACOA study participant Janice B. says she was eighteen when she became involved with a thirty-nine-year-old female neighbor who lived with another woman. *One afternoon, I was sunbathing outside in the backyard and drinking gin and tonics,* she says. *I was a bit drunk and feeling really good. The neighbor saw me over the fence and asked if I'd like to come over. I didn't think anything about accepting another drink from her. We joked, laughed, and listened to her stereo. After a while, we ended up holding one another and kissing. I went home feeling surprised and excited. I continued drinking and seeing her for about a year. Then I entered a treatment center and got sober. I started to question my sexuality. Was I a lesbian? A bisexual? Was I the one who initiated sex with my neighbor that first time? My treatment counselor kept saying my sexual orienta-*

*tion didn't matter. He told me to just focus on staying sober. But I needed to talk about my guilt and confusion. I needed to sort out my sexuality. In group, when other recovering women talked about their relationships with men, I felt left out. I had no idea getting sober would mean a sexual identity crisis for me.*

Questions about sexual orientation often occur for us as we recover in much the same way it did for Janice—we have sexual relationships before recovery and then question those relationships and what they mean about our sexual identity during recovery. Some of us have no same-sex relationships in our drugging years, then during sobriety we begin to notice affectional and sexual thoughts and feelings toward others of our sex. We may start having sexual dreams involving same-sex partners. Others of us may begin to reflect on the significance of our past intense relationships with same-sex friends. Many of us feel very confused about the possibility of being homosexual or bisexual and may be overwhelmed with thoughts and feelings that it is sick, wrong, immature, or sinful for us to feel sexual toward someone of the same gender.

Without the support and safe space we need to explore our conflicting feelings, we're highly susceptible for relapse into chemical dependency. Some of us have spent our drinking and drugging years denying our homosexual orientation. While we may have sensed emotional, affec-tional, and sexual attraction towards others of the same sex at some point in our lives, many of us reacted to these feelings by forcing ourselves into heterosexual activity. Denying our true sexual identity, however, may have necessitated that we chronically use chemicals to mask the truth. When the fog of drugs and alcohol begins to lift, old, partially formed questions about sexual orientation may reemerge.

Rather than confront our sexual orientation as we recover, some of us choose to deny any sexuality and become celibate. We may go through years of recovery while avoiding all intimate relationships. Instead, we often create "coping" methods such as compulsive work or compulsive service to others to postpone facing this powerful issue.

***Post-sobriety Sexuality.*** Regardless of our sexual orientation or child-hood sexual trauma, many of us who have just recognized and identified ourselves as alcoholic and/or drug dependent face changes in our sexual-ity. Recovering alcoholic ACOA Linda F. says, *As my drinking progressed, I got into the habit of faking orgasm. With booze, it was easy to fake it. I was con-stantly trying to meet the man's expectations. Now that I'm having drug-free sex, I can't fool myself into thinking that faking orgasms is okay. I can no longer tell myself that my sexual needs don't matter. In AA, I learned about being "rigorously honest" in my life. That honesty has crept into my sex life. I want to know where do I go from here with it?"*

Sexologist Mickey Apter-Marsh interviewed sixty-one recovering women alcoholics about their drinking histories, their sexual behavior, attitudes, and their sexual dysfunction. She examined three time periods for each woman: before drinking addictively, during addictive drinking, and during the beginning of sobriety (the first three months, nine months, and twelve months). She found that their sexual behavior changed dramatically depending on whether they used or didn't use alcohol. She also found that the changes that occurred weren't necessarily permanent. Most of the women reported they had more partner sex during drinking periods than they had during the first three months of their recovery. However, in time, most women regained their pre-addictive sexual frequency levels. After one year of sobriety, the women said they orgasmed more frequently with their partners than they had prior to sobriety.

Apter-Marsh's research offers reassurance to those of us who are recovering and struggling with post-sobriety changes in our sexuality. *Although sexual interest may decline in early sobriety, sexual functioning appears to gradually recover and sex becomes more satisfying than ever.* This is especially true for those of us willing to investigate our entire sexual relationship history and our feelings about that history and share those thoughts and feelings with trusted friends and professionals.

*Exploring Sexuality Anew.* Many of us who become clean and sober may feel "young" and "naive" about initiating or responding to sexual advances. Often recovering ACOAs in their thirties, forties, fifties and sixties say they don't know the "rules" governing sexual relationships. To a certain extent, those of us who are newly recovering are much like adolescents just beginning to relate intimately and explore our sexuality. It's the first time many of us have experienced our sexuality and ourselves without mood or mind-altering drugs and/or alcohol and often we haven't yet figured out what we really want or expect in a sexual relationship.

Learning to become comfortable with our sexuality without chemicals takes time. Often we are faced with years of powerful negative messages about ourselves and about sexuality which need to be overcome. Healing is possible. One of the most effective ways to begin to acquire the assertive skills you'll need for sexual healing is to join a women's recovery group with a therapist who encourages the open discussion of sexual issues and feelings. For most of us, this feels safer to do in a same-sex group, rather than in a mixed group. The group can provide feedback for you and let you know you're not alone in the fears and insecurities surrounding your sexuality.

Women's recovery groups can help you develop the assertive skills required to establish and maintain a healthy, addiction-free sexual relationship. Some of these assertive skills include learning to:

- Say no to sexual advances you don't want.
- Initiate sexual behaviors you desire.
- Ask directly and assertively for affection and sexual touching that arouses you.
- Communicate openly and clearly about your sexual experiences and your sexual feelings with your partner(s).

At first, you may feel scared and uncomfortable and very visible using these new assertive sexual relationship skills. Take time to practice the new skills and behaviors at a pace that won't overwhelm you. Incorporating these skills takes much repetition and reinforcement. As you begin to acquire these assertive skills, you can learn to view yourself more positively as a sexual being and you can begin to value your right to sexually assert yourself.

As in all other areas of your recovery from chemical addiction, the focus of sexual healing needs to be gentle and self-loving. Progress, not perfection, is the goal. To abandon your right to sexually relate to a partner in a healthy way is to experience an unnecessary loss. Deciding to live your life without an unhealthy dependency on drugs and/or alcohol is a positive, self-affirming step. This step toward a drug-free relationship with yourself and others does not have to include a life without sex. Your past sexual decisions and behaviors under the influence of drugs do not require current sexual abstinence. Recovery from chemicals can bring recovery of your healthy sexual self. Sex without chemicals can bring a type of intimacy that sex with chemicals could never allow. Your emotional, physical, and spiritual recovery includes reclaiming and celebrating your own inherent sexuality.

# CHAPTER 10

# Straight? Bisexual? Gay? I'm Confused

*My first relationship occurred when I was seventeen and Suzanne was eighteen. I thought I was in love with her. The following year, she married some guy she'd met in college. Can you believe that I agreed to be her maid of honor? She told me she loved me, but she had to do what was right and proper in the world.*

*I didn't have another relationship for ten years. I became involved with another woman and we were together for three years. Then her mother convinced her to come back to the Midwest and see a psychologist about her "lifestyle." I drove her back there. While there, she became involved in AA and got sober. I got into AA too, but we never got back together as lovers.*

*After about six months of sobriety, I found myself cutting my own arm with a razor blade. It seemed the only way I could feel anything. I was successful in my career, made tons of money, but I felt such loneliness inside. The day I cut myself, I'd received a letter from my ex-lover's mother calling me a lesbian and telling me how much she hated lesbians. No one at work knew about my lifestyle and she threatened to tell my boss. I didn't start drinking again, but I'd cut myself when I felt under tremendous pressure.*

*Eventually, I met a woman in AA and we became involved. She was vivacious and likeable. I constantly tried to please her. I'd bring her breakfast in bed, even turn down the covers for her. I'd cling to the smallest bit of affection from her. But no matter what I did, I never felt I mattered to her. I never felt any sexual satisfaction with her either. I'd cry when we made love because I couldn't ask her to touch me in the ways I wanted. After a while, I felt like I was sexually "servicing" her. Finally, she left the relationship and I felt devastated.—Michelle H.*

We asked the ACOAs in our research whether they'd experienced past or present sexual orientation confusion. A majority—56 percent—said they had. We all have questions about our sexuality. What makes us heterosexual, bisexual, or homosexual? Can we change our sexual orientation? How can we find our true sexual orientation? If a woman can have an orgasm with a man, is it possible that she could be a lesbian? Can lesbians become mothers and have kids? How does growing up in an alcoholic family affect our sexual orientation — or does it?

When we asked ACOA participant Michelle H., the woman whose story began this chapter, about her sexual orientation, she said she was homosexual. At age fifty-four, Michelle has never been married, never been pregnant, and has been clean and sober for the past nineteen years. She's had sex with three men and eight women and she says she's gay. How does she know? If she's been sexual with both men and women, doesn't this make her bisexual? How does anyone know their true sexual orientation?

## Determining Your Sexual Orientation

The term *sexual orientation* means erotic attraction toward people of the same gender (homosexual), the other gender (heterosexual), or both genders (bisexual). The original Kinsey reports on sexuality published in 1948 and 1953, the first attempts to scientifically identify peoples' sexual orientation, contained data collected from face-to-face interviews with more than ten thousand Americans. Interviewers in this study asked participants questions about their sexual behaviors including fantasies and masturbation in childhood, adolescence, and as adults. They also asked a series of questions designed to measure sexual arousal toward women and/or men.

Based on the responses, Kinsey devised a seven-point rating scale to describe the sexual attitudes and behaviors of people — their sexual orientation. His continuum ranged from zero, which indicates exclusively heterosexual behavior, to six, exclusively homosexual behavior.

---

*The Kinsey Scale*

0. Exclusively heterosexual behavior
1. Primarily heterosexual, but incidents of homosexual behavior
2. Primarily heterosexual, but more than incidental homosexual behavior
3. Equal amounts of heterosexual and homosexual behavior
4. Primarily homosexual, but more than incidental heterosexual behavior
5. Primarily homosexual, but incidents of heterosexual behavior
6. Exculsively homosexual behavior

Kinsey found that most people are neither strictly homosexual nor heterosexual. Instead, he concluded that most people exist along a *continuum* of sexual orientation, some leaning more heavily toward homosexual behaviors, others leaning more heavily toward heterosexual. Bisexuals, he said, exist more toward the middle of the scale and include women and men who are attracted to and who usually, but not always, engage in sex with partners of both genders.

Kinsey's findings challenged the world of sexology. According to Kinsey, 10 percent of white men are exclusively homosexual for at least three years during the ages between sixteen and fifty-five and 4 percent are exclusively homosexual all their lives. He further discovered that by age forty, nearly 20 percent of women experience erotic contact with a same-sex partner and that 3 percent of the women studied are exclusively homosexual all their lives.

The most frequently quoted Kinsey finding is that 37 percent of men and 13 percent of women experienced at least one homosexual encounter leading to orgasm by age 45. What's surprising about these statistics is the substantial number of people who engage in same-sex behaviors, but do not become exclusively homosexual. Kinsey found some women who had same-sex experiences considered themselves heterosexual, not homosexual or bisexual. Other women, he said, are homosexual and experience high levels of sexual arousal toward women, though they've never experienced sexual contact with another woman.

Kinsey recognized that, over a lifetime, people change positions on the sexual orientation scale. Most Americans, he said, fall somewhere between one and five on the scale—neither exclusively heterosexual or homosexual.

Sexology Researcher Fritz Klein developed a grid to measure seven interrelated aspects of sexuality: sexual attraction; sexual behavior; sexual fantasies; emotional preference; social preference; lifestyle; and self-identification. To determine sexual orientation, Klein has people use the Kinsey numerical scale for the seven variables in one's past, present, and ideal future.

To determine your own sexual orientation using Klein's grid, use the Kinsey numerical system (0-6) to accurately describe your sexuality in each box.

Add the numbers in the boxes and divide by twenty-one. If you put dashes in any boxes to indicate no sexual behavior, no experience, or no fantasy in any of the categories, divide the total by one less for each dash. The resulting number indicates your position on Kinsey's scale.

| | Past | Present | Ideal Future |
|---|---|---|---|
| Sexual attraction | | | |
| Sexual behavior | | | |
| Sexual fantasies | | | |
| Emotional preference | | | |
| Social preference | | | |
| Self-identification | | | |
| Lifestyle | | | |

From the work of Kinsey, Klein, and others, it's apparent that people display a wide range of human sexual behavior, attraction, and affection. This continuum of sexuality more accurately reflects reality than the extreme polarity of identifying oneself as 100 percent heterosexual or 100 percent homosexual.

Sorting our sexual feelings and identifying sexual orientation isn't easy, but it's an important step in the journey toward our real selves. What is it that keeps us from embracing our true sexual orientation?

Three factors make identifying sexual orientation especially difficult for ACOAs:

· Confusion over sexual orientation, gender identity, and sex roles.
· Addiction to chemicals and eating disorders.
· Externalized and internalized homophobia.

## Sexual Orientation, Gender Identity, Sex Role Confusion

The first factor which interferes with identifying our sexual orientation is confusion between the terms *sexual orientation, gender identity*, and *sex roles*. As mentioned earlier, *sexual orientation* refers to erotic attraction to same-gender partners (homosexual), different-gender partners (heterosexual), or both genders (bisexual).

*Gender identity* refers to the feeling or conviction that one is either female or male. *Sex roles*, also called *gender roles*, are the traits and behaviors a given culture expects of its females and males.

Most often gender—femaleness or maleness—is determined at birth through a complex set of chromosomal, hormonal, and physiological differences. The female determinants of gender are the XX chromosome, a preponderance of female hormones estrogen and progesterone, and female reproductive and sexual organs. The male determinants are XY chromosomes, a preponderance of the male hormones androgen and testosterone, and male reproductive and sexual organs.

Unlike gender, which is predetermined at birth, sex roles are behaviors that are acquired after birth through socialization. Sex role socialization occurs through parents, peers, and social institutions teaching children to behave in "gender-appropriate" ways—how to act like a "girl" or act like a "boy."

Traditional gender role stereotypes have long been a powerful characteristic of the American culture. Women and men are often assigned opposite and differing traits. Traditional masculine traits include being brave, strong, proud, stoic, decisive, athletic, logical, rational, practical, mechanical, aggressive, scientific, ambitious, confident, unemotional, adventurous, uninhibited, sexually experienced, sexually aggressive, and being the provider.

In contrast, traditional feminine traits in our culture include being sensual, shallow, gentle, tender, quiet, weak, tardy, romantic, domestic, nervous, insecure, fearful, graceful, seductive, virginal, expressive, religious, helpless, affectionate, sentimental, impractical, inconsistent, idealistic, a follower, submissive, noncompetitive, self-conscious, easily intimidated, and sexually passive and uninterested.

You may notice that there are fewer positive words and more blatantly negative words used to describe femininity than masculinity. Many gender stereotypes persist in our culture, despite the numerous role models to refute them.

Many of us, in attempting to identify our sexual orientation, think that the best orientation indicator is our gender role. Our gender role, however, does not determine our sexual orientation. We may engage in a number of "feminine" traits or behaviors, possess a female gender identity, and still be homosexual. Likewise, we may engage in many "masculine" sex role behaviors and be heterosexual.

As more and more women and men challenge the traditional stereotypical sex roles, people feel even more confused about sex roles and sexual orientation. Many of us are becoming more "androgynous," behaving in ways that are stereotypically both masculine, such as athletic and assertive behavior, and stereotypically feminine, such as being tender and nurturing of others. It's possible for a woman to be a "masculine" heterosexual; a "feminine" lesbian; an androgynous bisexual, heterosexual, or homosexual—or any combination of sex role and sexual orientation. How stereotypically "masculine" or "feminine" we are *does not* determine our sexual orientation.

Confusion over sex roles and sexual orientation has become even more complicated with the concepts of "butch/femme" in the lesbian culture. Many years ago, when lesbians formed partner relationships, they used heterosexual couples as role models. Consequently, lesbians assumed that couples must have one person who had to act out the masculine role, the "butch," and one who acted out the feminine role, the "femme." Gradually, under the influence of the Feminist movement, lesbians began challenging and refuting the notion that human behavior had to be divided so rigidly. Younger lesbians began exploring androgynous behaviors. Although they were confronting the traditional standards of relating as a couple, many began to feel better about themselves and they began to see their self-esteem increase. Today, as with men, women of all sexual orientations span the continuum of gender-stereotyped traits.

Taking on or rejecting traditional sex roles *does not* determine sexual orientation. Likewise, identifying your sexual orientation does not determine your sex role behaviors.

### Addiction and Sexual Orientation

The second factor which interferes with discovering our sexual orientation is the abuse of chemicals. If we're under the influence of mood- or mind-altering chemicals, we are unable to rationally examine factors that point to our true sexual orientation. Drugs and alcohol anesthetize feelings. Without such feelings, we lack the emotional feedback which could help clarify our sexual orientation.

Psychotherapist and Chemical Dependency Expert Stephanie Covington studied the sexual orientation of alcoholic and nonalcoholic women. She explored the sexual orientation of alcoholic women before they became alcoholic, during active alcoholism, and after being sober for at least three to twelve months (see table).

|  | **Before Alcoholism** | **Active Alcoholism** | **Sobriety** |
|---|---|---|---|
| Heterosexual | 74% | 57% | 66% |
| Bisexual | 20% | 37% | 17% |
| Homosexual | 6% | 6% | 17% |

On the one hand, the abuse of alcohol may have allowed the women in Covington's study greater freedom to explore their sexual orientation. However, the increase of women identifying themselves as lesbians from 6 percent before alcoholism to 17 percent in sobriety underscores the role that alcohol and drugs may play in the lives of some women while they are attempting to define their sexual orientation. The numbing effect of drugs and alcohol may help many ACOAs deny their same-gender feelings and attractions. This may explain why so many women never confront the issue of their sexual orientation until they become chemical free.

Obsessive and compulsive behaviors around food—whether it's over-eating, anorexia, or bulimia—help some of us deny our sexual orientation. Some of us who abuse food have histories of sexual abuse. Although sexual abuse does not always result in eating disorders, we may use eating disorders to avoid the feelings surrounding our sexual abuse, to exert some degree of control in our lives, and to conceal the pain and shame we feel.

If we've been sexually abused and develop eating disorders, we may suffer body image distortions and negative feelings about our overall sexuality. We may be reluctant or unable to examine any underlying questions regarding our sexual orientation. Just as chemically depen-dent women must first become clean and sober before exploring their sexual orientation, those of us with eating disorders must recover from our food compulsivities in order to achieve any accurate examination of our sexual orientation. Like chemically dependent ACOAs, those of us who recover from eating disorders may, for the first time, be confronted with our own sexual orientation confusion.

Others of us with no sexual abuse history may also abuse food com-pulsively to protect ourselves from sexual feelings. Anorexia, bulimia, and compulsive overeating can lessen the sexual interest and sexual fears that surround sexual orientation confusion.

## Homophobia

"Homophobia" refers to the fear of homosexuals and fear of any form of same-gender intimacy. Some people believe that homophobia is an archaic issue that the Gay Rights movement has all but eliminated. But research indicates homophobia is widespread. A nationwide survey con-ducted in 1974 showed that 81 percent believed homosexual acts were always or almost always wrong. Ten years later, in 1984, this same survey was repeated and 78 percent still believed homosexuality to be wrong.

Although not rated as harshly as homosexual men, lesbians are not seen by most people as normal, healthy adults. Since the AIDS epidemic, hatred, prejudice, and oppression of homosexuals and homosexuality has increased.

Surveys indicate that men's attitudes about homosexuality are more negative than women's. Studies show those who are most homophobic tend to be dogmatic, authoritarian, status conscious, intolerant of ambiguity, sexually and intellectually rigid, and guilty about their own sexuality. Homophobic individuals express their disapproval of homosexuals through degrading jokes and derogatory terms like "lezzie," "faggot," "queer," or "fairy."

Just as there is a cultural stigma against alcoholism, a more powerful stigma exists against homosexuality. A stigma is an attribute that is deeply discrediting. A stigma may not be readily observable, but is viewed as a character fault, an unnatural behavior, or a mental health problem.

Even though the American Psychiatric Association voted in 1973 to remove homosexuality from its list of mental disorders, many homosexuals continue to experience social, economic, and vocational oppression. Like any oppression, it causes homosexuals fear and anger, and often leads to depression and low self-esteem. Some churches, schools, and the media tell us that homosexuality is sick, sinful, and even criminal. The negative reactions to homosexuality by the largely heterosexual culture become internalized by lesbians and gays contributing to self-hatred and low self-esteem. When these negative and oppressive attitudes become part of the consciousness of homosexuals they feel alienated and isolated within their own culture.

Because of homophobia, many ACOAs choose to deny part of themselves by keeping their sexual orientation a secret, often hidden from themselves. Hiding the socially induced stigma leads to a double life. At church, on the job, or with relatives, the lesbian or gay male ACOA is thought of as heterosexual. At home, away from the eyes of the public, she or he can be close with a same-sex lover. Homosexuals who choose to conceal their identity often suffer anxiety about being "found out." Continual "passing" as straight in the heterosexual community— pretending to be heterosexual—prevents the homosexual from feeling personal integration, prevents her or him from feeling whole and is a betrayal of the real self. Neither being "out" as a gay person, nor being "closeted" provides a sense of safety.

Every individual in this culture, including homosexuals, has acquired homophobic thoughts, feelings, and behaviors. As long as we maintain these homophobic attitudes, we aren't free to *objectively* assess our sexual orientation. Homophobia leads many of us to reject any thought that we might be gay and may push us into early heterosexual marriages or cause us to date one man after the other.

If you lived in a culture where all three sexual orientations were valued and where homophobia didn't exist, the process of accurately determining and accepting your sexual orientation would be much easier.

*Causes.* So what determines sexual orientation? The most frequently asked question is what "causes" someone to be homosexual or bisexual. Unfortunately, too often the intent behind such questions is to know what causes sexual orientation differences in order to "cure" or change them. Most people do not view bisexuality or homosexuality as normal variances from the norm of heterosexuality. Instead, such differences are seen as deviant, abnormal conditions which must be condemned and/or eliminated.

Sexual research shows that the incidence of homosexual and bisexual behavior has remained fairly constant throughout history. Although homosexuals and bisexuals may be more visible today, the actual numbers of people of such sexual orientations remains largely unchanged.

Why do a certain percentage of people become bisexual or homosexual while the majority become heterosexual? Much of the debate has centered on whether homosexuality and bisexuality are conscious choices or inherited behaviors for which there exists little or no choice. Although much time, energy, and money has been spent investigating the "why" of sexual orientation, the truth is that sexologists simply do not know what causes the development of any sexual orientation whether homosexual, bisexual, or heterosexual.

Researchers have extensively studied sets of identical and fraternal twins in which one twin was heterosexual and the other homosexual. The search for a genetic determinant for sexual orientation has lead to inconclusive results. Hormonal research has yielded no simple cause-effect relationship between hormones and sexual orientation. Psychological theories which attempt to explain homosexual behavior lack sufficient evidence to show that homosexuality or bisexuality results from inadequate parenting. The one thing on which sexology experts seem to agree is that there is no agreement about what causes sexual orientation.

### Bisexuality

As we mentioned earlier, bisexuals are sexually attracted to people of either gender. Usually, they've had overt sexual experiences with partners of both genders. As a bisexual, one finds oneself attracted to and able to enjoy sex with either gender.

People who are bisexual have received little social or scientific attention. In a world that tends to polarize people into heterosexual or homosexual camps, bisexuals have been largely ignored. Bisexuals are generally viewed by the homosexual subculture as individuals unwilling to come to grips with their "true" homosexual orientation. Some members of the homosexual community condemn bisexuals for exercising their "heterosexual privilege," protectively hiding behind heterosexual assumptions or heterosexual partners in order to avoid the oppression of being labeled homosexual, while engaging in sex with homosexual lovers.

Bisexuals receive even less support from the heterosexual world. Many heterosexuals view bisexuals as simply "mixed up" heterosexuals who need "guidance." The fact that recent evidence indicates that bisexuals carry an increased risk for developing AIDS has served to alienate them even further from the heterosexual community.

Some homosexuals and heterosexuals believe that bisexuality is merely the middle ground or transitional point for those "fence-sitters" who are unwilling to commit to either a homosexual or heterosexual lifestyle. However, Kinsey, along with many sexologists today, believed that bisexuality can be a separate sexual orientation which represents, for some individuals, a definite place on the Kinsey sexuality continuum.

## The Alcoholic Family and Sexual Orientation

For anyone struggling to identify their sexual orientation, confusion over one's gender identity, gender role behavior, one's own addiction to food or chemicals, and externalized and internalized homophobia are powerful obstacles. Additionally, for many of us, the extraordinary pressures of growing up in an alcoholic family make identifying our sexual orientation even more complicated and anxiety-producing.

When we were children, our alcoholic families with their rigid rules and roles created little space for us to risk exploring or disclosing a sexual orientation that differed from the norm. The continual chaos and crises in our families, the pressure to maintain family secrets at all costs, and the limited problem-solving skills among our family's members all worked to make identifying a homosexual or bisexual orientation more traumatic for us.

One example of this difficulty can be seen in the bisexual and homosexual "coming out" process. "Coming out" refers to the process of telling others about our nonheterosexual sexual orientation. It is a lifetime process which begins for most of us by cautiously telling a trusted friend and slowly progresses to include other friends, family members, colleagues at work, and sometimes, even casual acquaintances. Some of us choose not to come out and risk the potential rejection from our families. Instead, we live hidden lives in an effort to maintain our family connections.

Some of us who are bisexual or homosexual, choose to "pass" as heterosexuals to avoid condemnation as "crazy" or "sick," and to prevent family disapproval or familial economic repercussions, such as being cut out of wills or having financial support cut off. The cost of passing, however, often includes feeling dishonest with family members and/or may result in distancing from our families to avoid being discovered. Passing as heterosexual with family, friends, and co-workers can cause us much pain and anxiety. When we conceal our true sexual orientation, we can only guess the degree of real acceptance by our families and friends. We never know for certain whether the intimacy and closeness we feel with them will disappear or turn into cool tolerance if our homosexual or bisexual identity becomes known. *"Not out" always means "not sure."* Many of us prefer to allow family and friends to fully know us, along with our sexual orientation. The degree of continuing support, respect and love we receive then determines how we choose to relate with them.

Others of us, perhaps sensing little or no hope for support or understanding from our alcoholic families for our alternative sexual orientations, cut ourselves off entirely from family interactions. Many of us move geographically far away to protect ourselves from the abandonment we fear. For some of us, the pain and stress from these decisions lead to seeking comfort through drugs, alcohol, food, work, addictive relationships, or other compulsions.

## What Contributes to Sexual Orientation Confusion?

*Denial.* One of the ways the alcoholic family environment contributes to our sexual orientation confusion is through denial. We're raised in families whose primary defense mechanism is denial. According to Dana Finnegan and Emily McNally, coauthors of *Dual Identities: Counseling Chemically Dependent Gay Men and Lesbians*, many people use denial to "prevent themselves from knowing about something which, if they did know about it, would threaten their self-concept and create unbearable anxiety." With denial, we can:

· Engage in homosexual behavior without defining that behavior as gay.

- Be asexual or celibate and remain unaware of our homosexual feelings.
- Live as heterosexuals and unconsciously deny any indications that we may be homosexual.

*Traditional Sex Role Expectations.* Another factor which contributes to our sexual orientation confusion is the fact that many of our alcoholic families required us to enact traditional sex role behaviors and attitudes. Alcoholic families generally operate within rigid sex role expectations. Both females and males are usually expected to behave in stereotyped ways with little room for variance or exploration. If we stepped outside our proscribed sex role, we may have been abused or rejected by our parents. Given this familial inflexibility, many of us who wanted to examine our own sexual orientation confusion were unwilling to take the risk.

*Lost Child.* One of the sibling roles in alcoholic families is that of the "lost child," the one who receives little or no family attention. According to Therapist Sharon Wegscheider, author of *Another Chance,* these lost children do not learn to develop intimacy with others and may be prone to confusion over their sex roles and sexual orientation.

*Same-Gender Boundary Invasion.* Those of us as children who were expected to emotionally care for an alcoholic parent of the same gender may have experienced sexual energy from that parent. One woman from our research said she felt confused when her drunken mother would dance suggestively with her and touch her in inappropriate ways. When the daughter began to question her own sexual identity, she had no one to talk with and her confusion and self-doubt remained unresolved.

*Parents' Sexual Orientation Confusion.* Our sexual orientation confusion may be passed onto us by parents who have never confronted or explored their own sexual orientation confusion. They may have conveyed ambivalence or contradictory sexual identity messages about themselves to us.

ACOA Sharon K.'s behavior gives her two teenaged daughters confusing sexual orientation messages. *The longest relationship I ever had was when I was with a woman who was at the same time in a relationship with a man. I've often been sexual with men and with women during the same period of time. Sometimes I'd go to a party and would wind up sleeping with someone and wonder why. Sometimes it was a man, sometimes a woman. I enjoy sex with women a lot, but I keep thinking I should be with a man.*

*Incest.* In *Incest and Sexuality,* coauthors Wendy Maltz and Beverly Holman say that incest can influence sexual preference. They say that some heterosexual women who are incest survivors find it easier to relate sexually to women because of their past sexual abuse from men. In contrast, they say some lesbian incest survivors may block their preference for female partners and relate exclusively to men due to years of repressed anger they feel toward their mothers who failed to protect them.

Incest survivor Martha T. feels confused about her sexual orientation. *I felt dissociated when I had intercourse for the last time. I felt like I was there because I was supposed to be. I had sex with him only once. I knew that it just wasn't there for me. Three months later, I had sex with a woman.*

***Adolescent Sexual Identity and Parents' Unavailability.*** A final contributor to our sexual orientation confusion is the lack of support and guidance most of us received from our parents during adolescence when we were clarifying our sexual identities. As adolescents, we needed to be able to talk with our parents about the confusing emotions and conflicts we felt during that time. When this kind of openness is available to adolescents, they can more securely explore their own sexual orientation issues. Unfortunately, few of us received this kind of support from our parents.

ACOA Theresa P. says lack of support from her family around her ambivalent sexual feelings caused her to turn to drugs and alcohol for relief. *When I was a teenager, I dated boyfriends but I never felt the sexual excitement they felt. I knew I was gay and I set out to cover up and hide it. When I was nineteen, I started working as a barmaid drinking heavily. I had a couple of brief affairs with women and men, but the sex was always under the influence of alcohol. The alcohol and pills quieted my questions about what I was doing having sex with both men and women.* Theresa remembers that there was no safety in discussing her confusion over being heterosexual or homosexual with either of her alcoholic parents. Daily binges, hangovers, and marital fights made them unavailable to respond to her growing questions about her true orientation. Theresa eventually turned to drugs and alcohol in an effort to medicate her sexual orientation confusion.

## Sorting It Out

Common in alcoholic families, these variables confuse and compound the issue of determining sexual orientation. While they influence the process of identifying our sexual orientation, they don't in and of themselves cause us to become heterosexual, homosexual, or bisexual. They do, however, interfere with our ability to discover and accept our true sexual identity. Sexual orientation involves much more than a decision about whether to relate sexually with men and/or women. It also includes our emotional and affectional attraction to members of the same or other sex.

Many sexologists now believe that our sexual orientation is formed between the ages of three and five years. Although researchers have yet to discover the exact process of developing sexual orientation, we know that while people have a choice of sexual behavior, they do not have a choice of sexual orientation. We can act in congruence with or in opposition to our real orientation. It's possible for us to have a true homosexual orientation, yet never engage in affectional, emotional, or sexual behaviors with someone of the same gender. If we act in opposition to our real sexual identities, we're likely to experience conflict and distress and may resort to drugs/alcohol, or other compulsions to ease those feelings and prevent our awareness of our sexual identity conflict.

In the process of talking with women who identified their orientation as homosexual, many described the feeling they experienced when they began acting in accordance with their true orientation as "finally coming home to myself." You have a right to discover and accept your sexual orientation, whether it is heterosexual, homosexual, or bisexual. As you free yourself from addictions and compulsions and develop a stronger sense of yourself, living from a false sexual orientation feels less satisfactory. Living in congruence with your true sexual orientation and coming to accept and love that orientation can help you develop a stronger sense of yourself and can increase your self-esteem.

# CHAPTER 11

# I Think I'm Sexually Happy, But I'm Not

Throughout this book, we've talked about the ways in which we experience limitations in our sexuality—difficulty achieving orgasm, sexual orientation confusion, lack of sexual desire, compulsive masturbation and partner sex, the need for rigid rules governing sex, and participation in sexual behaviors that can leave us feeling degraded and embarrassed. We've also discussed the problems many of us have with our intimate relationships—the inability to trust and be intimate, repeatedly selecting unavailable partners, giving more than receiving, being unable to distinguish ourselves from our partners, and difficulty asking to have our emotional and physical needs met. We wondered how ACOAs perceive their sex lives. How do we evaluate our intimate sexual relationships? Can we determine when we're sexually happy or unhappy?

To find out, we asked our ACOA research participants four questions:

1. How would you rate your current level of sexual adjustment? ("Very adjusted" to "very unadjusted.")
2. In comparison to other women, what is your perceived level of sexual responsiveness? ("Very much above average" to "very much below average.")
3. How would you rate your overall personal physiological level of sexual satisfaction? ("Very much satisfied" to "very much dissatisfied.")
4. How would you rate your overall personal level of psychological sexual satisfaction? ("Very much satisfied" to "very much dissatisfied.")

Additionally, we asked the women to describe in their own words and with their own examples the extent of their current sexual functioning and satisfaction.

We then reviewed the women's entire sexual histories, both statistical and anecdotal, and formed an independent rating of each woman's level of sexual adjustment, a rating based on a variety of issues known to contribute to overall sexual health:

- Sexual attitudes and behaviors.
- Issues surrounding the family of origin.
- The emotional, sexual, and physical availability of the woman to herself and the availability of her partner(s) to her.
- Codependent attitudes and behaviors.
- Chemically addictive attitudes and behaviors.
- Eating disorder attitudes and behaviors.
- Communication skills around sex.
- Sexual-interpersonal intimacy dynamics between the woman and her partner(s).

To determine our ratings, we reviewed basic information about each woman's body image, her sexual orientation confusion, frequency of masturbation, sexual abuse history, sexual compulsivity, oral sex, genital sex, and sexual fantasies, as well as her attitudes surrounding her sexual behavior. We watched for evidence of multigenerational shame, her attempts to individuate from her childhood family, her ability to establish and protect personal boundaries, and for examples of triangling and inability to separate herself from her partner (fusion) in her relationships. We observed the extent to which she and her sexual partner were "available" for a physically, emotionally, and sexually intimate relationship. We looked for examples of compulsive and addictive food and chemical use and for patterns of codependent behavior in herself and her partner(s). We examined the degree to which she had developed and used sexual assertive communication skills: sexual requests, sexual refusals, sexual limit-setting, active listening, conflict-resolution behaviors, sexual self-disclosure, and identifying and expressing intimate feelings. Finally, we looked for evidence of intimacy skills—the ability to give and receive affection, tenderness, empathy, trust, and the willingness to risk being emotionally and sexually vulnerable.

When we compared our ratings with the women's self-ratings, we found extreme discrepancies and differences. *More than one-third of the ACOAs in our study rated their sexual adjustment and satisfaction much higher than we rated them.* None of the women rated themselves lower than the rating we gave. Although it's difficult for anyone to evaluate another's sexual satisfaction and adjustment, our ratings were based on our experience as trained sexologists and on factors known to affect sexual satisfaction. We believe our ratings *may* more accurately reflect the actual levels of sexual health. The implication is that as ACOAs we may have difficulty determining our own level of sexual satisfaction or dissatisfaction. In other words, we may not be able to identify when we're sexually happy or sexually unhappy.

One of the ways to understand the discrepancy between the research participant's self-rating and the interviewer's rating of her sexual adjustment and satisfaction is to examine several cases from our research.

### Hating My Body

Paula W. says, *I'm twenty four and I still live with my alcoholic mother. Since everyone else in my family has turned their back on her, I feel it's my primary responsibility to take care of her.*

*My partner lives out of town and we commute to see each other. We don't have intercourse often because we see each other only once or twice a month. When we do, I never achieve orgasm through intercourse. I used to fake it, but now he's learned to stimulate me clitorally. I masturbate a couple of times a month, but I don't always experience orgasm when I do.*

*I'm bulimic. I binge, then fast and use laxatives. I know the bulimia has a lot to do with not feeling much in my relationship. I also know it has something to do with my sexuality and how I want people to see me. I hate my body and I feel embarrassed having it touched. When I think about my partner looking at my body and touching me, I can't come at all.*

| *Paula's Self-Rating:* | |
| --- | --- |
| Level of Sexual Adjustment: | Adjusted |
| Level of Sexual Responsiveness: | Above average |
| Physiological Sexual Satisfaction: | Satisfied |
| Psychological Sexual Satisfaction: | Satisfied |

*Interviewer Rating.* Paula's self-rating is higher than what she would have received from either interviewer. Let's look at why. Paula and her partner's geographical distance create some of the "unavailability" we discussed in chapter 2. Distance, in and of itself, does not create sexual dysfunction. It is, however, one contributing factor in overall sexual adjustment and sexual satisfaction. Selecting a partner who lives out of town is selecting someone who is only partially available. Some of us who have long-distance relationships might receive a higher rating than Paula because other aspects of our sexual history might indicate more adjustment and satisfaction.

Paula has a relatively low frequency of both masturbation and intercourse. Her ability to orgasm consistently through masturbation and with her partner is lower than expected. For someone of Paula's age group, the average frequency of masturbation is thirty-seven times per year. Paula masturbates about twenty-four times a year.

The fact that Paula engages in premarital sex puts her in the norm with her age group. Two-thirds of women Paula's age have premarital sex. Most of these women have intercourse once a week or more, a figure higher than Paula's once-a-month frequency. Sexual adjustment isn't determined solely by how often one has sex or how often one achieves orgasm. Again, sexual frequency and ability to experience orgasm are pieces that make up the picture of Paula's overall sexual interaction.

From a sexologist's point of view, Paula's progressive eating disorder is likely to produce sexual symptoms. She's 5'8" and weighs ninety-seven pounds. Her addiction allows her to dull her senses and momentarily relieve her psychological pain. The obsessive thoughts she has about fat and dieting occupy most of her time. Her need to control her body serves to feed her hatred of it.

As her alcoholic mother's caretaker, Paula's untreated codependent behavior increasingly prevents her from taking constructive action for herself. It's likely that Paula is beginning a predictable downward spiral that will, without help, end in isolation. She is likely to feel less and less desire for sex and her already infrequent sex life may become even less frequent. Her self-rating of "above average sexual responsiveness" reflects Paula's denial, a product of her eating disorder.

### What Is an Orgasm?

Lesbian ACOA Nancy F. describes her current sex life: *During the past four years I've been with my partner, I've never masturbated. It never occurs to me to masturbate even when I'm single. For me to reach orgasm with my partner, we must be touching each other at the same time. I couldn't have an orgasm if I just lie there and let her touch me. I can't have an orgasm with oral sex because I try too hard. I can feel good and even have an orgasm by just wanting to please her, or by thinking loving thoughts about her. An orgasm is a warm feeling in my body that feels like a nice embrace—a calm, quiet, relaxing feeling. I don't know how long an orgasm lasts because most of the time I can't tell exactly when it starts and when it ends.*

| *Nancy's Self-Rating:* | |
| --- | --- |
| Level of Sexual Adjustment: | Adjusted |
| Level of Sexual Responsiveness: | Above average |
| Physiological Sexual Satisfaction: | Very much satisfied |
| Psychological Sexual Satisfaction: | Very much satisfied |

*Interviewer Rating:* Nancy's brief sketch illustrates another case of discrepancy between our ratings and her self-rating. Most lesbians have masturbated to orgasm at some time and most continue to masturbate even when they're in committed relationships, according to Therapist JoAnn Loulan, author of *Lesbian Passion.* Loulan surveyed more than fifteen hundred lesbians and found that 89 percent of them masturbate. Ninety-two percent of single lesbians in her study masturbate; 92 percent of those casually involved with someone; and 88 percent who are involved in a couple relationship. Nancy does not masturbate when she's single nor when she's involved in a relationship. Although a woman who never masturbates differs statistically from the norm, it does not make her sexually abnormal. Her choice to exclude masturbation is important only if not masturbating negatively affects her in some way or if she wants to masturbate but is somehow blocked from doing so. We don't know whether Nancy has decided not to masturbate because of religious prohibition, early childhood anti-sex messages, an inability to give herself permission to touch her body, or a lack of sexual desire. We do know that masturbation can teach women about their own pattern of sexual arousal, about what type of touch is most likely to produce orgasm, and about how orgasm feels.

Nancy's discrepancy revolves around her experience of "orgasms." From her description of orgasm—"a calm, quiet, relaxed feeling like a nice embrace"—it's likely that Nancy has never experienced a physiological orgasm. Her definition of what occurs in her body during orgasms, the fact that she has never masturbated, and the limited circumstances under which orgasm occurs—"we must be touching each other at the same time"—leads us to conclude that Nancy believes she experiences orgasm when in fact she may not.

The physiology of female orgasms is such that it would be difficult to describe them as "calm, quiet, relaxed" feelings. Women's orgasms are marked by simultaneous rhythmic muscular contractions of the uterus, the outer third of the vagina, and the anal sphincter. The first contractions are usually rapid and intense and slowly decrease in force and frequency. Most orgasms consist of three to fifteen contractions and the whole body, not just the pelvic area, becomes involved. When most women describe an orgasm, they say it's an intensely pleasurable physical sensation, one that begins with muscle contractions in the vagina that spread out through the pelvis. Orgasms vary considerably from time to time and include the subjective feelings we attach to them as well.

Nancy's sexual history indicates she's not "faking it," but that she truly believes she's having an orgasm when in fact she may not. The fact that Nancy has never reached orgasm through masturbation increases the probability that she may be defining sexual arousal as orgasm. If Nancy chooses to work on becoming orgasmic, some basic sex information about masturbation might help. Her wishes and her timing around working to alter her orgasmic experience belong solely to Nancy and deserve to be respected. As with Nancy, it's important for us to realize that we have the right to decide what we do or do not want to work on in our sexual lives.

### Avoiding Sex Feels Safer

Jane D. is twenty-nine and divorced from her addict husband after a brief, one-year marriage. For the past five years, she says she's been dating casually. Both Jane's parents are practicing alcoholics who still live in the same house after thirty-four years of a tumultuous marriage. Since Jane's divorce, she's been involved sexually with three men and she's ended each of these relationships after about six months.

In the past year, Jane says she's never masturbated—*I never even considered it,* she says. Between relationships, she goes without sex for long periods of time. Most of the time, she doesn't allow herself to think sexual thoughts. When she becomes involved in a relationship, she says it's difficult for her to resume being sexual. *Allowing someone into my space and letting them come close to me after long periods of celibacy is hard,* she says. *I become increasingly nervous about having someone see my body. I even feel anxious about having them see me in my bathing suit. I've always been tall and thin with no breasts. As a kid, I was teased about being nobby-kneed and flat-chested. My sisters are both short and have darling figures.*

Jane works and goes to school sixty to eighty hours each week. She's adhered to this grueling schedule since she was fifteen. *I use work and school as a great excuse not to go out with men,* she admits. *That way, I don't have to lie to them. People want to take up too much of my time. I want to be solely independent. I want to just take care of myself, not to have to ask help from anyone.*

Jane says she's never experienced orgasm through oral sex and she's given up trying. She doesn't reach orgasm through intercourse either. In the midst of telling us about her inablility to orgasm, Jane says, *When I was in high school, my mother had gorgeous legs and a great figure. Boys would come over to pick me up for a date and comment on her legs and body. My mom would be drunk and she'd bend over wearing these short skirts. It embarrassed me. At the same time, my dad was having affair after affair. I'd find strange women's underwear in our car and women would call him at night. When they'd call, he'd just wink at me and take the calls up in my room. Other nights he'd be gone out at the bars.*

---

*Jane's Self-Rating:*

| | |
|---|---|
| Level of Sexual Adjustment: | Average |
| Level of Sexual Responsiveness: | Average |
| Physiological Sexual Satisfaction: | Very much satisfied |
| Psychological Sexual Satisfaction: | Very much satisfied |

---

*Interviewer Rating.* Jane self-rates her sexual adjustment as "average," yet we see a woman who does not masturbate, does not experience orgasm with her sexual partner, ends her intimate relationships within six months, has a negative body image, and works compulsively, most likely to avoid intimacy with others.

It's not accidental that Jane finds herself with little or no time to date. Although her motivation may be unconscious, Jane intentionally structures her life so that she's protected from sexual involvement. Her need for such protection has its roots in an alcoholic childhood filled with a mother who made sexual advances toward Jane's dates and a father whose extra-marital affairs were common knowledge. Jane did not witness sexual intimacy between her parents. Instead, the relationship between her parents was filled with deception, disappointment, and sexual tension, which contributes to Jane's need to avoid rather than seek out sexual relationships as an adult.

## Safety Through Affairs

In reviewing Alice M.'s history, you might reflect on the criteria we used to determine ACOA sexual adjustment ratings—sexual attitudes and behaviors, issues surrounding the alcoholic family, availability of self and partner, compulsive use of food and chemicals, codependent behavior, and assertive intimacy and communication skills.

Alice is a thirty-four-year-old ACOA, the youngest of six children raised by her two alcoholic parents. When Alice was six, her father moved out of their home. He died from alcohol-induced liver damage when she was twenty. When recalling her father, Alice says, *I only knew my dad when he had the shakes, when he was drunk, or when he had a hangover. He was never violent with me, but he often beat up my mom. After he left, I rarely saw him. He tried to visit me at first, but he and Mom fought whenever he came over. After a while, he just kind of faded away.*

Nearly two years ago, Alice married. At the time of the interview, Alice was thirty-two days sober through Alcoholics Anonymous. She says her marriage is "neither happy nor unhappy" and she regrets getting married and thinks about divorce "frequently." About six months into her marriage, she began to have affairs. *I'm bored in my marriage,* she says. *Most of my relationships are short-term. Now I have sex periodically with a married man. Most of my lovers have had numerous sexual partners. My husband, however, hasn't had much sexual experience.*

During Alice's month of sobriety, she's not had any intercourse with her husband, although she continues to have sex with her extra-marital lovers. *I've never enjoyed making love with my husband,* she says. *I've never really been in love with him. I cared about him and I thought that caring might grow into something else. It hasn't. The man I'm having an affair with now is an ACOA who smokes pot every day. He has several other lovers. I'd like to have intercourse with him more often, but I don't ever want to do it again with my husband. I've never experienced orgasm with him and I always fake it. I can have orgasms with men I have affairs with, but my sexual feelings for my husband are dead. He's emotionally dependent on me and I hate it. When I first got sober, I told him I was going to leave him. He says he'd kill himself if I left so I can't leave him.*

Alice says she's had intercourse with at least fifty men and has been in love with four of them. Three were married and the fourth, although single, was compulsively sexual with other women. Alice acknowledges she feels confused about her sexual orientation. She says she masturbates to orgasm about once a month.

| *Alice's Self-Rating:* | |
| --- | --- |
| Level of Sexual Adjustment: | Adjusted |
| Level of Sexual Responsiveness: | Average |
| Physiological Sexual Satisfaction: | Satisfied |
| Psychological Sexual Satisfaction: | Satisfied |

*Interviewer Rating.* Alice gave herself the second highest rating on both psychological and physiological sexual satisfaction — a higher rating than we expected to find. From our perspective, the most crucial factor in Alice's sexuality is her new-found sobriety. Although she's been clean and sober for thirty-two days, she's still detoxing from the multiple drugs she's used since high school — pot, speed, hash, cocaine, LSD, alcohol, and Percodan. For many years, she says she never went more than two days without drugs and/or alcohol. She states she has no clear concept of drug-free sex.

Factors which lead us to rate Alice's sexual adjustment lower than her self-rating include: codependent behavior; compulsive sexuality; inadequate sexual communication; and confusion over her sexual orientation. Although Alice acknowledges she feels confused about her sexual orientation and says she's had same-sex partners, she identifies herself as heterosexual and says she has no desire to explore her sexual orientation confusion further.

Alice says her relationship with her husband is "neither happy not unhappy," yet the description of her marriage indicates frustration, disappointment, and repressed anger. The lack of assertive communication between Alice and her husband interferes with her ability to make responsible decisions about what she wants from that relationship. She's unable to tell her husband she has trouble reaching orgasm with him and cannot ask him to change his style of lovemaking. Her codependent behavior makes it difficult for her to accurately assess her marriage. Instead of being able to determine whether or not the relationship can meet her needs, her codependency facilitates her staying in the relationship to "take care of" her husband's emotional needs.

Because of a chaotic, alcoholic childhood, Alice has several unresolved family of origin issues that interfere with her sex life. She never experienced the relationship she wanted with her father — he was there infrequently and when he was, he fought with her mother. Each visit from her father brought her the hope for closeness, always followed by disappointment. As an adult, Alice's affairs with emotionally unavailable men seem to offer her a sense of control. She decides on who she will see, how much time they'll spend together, and what they'll do together sexually. While living in her alcoholic family, Alice experienced few things she could control. Things happened to her without her feelings or her wishes being considered. Her father moved in and out of her life at will. Now she moves in and out of the lives of others at will. Her affairs provide Alice with the "illusion of control" she actively seeks. Alice says she's "adjusted" sexually and her sexual responsiveness is "average."

A major risk for Alice at the moment is the fact that she's involved with a man who uses pot daily. His drug use puts her in danger of relapse. If Alice relapses, she loses the opportunity and her ability to sort out her sexual life.

## Alcoholic Families and Sexual Satisfaction

What does this all mean? How does growing up in an alcoholic family impact our ability to realistically assess our sexual relationships? When we began our research, we selected a sample which had equal numbers of ACOAs with alcoholic mothers, alcoholic fathers, or both. The women with fathers who were alcoholic reported the highest incidence of childhood sexual molestation. Women with two alcoholic parents had the next highest incidence of incest and ACOAs with alcoholic mothers the lowest.

From the more that one-third of ACOAs in which there was an extreme disparity between their sexual self-rating and our rating, fourteen had alcholic fathers, eleven had two alcoholic parents, and nine had alcoholic mothers. Surprisingly, the women who were incest survivors—and most likely to have alcoholic fathers—reported the highest level of sexual satisfaction. One might suspect the opposite to be true. What might contribute to ACOAs with the highest level of childhood sexual abuse saying they felt the most sexual satisfaction as adults? Could it be that sexual trauma in childhood impairs our ability to assess our own sexual adjustment and satisfaction?

While we can't definitely answer that, we can examine what we know about how those of us who grew up in alcoholic families develop relationships with ourselves and with others and perhaps find pieces to this puzzle. Factors such as denial, codependency, lowered expectations, partner selection, the effect of the false self on perception, and actual versus ideal self-rating may contribute to our inability to accurately assess our own level of sexual adjustment and sexual satisfaction.

*Denial.* Growing up in an alcoholic family, each of us learned to deny, minimize, and rationalize what was really going on. We learned how to ignore problems, how to convince ourselves that things will be better tomorrow, and how to stay preoccupied with other things so we don't have to assess what's going on with ourselves and with others. In sexual relationships, we can and do use these learned behaviors to keep the painful truth about our sexual disappointment at bay.

Denial is so engrained in many of us that it can prevent us from ever allowing ourselves the "right" to think about our own sexual needs and sexual adjustment. During the interviews, many of the ACOAs were surprised that we asked them about their sexual satisfaction. Many had never thought about how sexually satisfied or dissatisfied they were. Most of them seemed to be more comfortable talking about their partners' sexual behaviors, attitudes, and satisfaction than about their own sexuality.

*Codependency.* Melody Beattie, author of *Codependent No More*, defines a codependent as one who allows another person's behavior to affect her or him and who becomes obsessed with controlling that person's behavior. Codependents often take on the responsibility for how others think, feel, and behave. Primarily, they want to please others to keep the focus off themselves.

If we're codependent and we think about our sexual adjustment and satisfaction with our partner, we're likely to "protect" our partner's feelings. If we feel disappointment in our sex life, we may believe that acknowledging our dissatisfaction would somehow injure, embarrass, or humiliate our partner. Telling the truth about our level of sexual adjustment and satisfaction would "betray" them.

Some of us believe if our partner thinks our sex life is adequate, then everything must be fine. We take on our partner's sexual evaluation and dismiss our own. If we begin to acknowledge our dissatisfaction and see that our evaluation of our sex life is different from our partner's, we may feel guilty or selfish. Valuing our partner's opinion more than our own feelings, we deny our own ability to assess our sexual relationship and, consequently, we deny and discount our own needs.

Untreated codependents are usually perfectionists. We want to please everyone—and do it without making any mistakes. To identify any sexual dissatisfaction means we've failed. We're not perfect. We also know if we admit a problem exists, we'll need to do something about it, but we may be unsure what to do. For many of us, it's easier to refuse to acknowledge sexual relationship problems and continue to "hint" and "hope" that things can improve.

*Lowered Expectations.* We learn how to interact with others through our families. For most of us, our alcoholic families taught us damaging and ineffective ways of relating. We may have witnessed physical, emotional, and sexual abuse between our parents. We may never have learned that two people develop trust *gradually* over time through a process of open communication. From carefully watching our alcoholic parents, we may have come to believe that the primary goal in a sexual relationship is to merely *survive.*

Many ACOAs, especially those of us who've been sexually and physically abused, believe that a "satisfactory sexual relationship" is simply one without obvious abuse. A woman who has been raped, beaten, or sexually degraded in relationships, may define her relationship as "happy" as long as there are no beatings or sexual assaults. For her, the *absence of abuse* may become the criteria for a sexually adjusted and satisfying relationship.

The ACOAs we interviewed tended to evaluate their happiness and satisfaction by what was *not* happening in their relationships rather than by what was happening. One ACOA told us, *My partner never showed explicit porn magazines to our daughter like my dad and brothers did to me.* Others said their relationship was satisfactory because they didn't divorce or separate. *At least I didn't divorce, remarry, and divorce again like my parents did,* said another. Several indicated they were happy because they and/or their partner never participated in sexual affairs. *My kids never come home to find me in bed with strangers like I did with my mom,* said one interviewee. In all these cases, the focus—and the criteria for satisfaction —becomes negative things that occurred during childhood, things that are *not* happening in the current relationship.

Many of our definitions of sexual adjustment originate from emotional, behavioral, and attitudinal *reactions* to what we remember from childhood about our parents' sexual interactions. Because we define satisfaction by the lack of abuse or by the opposite of what we experienced as children, we may have lower expectations for our sexual relationships—we simply don't expect much from our sexual relationships and, as a result, are "satisfied" with very little. *We tend to settle for much less satisfaction in our sexual relationships than we deserve..*

When asked to rate our sexual adjustment, most of us use different criteria than people who grew up in nonalcoholic homes. From the research conducted by Dolores Curran, author of *Traits of a Health Family,* we know that couples from more functional families define satisfying relationships as those having mutual trust and respect, support for one's own and one's partner's sexual needs and desires, respect for individual and couple sexual privacy, and open sexual communication. Many of us do not even consider such criteria in defining our level of sexual satisfaction. For us, such expectations may be regarded as futile and impossible.

*Partner Selection.* As we discussed in chapter 2, we tend to select intimate partners who are emotionally, physically, or sexually unavailable to us. We also select partners who have similar levels of autonomy and a similar sense of self. As a result, we often select partners who share similarly low expectations for sexual relationships. Many ACOA couples may have an unexpressed agreement that "all you can expect in an intimate relationship is . . . " or "the best you can get sexually is. . . . " Unfortunately, both partners reinforce one another's low expectations for sexual satisfaction.

*The Effect of "False Self" on Perception.* Living from our "false self" prevents us from knowing the truth about our real self. It prevents us from seeing ourselves clearly, from being able to accurately assess our real level of satisfaction. Discrepancies we see between ACOA self-ratings and interviewer ratings may originate from may of us having limited access to our real selves.

*Actual Versus Ideal Self-Rating.* When measuring behavior or personality, therapists often ask clients to rate themselves both as they are and how they would like to be. Then they make comparisons between these "actual" and "ideal" ratings. When there's a large gap between how we perceive ourselves and how we'd like to be, we're likely to feel anxious and suffer from low self-esteem. A possible explanation for the large gaps between how our ACOA research participants see themselves sexually and how we see them is that the ACOAs may be using "ideal-self criteria" rather that "real-self criteria"—rating themselves on behaviors, thoughts, and feelings they "should" or "want" to have rather than what they actually experience. Some ACOAs may rate their sexual adjustment on what they believe is "good" or "right" rather than what is actually present in their lives.

In therapy, it's often helpful to find out a person's ideal and actual sexual adjustment to see how much internal discrepancy exists between the two. While individual therapy and/or group therapy is probably the most effective way to explore such discrepancies, you can begin the process yourself with your own self-examination. Ask yourself: What's my *ideal* level of sexual satisfaction—what do I really want from my sexual relationship? What's my *actual* level of sexual satisfaction? You can also ask your partner the same questions. Is there a large gap between your ideal and your actual level of satisfaction? Is there a large gap between your partner's level of sexual satisfaction and your own? This process can help you begin to look at any discrepancies between what you perceive is going on in your relationship and what is actually going on.

# CHAPTER 12

# Please Love Me

*I feel a hunger inside me that's not satisfied. I have a sense of wanting something more, something different. When I have sex I want something different, but I'm not sure what it is. It makes me feel ashamed because I think I want something that another can't give me. I look to my husband to give whatever it is I'm looking for through our lovemaking. I keep wanting him to make things different, but I think the key is really inside me. —Janet S.*

In all of our interviews with ACOAs, we sensed a longing—a "hunger" as ACOA Janet calls it. What is it that we long for in our intimate lives? What is it we want that we're not receiving?

## What Do ACOAs Long For?

We asked the women in our study, "What changes do you seek in your sexual lives?" The answers we received were honest, painful, touching, and revealing. First, we asked them to answer "yes" or "no" to a list of potential changes in their sexual relationships. Then we asked them to explain more fully in their own words what they want from their relationships. We provide the list of original questions here with the number of ACOAs (in parenthesis) out of the hundred participants who desired each change. You might use this list to determine what changes you'd like in your own sexual relationship.

*Desired Sexual Changes*

Answer "yes" if you desire the change and "no" if you don't.

— 1. More foreplay? (48 yes)
— 2. Use of vibrator during foreplay by partner? (12 yes)
— 3. Self-masturbation during foreplay? (15 yes)
— 4. More tenderness by partner? (42 yes)
— 5. Less tenderness by partner? (2 yes)

-   6. Manual stimulation of breasts by partner? (12 yes)
-   7. More manual stimulation of breasts by partner? (20 yes)
-   8. Oral stimulation of breasts by partner? (11 yes)
-   9. More oral stimulation of breasts by partner? (24 yes)
- 10. Manual stimulation of clitoral area by partner? (11 yes)
- 11. More manual stimulation of the clitoral area by partner? (32 yes)
- 12. Oral-genital stimulation by partner? (13 yes)
- 13. More oral-genital stimulation by partner? (20 yes)
- 14. Sex partner with smaller diameter penis? (0 yes)
- 15. Sex partner with larger diameter penis? (4 yes)
- 16. Sex partner with longer penis? (1 yes)
- 17. Ability to achieve orgasm through masturbation? (5 yes)
- 18. Ability to achieve orgasm during petting? (22 yes)
- 19. Ability to achieve orgasm during sexual intercourse? (25 yes)
- 20. More frequent orgasms? (43 yes)
- 21. More orgasms during sexual intercourse? (26 yes)
- 22. The ability to have multiple orgasms? (38 yes)
- 23. The ability to experience a different kind of orgasm? (49 yes)
- 24. Acceptance of masturbation while alone as a sexual outlet? (19 yes)
- 25. Available sex partner? (18 yes)
- 26. More availability of current sex partner? (24 yes)
- 27. Find a new sex partner? (24 yes)
- 28. End current sexual relationship? (9 yes)
- 29. Petting with mutual love between self and partner? (45 yes)
- 30. Sexual intercourse with mutual love between self and partner? (40 yes)
- 31. Feeling less fatigued, in general? (49 yes)
- 32. More time for sexual activity? (48 yes)
- 33. Elimination of fear of pregnancy during sexual intercourse? (19 yes)
- 34. Less frequent sexual intercourse? (6 yes)
- 35. More frequent sexual intercourse? (47 yes)
- 36. Less painful sexual intercourse? (10 yes)
- 37. Ability of partner to maintain an erection for a longer period of time? (22 yes)
- 38. Greater length of time before ejaculation by partner? (28 yes)
- 39. Shorter length of time before ejaculation by partner? (2 yes)
- 40. More aggressive role by self during sexual activity? (30 yes)
- 41. More aggressive partner in sexual activity? (24 yes)
- 42. Different positions for sexual activity? (27 yes)
- 43. More verbal communication by partner immediately before sexual activity? (48 yes)

— 44. More verbal communication by partner during sexual activity? (42 yes)

— 45. More verbal communication after sexual activity? (44 yes)

— 46. More physical affection after sexual activity? (36 yes)

— 47. Use of contraception by partner instead of self? (9 yes)

— 48. Change form of contraception used by self and/or partner? (5 yes)

— 49. Ability to conceive during sexual intercourse? (7 yes)

— 50. More romantic approach prior to initiating sexual activity? (55 yes)

— 51. Ability to experience sexual fantasies? (23 yes)

— 52. More privacy for sexual activity? (27 yes)

— 53. Fewer distractions during sexual activity? (33 yes)

— 54. More stimulation of parts of body other than genitals and/or breasts? (54 yes)

— 55. Lubricating more quickly for sexual activity? (19 yes)

— 56. Ability to achieve more intense orgasms during sexual activity? (31 yes)

— 57. Educational opportunities about sexuality for self and partner together? (50 yes)

— 58. More time spent in total sex experience during each episode of sexual activity? (52 yes)

— 59. Other changes you'd like, please specify.

After all the ACOAs answered the questions about desired sex changes, we placed the questions into types of categories:

· Desired body changes.
· Changes involving sexual behaviors.
· Changes in communication.
· Changes in the frequency and duration of sex.

**Body Changes.** Out of all the categories, the ACOAs we interviewed said they wanted the fewest changes involving their own or their partner's body. For example, very few women wanted any change in the size of their partner's penis. Only ten women said intercourse was painful for them. The most frequently desired change under the body category was a reduction in the amount of general fatigue they feel around their relationship.

Two questions immediately come to mind: What would contribute to a high rate of fatigue among female ACOAs? And how does this fatigue impact our sexuality? It's likely that one of our main sources of fatigue is codependent behavior in which we're overly focused on our partner and rarely focused on ourselves. Like alcoholic families, codependent relationships thrive on maintaining chronic drama, stress, and conflict. Consequently, such relationships drain both our energy and our spirits.

Another probable factor contributing to high fatigue among ACOAs is compulsive overworking. Many of us who work compulsively can often keep up an accelerated pace with little or no awareness of our fatigue level. After devoting grueling hours in our careers and homes, when it comes time to express ourselves sexually, we're mentally and physically exhausted.

Work burnout serves many functions for us. One of the most significant is that it allows us to avoid intimacy. Working until exhaustion precludes us from having the energy or giving ourselves permission to set work aside for affection, intimate self-disclosure, and tender exploration of ourselves and our partners.

Like other compulsive behaviors, overworking and codependency are often passed from generation to generation. If codependent behaviors and compulsive work are ways you avoid intimacy in your life, the following questions may assist you in more clearly identifying the origin and process of this pattern: Who used fatigue or overwork as a way to avoid intimacy in your childhood family? Can you recall conversations in which one parent complained, criticized, or attacked the other for using fatigue, or work as a way to avoid sex? How might you or your partner use fatigue, overwork, and codependency to avoid sexual intimacy?

In addition to fatigue caused from codependent behavior and overworking, many of us may feel tired because we don't know how to regularly nurture ourselves. Most of us continue to adopt the patterns we learned in childhood and practice few self-nurturing behaviors. Few of us have learned how to bring rest and comfort into our lives. ACOA Shari R., says she's struggled during the last year learning to take better care of herself. She fears if she becomes involved in a relationship, she'll lose those new-found, self-nurturing behaviors. *I have a life now that's fulfilling—a garden, a network of friends and neighbors, hobbies that interest me,* she says. *I'm not willing to give these things up for a relationship, out of the need to be with someone. I've had enough of one-sided relationships.*

What things do you regularly do that nurture you? Each of us is revitalized through different sources. For one, a few hours spent digging in a flowerbed is calming and nurturing. For another, it's a run in the park, a bike ride, or a drive in the country. You might want to list all the things you did this week to nurture yourself. Then write down all the nurturing things you might like to do for yourself and do not. Is there a large discrepancy? What interferes with doing all the nurturing things you would like? When was the last time you nurtured yourself? When you are in a relationship, do you continue to do things you enjoy, the things that nurture you? What beliefs, attitudes or feelings interfere with your doing so?

*More Touch.* In the sexual behaviors category, ACOAs overwhelmingly said they wanted more touching. They said they wanted their whole body touched, not just the mouth, breasts, and genitals. Many of the women we interviewed said the sexual touching between themselves and their partners had become predictable. For most couples, there was a set pattern of touching that allowed for little deviation or spontaneity. One woman said that if her lover kissed her on the mouth and then squeezed her buttocks hard, intercourse was always next. Another said it felt like her partner had designed a "map" of her body which he routinely followed. She said sex was so similar from one time to the next that she felt more like an object to him than a person.

The ACOAs we interviewed said they wanted partners who would delight in exploring their bodies in a random, yet curious and playful manner. Most said that being touched in the same way and making love in the same position time after time made them feel as if their partners weren't really interested in or aroused by them. All of us want to believe that our partners respond sexually to us in a unique and attentive way. ACOA Georgia D. put it this way, *I'd like affection from my partner—that means talking, touching, closeness, understanding. I want someone to give to me like I give to them.*

*More Foreplay.* The ACOAs we surveyed said they wanted more foreplay from their partners. Too often, our partners focus only on our genitals. Harriet D. said, *I want more tenderness, want more parts of my body explored than just having two areas—my breasts and genitals—zeroed in on.*

Most women said they felt as if foreplay had no meaning or purpose for their partners, that it was simply a means to an end. From a sexologist's perspective, this is curious because foreplay has several important functions including physiologically preparing the body for orgasm and exchanging intimacy-producing behaviors. One out of every two ACOAs we talked with said they'd like to be able to become vaginally lubricated more quickly, something that occurs with foreplay and makes penetration of the vagina more comfortable and enjoyable.

With foreplay, we can become sexually aroused through touch, smell, taste, sight, sound, kissing, and fantasy—all of our senses become involved in making love. Foreplay teaches us how to feel sexually aroused and how to emotionally and physically respond to that arousal.

It may be that in an effort to avoid the intimacy that makes us feel anxious and uncomfortable, we select partners who will give us less foreplay. If foreplay seems too personal and too intimate to share with another, we may give signals with our bodies to avoid foreplay. While many of us are not getting the foreplay we say we'd like, it may be a symptom of our underlying fear of intimacy.

Take a moment to examine your own sexual relationship. Does your partner touch you, caress you in places other than your mouth, breasts, and genitals? In what ways do you explore your partner's body? Would you enjoy more foreplay in your lovemaking? Does foreplay make you feel anxious or uncomfortable? What specifically would you like your partner to do in foreplay?

*More After-Sex Touching.* The third most frequently desired sexual behavior change ACOAs expressed was the desire for more touching after making love. ACOA Marsha L. says this about her lover, *I'd like him to hold me longer after intercourse. It embarrasses me that I have to ask him to put his arm around me and hug me.*

For many of us, after we or our partners reach orgasm, lovemaking comes to an abrupt halt. Our partners either immediately roll over and go to sleep, or get up and retreat to another part of the house. One minute we're being touched intimately, the next, with no explanation, our lover disappears.

This abrupt ending to sex leaves many of us feeling used, rejected, and abandoned. Many of the women in our survey said they wanted time after making love to cuddle, talk quietly, and maintain the closeness for a while that they felt during sex. Although they said they wanted this kind of time after sex, many admitted that they often feel vulnerable after orgasm and sometimes they themselves are the ones to leave.

What do those minutes after being sexual feel like for you? Do you feel in a hurry to leave your partner and get dressed, or resume work? By ending physical touching immediately after sex, what feelings do you think you might be avoiding? The next time you make love, you might experiment with staying for a few minutes longer.

*More Communication.* The majority of ACOAs we interviewed said they wanted more communication with their partners before, during, and after sex. For many of us, the "no talk" rule we learned from our alcoholic families governs sexual communication. We've learned from our families to keep sexual secrets, to express few sexual opinions, to guard, deny or exaggerate our sexual feelings, and to keep our sexual wants, needs, and longings to ourselves.

ACOA Jan F. says she wants more communication with her partner. *I'd like to be more verbal with her,* she admits. *I'd like to tell her what I like and dislike without worrying about my own sexual performance.*

Open communication about sexual feelings and behaviors can enhance our sex lives. In many ACOA relationships, however, sexual mindreading is common and often produces frustration, discouragement, and tension between partners. Openly communicating before, during, and after having sex can produce emotional vulnerability and sexual closeness.

In your sexual relationship, do you find yourself able to talk openly with your partner about what you want and need sexually? Do you find yourself able to tell your partner how you feel about sex? For most people in our culture, sex is a taboo discussion topic. For ACOAs, talking about sexual feelings and behaviors can be particularly challenging, especially at first.

We might begin by opening up the sexual communication in our relationship slowly. For example, we might tell our partner how we enjoyed a particular touch. "Jane, I really liked it when you rubbed your hand slowly up my thighs." Or tell your partner about something you'd like him or her to do. "John, I'd like you to touch my breasts and nipples more. It really turns me on." Or you can ask your partner specific questions. "How did you like by rubbing my breasts on your penis?" or "What's the touch that turns you on the most?" The idea is to become comfortable talking with each other about sex. As you practice, you'll likely become more comfortable in directing your partner more toward meeting your needs.

The following list, adapted from *Sex and Recovery: Straight Talk for the Chemically Dependent and Those They Love* by Jon R. Weinberg, Ph.D., can help you understand what assertive communication skills are and how to make them a part of your relationship.

*To Be Sexually Assertive Means:*

1. I tell my partner what I like sexually and what I dislike sexually.
2. I say out loud what I want sexually in specific behavioral terms. I demonstrate if necessary.
3. I say yes to my partner when I mean yes and no when I mean no.
4. I affirm that my wants and needs are really important. My partner's needs are also important.
5. I am comfortable with the idea of change. Today's no may become yes tomorrow for both my partner and me (and vice versa).
6. I can hear my partner's no in ways that don't damage my self-esteem.
7. I say no in such a way that my partner's self-esteem isn't diminished.
8. I look for alternatives and compromises when we have disagreements on important issues.

**More Sex, More Time.** A large number of ACOAs say they want to spend more time being sexual and they want to have sex more often.

Some of us have internalized the idea that to ask our partner to spend more time sexually is somehow selfish. Many of us spend a disproportionately small amount of time on our sexual/affectional life compared to the time we spend working, maintaining our homes, and relating socially to others. Certainly our sex lives deserve more time and attention than most of us give to them. Too often, we equate time for sex as time for orgasm. Equally important is time for affection.

What kind of time do you allow in your life for sex and affection with your partner? Do you plan romantic alone time or is sex squeezed in after the kids are in bed or between other "more important" things? If you feel you'd like to spend more intimate time with your partner, you might consider scheduling it into your week much as you plan other important events. Some ACOAs fear that scheduling this time alone may take the spontaneity out of their sex life. You may be pleased to discover how planning special time together—time for baths, massage, hot tubs, quiet music, erotic talk, and love making—can be stimulating for both of you.

*More Romance.* More than two out of three ACOAs said they'd like more "romance" in their sex lives. They'd like to feel more tenderness and mutual love during sex. However, trust and self-disclosure are prerequisites to expressions of love, tenderness, and romance. The absence of one affects the other.

In ACOA relationships where there's sexual, physical, or emotional abuse, there is little opportunity for the development of trust, personal safety, or self-disclosure. Without these, there's little love, tenderness, and romance.

Those of us who feel we must be vigilant in our intimate relationships, who expect to be left or hurt, don't often develop a sense of trust. In the past, ACOA Barbara S. says she's always emotionally and physically held back from lovers because she feared being left like she was as a child by her alcoholic father. *I hope to God I'll be able to take more risks with my next lover,* she says. *I want to be more emotionally open. I don't want to have to do the old withholding dance again.*

## Changing Behavior

How can we get the kinds of changes we want in our intimate relationships? Let's look at Jane T., an ACOA whose husband wants sex more frequently than she does, and examine how she can effectively work toward change in her relationship: *We have intercourse a minimum of six times a week at his insistence,* she says. *He'd like it if we had sex twice a day and three times on Sundays. I can't do it. I get physically sore having so much sex. I want sex only once or twice a week. Recently, I've realized that the only time we don't have sex is when we have a horrendous fight. Now I know how to get things to happen more the way I want them. You can bet we'll never talk openly about this together.*

On the surface, it seems like Jane's problem has a simple solution. She could tell her husband that having sex so often causes her pain and that she'd like to have sex less frequently. However, it's probable that Jane's reticence to talk directly to her husband about this problem isn't limited to just this topic. Jane may generally feel inadequate and may have difficulty asking for what she wants.

Rather than talk directly with her husband about reducing the frequency of their intercourse, Jane plans to use an old and ineffective pattern of problem-solving she probably learned from her alcoholic parents—she'll engage in a distance-producing fight with her husband to reduce their sexual frequency. This indirect solution further damages her relationship. Having witnessed the abusive relationship between her parents for years, Jane knows no other way to ask for what she needs.

A more effective method of asking someone to change their behavior is called a "behavior change request." Such an assertive request has three parts:

- Identifying the problem behavior.
- Expressing feelings the behavior evokes.
- Requesting specific changes in the behavior.

In the first part of the behavior change request, Jane begins by clearly identifying the problem behavior to her husband: "When you and I have intercourse nearly every day. . . ." Notice that Jane is *specific* about exactly what behavior causes the problem—intercourse, not just "sex." By describing the exact behavior she wishes to change, Jane can later discuss other sexual options to intercourse, such as oral sex, manually bringing one another to orgasm, and holding one another while each masturbates. This first step describes exactly in behavioral terms the behavior she wants changed.

In the second step, Jane tells her husband what she feels when intercourse occurs so frequently. It's important for Jane to identify her feelings about the too-frequent intercourse. While she experiences physiological pain or discomfort, she may also feel some sadness over missing other ways of being close. So she tells him, "When we have intercourse every day, I feel vaginal pain. I also feel some sadness that we are missing other ways of being close to each other." Notice that she uses "I" statements and keeps the message clear and simple, avoiding overwhelming him with an array of feelings to which he might respond defensively.

Jane does not say "You make me feel pain and sadness." Others do not control how we feel. "I" statements do not blame, accuse or condemn. They place the responsibility for the feelings with the person who feels them.

In the third step, Jane asks for a "behaviorally specific" change—that is, she states exactly the change in behavior she'd like to see. As in the other parts of the request, Jane must avoid being vague or general about what she wants. She might say, "For the next two weeks, I want us to have intercourse two nights a week and do some other type of sexual touching three days out of the week." Jane does not say ambiguous things like "you need to make it better for me," or "so things could be a bit easier somehow. . . ."

Instead of coming up with the solution by herself, Jane might request that they talk about specific changes that would incorporate what she wants. "I'd like for the two of us to take some time to talk tonight about how we can make some sexual changes." She does not say, "I hope we can talk someday about this." Rather, she asks specifically for a time and identifies the subject she wants to talk about.

Assertive behavior change requests do not employ apologies or defenses for feelings. Jane does not put herself or anyone else down in the process of asking for the behavior change. An effective behavior change request includes a clear description of what the behavior is, what feelings emerge around the behavior, and a specific suggestion for altering the behavior.

When Jane combines all three parts of the behavior change request, she says, "John, when you and I have intercourse nearly every day, I feel vaginal pain. I also feel some sadness that we are missing other ways of being close to each other. I want the two of us to take time to talk tonight about how we can make some sexual changes."

Notice that this behavior change request does not hint at a solution, does not avoid the issue, and is neither ambiguous nor attacking.

For some of us, such a behavior change request may sound mechanical or artificial, or even impossible to request. In healthy, growing relationships, this type of direct confrontation is respectful to oneself and one's partner. Such confrontations may initially leave us feeling vulnerable. This vulnerability may come from years of passive, indirect, "hinting" and "hoping" for changes in our alcoholic families. It comes from rarely seeing our parents use such direct, respectful requests. At first, making behavior change requests may feel foreign, even dangerous to many of us. It may feel dangerous because assertive behavior change requests make us quite "visible" in our relationships. It puts our feelings and needs right out where our partners can see them.

Healthy couple relationships make frequent use of behavior change requests. Practicing this effective tool for change can help improve your self-esteem. It means you're respecting yourself, your partner, and your relationship.

***Meeting Unmet Childhood Needs.*** If you listen carefully to the changes many of us say we want in our sexual/affectional relationships, more often than not, we're describing what we needed and wanted to have changed for us as children. Joan H., a thirty-nine-year-old ACOA, married fifteen years and the mother of three, provides a good example of these unmet childhood needs. *I never thought I was greedy about sex, but I know I somehow wanted physiological proof that someone loved me. That proof could only come through sex. Sex is my substitute for alcohol. I'm as compulsive around sex as I was with alcohol.*

*Besides my husband, I've only had sex with two people in my life—the first man I had intercourse with and a man I was dating who raped me. Even with my limited experience, I obsess about having sex with others, even with friends of my husband. I've never had a real affair in my life, but I've had hundreds of them in my fantasies. I fantasize in elaborate detail about what the person and I do together sexually. It's an exciting secret life. But sometimes I get afraid that I might actually seduce one of my husband's friends.*

*I find myself wanting sex more and more with my husband. It's probably no accident that he's plagued with impotence. Shortly after having a bout with pneumonia, he became very depressed, began to withdraw, and began having periodic impotence. He's never sought help for his impotence. He blames it on my wanting too much sex. He's probably right.*

*My husband has always doubted my faithfulness. The irony is that I left him years ago for my fantasy life. It's gotten to the point that my husband can only get an erection if he watches me masturbate. Now, unless I masturbate in front of him, we don't have sex. At the beginning, masturbating for him was fun and different. Now it feels as if I'm responsible for his erection and I resent it.*

*Sure I want changes in my sexual relationship. I want to be more at peace with myself and not feel so greedy about wanting sex. I'd like to be able to accept myself as a person who's not perfect. I never allow myself to make mistakes. I'd like to be able to trust my husband with more of the truth about myself. There's such a gap between my sexual fantasy world and what he thinks is going on. I want him to know about my hunger, my craving for sex. I want to lose my urgent and desperate need for sex and begin feeling closer to him.*

To understand how Joan's desired changes in her sexual relationship reflect some of her unmet needs as a child, it's helpful to know that Joan learned early to accept responsibility for the behavior and feelings of others—codependency—from her alcoholic family. She learned that vulnerable feelings are unsafe to disclose. She became the "parent" in her family and was given total charge of maintaining the household and her infant brother. She had to keep her mother's house "perfect" or face her mother's alcoholic rage. One day at age twelve when she was busy with household chores, she found her brother had crawled out to the family's pool and nearly drowned. She pulled him from the water and called the fire department and the child survived. Instead of commending her for saving her brother's life, her mother and father blamed her for the incident. Joan learned to hide the truth about this tragic family secret. To tell the truth about it, she says, would have required everyone "to face the alcoholism and neglect that was the foundation of our family."

From her father, who never confronted his wife's disease of alcoholism, Joan learned to deny reality, to avoid confronting the disappointing behaviors and attitudes of others, and to remain in a marriage no matter what emotional and physical toll it exacts.

Joan, like so many of us, wants the acceptance and love from her sexual relationship that she never received as a child. She wants to be able to let go of the compulsive behavior that keeps her from facing the painful memories and feelings from her childhood. She wants to be able to trust her husband with her innermost feelings and thoughts.

By examining our family histories and the changes we want in our relationship, we can come to a better understanding of the motivation behind our desired changes—and our resistance to those changes.

Most of us are particularly vulnerable to criticism. Often we and/or our lovers perceive "suggestions for change" as personal attacks. This defensiveness develops when, as children in alcoholic families, we received hostile or punitive feedback or no feedback at all. Assertively confronting and sharing our feelings with another are major steps toward developing true intimacy with ourselves and with others.

*Inability to Reach Orgasm with Partners.* The inability to reach orgasm concerns many of us and is one of the aspects ACOAs in our study said they'd like changed in their relationships. In our research, 63 percent of the women said they had difficulty achieving orgasm with their sexual partners. One out of every two women said they regularly pretended to have orgasms. This was true for heterosexual, homosexual, and bisexual women alike. Two-thirds of them said they privately masturbate to orgasm after not experiencing orgasm with their partner.

When we asked these women what prevented them from reaching orgasm, most identified conflicts unrelated to sex and preoccupation with nonsexual thoughts. ACOA Mary J. says past and present conflicts within her relationship inhibit her ability to orgasm. *So many things keep me from experiencing orgasm with my partner,* she admits. *We fight constantly, tear each other apart with verbal insults and put-downs. We both know how to go for each other's emotional jugular vein, go to the place that really hurts. When we have sex, the words we've thrown at each other during our fights come flooding back to me. By reliving our battles during sex, I can keep from acknowledging that someone is touching me. It's like my body isn't there. How can two people who wound each other so deeply ever relax and enjoy each other sexually?*

**Conflict Resolution.** *Facing Shame* authors, Merle Fossum and Marilyn Mason, believe that shame-based, alcoholic families establish a pattern of never resolving conflict between family members. Disagreements between family members may last for months, years, even lifetimes without resolution. Members learn how to continue conflict, aggravate existing conflict, and ensure lack of closure around conflicts. Alcoholic family members rarely exhibit effective conflict resolution skills—they simply don't know how to resolve conflicts. Instead of being resolved, relationship issues either continue to be a source of open conflict or they are dropped.

Most of us from alcoholic families don't understand the *process* of completing an exchange with another to the point of resolution. Fossum and Mason say that in the first step of a healthy interaction someone initiates the interaction and the other person responds. Then the first person responds to the second person's response, which clarifies and assists in the decision-making. This second step exchange between the two goes on until each person is able to completely state her or his position and each accurately hears the other's position. "Are you saying . . . ?" "Do you mean . . . ?" "I think. . . ." Healthy interactions require many clarifying responses between two people.

The third and final step of the interaction is resolution, coming to a place of agreement. However, in shame-based, alcoholic families, resolution rarely takes place between people. Instead, life becomes filled with chronic tension from hidden disagreements and an overwhelming feeling of discouragement and emotional exhaustion.

An example of this process might look like this: Jennifer wants to tell her lover of three months that she's been pretending to have orgasms with him. She tells him honestly and clearly about this (first step) and then answers his questions about what might be interfering with her ability to orgasm (second step). Then they discuss and decide on what changes each will make (third step). In the resolution, she agrees that she will not pretend to have orgasms and that she will show him how she stimulates herself during masturbation and what feels especially good to her. He agrees to touch her that way and to ask questions about their lovemaking when they come up. *Both* partners agree to express any feelings that emerge during these changes. The last step, committing to specific behavior changes and discussing the feelings surrounding those changes, is the most important part of the resolution process.

Just as unresolved relationship conflicts can inhibit orgasm, the unexpressed anger that accompanies the ongoing conflict further reduces the possibility of orgasm. Donna L., a thirty-three-year-old ACOA says the anger in her relationship prevents her from achieving sexual satisfaction. *The high degree of conflict in our relationship robs me of having orgasms,* she says. *How can we be so angry with one another one minute and the next let go and climax with each other? It just seems hypocritical.*

Donna wants to be able to have orgasms with her husband more frequently. To accomplish this she'll need to examine the unexpressed anger and conflict in her relationship. She and her husband will need to begin discussing the resentments that each harbors. Like many of us, Donna feels consumed by her anger. She fears if she releases it, her relationship will end. Contrary to what Donna and many of us believe, conflict doesn't have to mean the end of relationships or the end of loving. People *can* work through conflict and anger, rather than reenact those feelings within the relationships in endless, futile conflict.

Donna's relationship is a good example of how one kind of change often requires other changes. One change can set off a chain reaction of other needed changes. To be able to orgasm, Donna needs to examine the conflict and anger and needs to learn effective ways to resolve the conflict, while appropriately and assertively expressing her anger.

*Preoccupation with Nonsexual Thoughts.* The ACOAs in our interviews said preoccupation with nonsexual thoughts was the most common cause of not being able to achieve orgasm with their partners. The first step in changing this pattern is to identify those nonsexual thoughts. The ACOAs in our research said their thoughts fit into three categories: work-, school-, child-related thoughts; flashbacks of sexual or emotional abuse which contain negative body-image messages; and thoughts/fears about sexual performance.

ACOA Jan Y., a nurse in a major hospital, describes the thoughts that interfere with her orgasms: *My occupation is my biggest inhibition to orgasms. When I get home from work, I'm still thinking about my patients. I keep replaying conversations I had during the day, reviewing each decision I made. My job demands a great deal and involves a tremendous amount of stress. It's nearly impossible for me to unwind. The other thing that interferes with orgasm is that when I shut my eyes when I'm with my boyfriend, I see my ex-husband in a drunken stupor. I have vivid flashbacks of what sex with him drunk was like. It all seems so real that I forget to notice that I'm with someone new.*

To reduce those interfering thoughts, Jan might ask her new lover to talk to her while they are having sex. Hearing the sound of her lover's voice may help her feel more grounded in the present. Ellen Bass and Laura Davis, authors of *Courage to Heal*, offer these suggestions for those of us plagued with abuse flashbacks:

- Use a code word like "ghosts" to say to your partner when flashbacks occur.
- Stay with the flashbacks to gather information about past abuse.
- Keep your eyes open during sex so you can fully see your partner in the present.
- Stop if you need to and talk with your lover about the emerging feelings and memories.

Negative body image messages can also interfere with sexual pleasure. Sharon Q., a newly recovering alcoholic, was sexually abused by her father between the ages of seven and twelve. Her father forced her to engage in intercourse and anal sex with him. She says she wants to be able to eliminate the negative thoughts she has about her body that keep her from having orgasms with her lover. *In the six years we've been together, I've never been able to have an orgasm with my lover,* she says. *One thing that interferes is how I feel about my body. I hate my body from the waist down. My legs are too hairy and my thighs and butt are too big. Maybe if we kept the lights off while we made love it would be easier. I just can't stand someone seeing my lower body without any clothes on.*

Changing a negative body image takes time and patience. To help you begin the process of accepting your body, authors Bass and Davis, *The Courage to Heal*, devote the chapter "Your Body" to discussing the importance of healing those bodies that were abused so long ago. They provide valuable exercises, affirmations, and suggestions for learning to listen to and nurture our bodies.

When we feel sexual anxiety, we often remain outside ourselves, detached, objective, removed from what is happening in the present. Anxiety causes many of us to tightly control our feelings. By detaching from the present and controlling our feelings, we become "spectators" in our own lovemaking. When we become spectators, we become less involved in the sexual activity because watching and evaluating what's going on is distracting. In the spectator role, we become less intimate and spontaneous. When combined with our preexisting fears and doubts about our sexual performance, this obsessive self-observation can easily rob us of orgasms. Sexologists Masters and Johnson found that those who become sexual spectators are most often perfectionists who are hesitant to trust others and who fear being rejected in their love relationships.

Those of us who develop an excessive need to please others, to serve others, and who strive never to disappoint those we love are particularly susceptible to sexual spectatoring. The roots of sexual spectatoring may begin for us in our childhood alcoholic families where we received love and affection only when we pleased and performed well.

### Achieving the Changes You Want

To assist you in the initial process of identifying and achieving the changes you desire in your sexual life, writing out a general inventory of your current sexual health and sexual relating can be beneficial. Categories to explore include:

- Your overall health status.
- Your body image.
- Sexual fantasies.
- Sexual values.
- Sexual orientation.
- Contraception use.
- Partner pleasuring.
- Self-pleasuring patterns you engage in.
- Sexual expectations of yourself and your partner.
- Sexual communication level between you and your partner.
- Sexually transmitted diseases (include your symptoms, treatment, and prevention strategies).

It might also be beneficial to include in your sexual inventory specific areas of satisfaction, dissatisfaction, and confusion you might feel. What changes do you want in your sexual relationship? Describe specific steps you'd be willing to take in order to achieve those desired changes. This written inventory may help you become aware of your sexual beliefs, feelings, and patterns. Once you become aware of your own sexual process, you can gradually begin to make constructive changes.

# CHAPTER 13

# The Emergence of Self

Clara T., thirty-eight years old, came from a family in which both parents were alcoholic. Clara, the youngest of seven children, had a father who was a compulsive worker and high achiever. Her father had a professional occupation in which he traveled extensively. He was absent from the home approximately three out of every four weeks.

Clara's father was verbally abusive with her mother and with the children. *He was like a dictator in our home. Anything that wasn't done as he wanted, he would explode. He beat my brothers almost on a daily basis with a huge leather strap. The beatings came when they didn't do something to his specification. Everyone in my family was terrified of my father.*

*My father seemed to favor me. My mother and my siblings did not like that. I am the only one in the family who was never beaten by him. My father was more benevolent with me with material possessions as well. My brothers and sisters seemed jealous and sometimes hostile toward me because of his attention toward me.*

*When my father was alive, everyone just tried to stay out of his way. I remember hiding a lot. I hid in closets and under the bed. It seems as if everyone in my family beat each other up. My father died from alcoholism when I was seven and my mother never remarried. After my father died, my brother took over his tyrannical role. My mother would grab my hand and run me into her bedroom. She'd pull the dresser in front of the door so that my brother could not get in. This happened several times a week. When my father was alive, he would yell at my mom, loud fights with him swearing and her never yelling back. She always tried to pacify him.*

*After my father died, my mother couldn't leave the house without me getting hysterical. I wanted to be with her. She wasn't available because she was now either working outside the home or drinking inside our home. I spent a lot of this time trying desperately to get her to want to be with me. I made excellent grades in school.*

*When I was eight, my mother overdosed on librium and valium. When I was fourteen, I came home from school and found my sister at the dining room table with an empty Jack Daniels bottle. She had slashed both her wrists. My mom wrapped it up for her. Two days later my mom overdosed again. With all these suicide attempts, she never received psychiatric help.*

*When I was eight, the same brother who took over my father's role began sexually abusing me and would periodically beat me up. He continued to molest me for years. I hated this brother. I used to dream about killing him.*

*Though I hated this brother, I had always liked the brother who was thirteen years older than me. He and I had always been very close. When I was eleven and he was twenty-four, he took me to the county fair. When we got in the car to go home, he gave me some beer and he told me I should drink it. He was drunk but was playful. I drank several beers and he started fondling me. In the car, he kept touching me. I was afraid if I didn't do this with him, he'd leave me. He was like my "special person." He had always been there for me. He cared about me. I knew he loved me. When I used to come home from school, he would take me out to places. When this happened in his car, he was married. I was totally afraid that he would leave me if I stopped. He was real gentle with me, telling me that he wanted to be closer to me. He had intercourse with me in the back seat of the car. Afterwards, it was like it never happened. He and I never discussed it. I never told anyone about it until just a few years ago. He and I never touched sexually again.*

### The Interrelationship Between Past and Present

Clara's entire history affects her sexual functioning today. It is from her whole history that her present sexual life develops meaning. Clara has just described what it looked and felt like growing up as a child and as an adolescent in her alcoholic family system. Clara now discusses what her sexual and intimate relationship experiences have been like as an adult.

*I've had sex with about twenty-five men and about forty women. I have never had even one long-term committed relationship with a man. I've never lived with a man. Ten of the men I have had sex with paid me for it. With all of the women, there were only three committed relationships. Most of the sex I had with men was between the ages of sixteen and twenty-one. I had sex for the first time with a woman when I was twenty-two. She and I began living together. I left her for another woman. I was with that woman for four years, living together. During that relationship, I had two affairs. I left this relationship for another woman. I only stayed with this person for two months and then I left.*

*My pattern has always been to get out of a relationship only when I had another one. I have ended every relationship I have been in. My last relationship was with a woman and lasted three years. We got into a lot of heavy S & M. I got addicted to the S & M and was using pot and alcohol heavily. I had an affair and then left this relationship. From then on, I've only had casual sex.*

*I'm very uncomfortable with a woman making love to me. I have not allowed myself to have an orgasm for the past five years. With all the women partners I have had, I rarely allow the woman to touch me. I have a fear of letting anyone be too close. I can be close if I am in control. If I lose control by letting them touch me to orgasm, I'd feel vulnerable. I don't know quite how to explain this. I'd be afraid that I'd lose myself. They would know something. I don't even know what they'd know. Even the very idea of this is frightening. I'd have to do something or I'd have to give something up. Maybe that's it. Maybe I'd have to give myself up. In all my relationships with men and women, I have faked orgasm.*

*Sometimes I'll masturbate alone after the sex with a partner is over. Most of the time I don't even do that. I've never allowed men or women to have oral sex with me. Every time I think about it I feel claustrophobic, panicked, and too vulnerable. The S & M continued with the casual affairs until eighteen months ago. At that time, I stopped dating and having sex with anyone.*

Clara decided that several parts of her life needed to be changed. In her last relapse, she recognized that she had moved from being a periodic alcoholic to drinking on a daily basis. She also found it far more difficult to stop drinking and get back to AA.

*I've had no sex and no relationship for the last eighteen months. This decision has a lot to do with my drug history. I got sober for six years and then went out for a year on pot and alcohol. I got back into recovery and stayed sober for another three months. Things got very bad. I am so addicted to relationships, so compulsive in them. Relapse on drugs has always been over a relationship. I somehow pick partners who don't really want a relationship with me. Then I get obsessed with them and try to convince them to have a relationship with me. The more I think they are going to leave me, the more crazy I get. I always get to a place where I suddenly decide that I am not going to be abandoned and I develop an affair. The pain in talking about this is excruciating because I now recognize that all my involvements have been like this.*

*I've been sober for eighteen months. The last time I drank I found I had moved from being a periodic drinker to a daily drinker. I cannot afford to drink again. I decided I did not want any more affairs in my life.*

Clara is beginning to develop a new way of examining the sexual relationships from her past. Four weeks before the interview she joined an eight-week ACOA educational group. She spoke enthusiastically about all that she was learning and of the enormous risk she had taken. She further mentioned that prior to this group, she had never looked at any of her childhood history in an alcoholic family.

*I came to the conclusion that this time I needed to begin to find out who I really was. I'd like to develop a close, intimate relationship with someone without any of the addictive sex. I'd like to learn to love, to discover how to get to know another person, to be able to spend time with someone and get to know their values before having sex. I'd like to be close and experience intimacy. I'd like all of this stuff to be different. I want to be open and vulnerable and sober.*

When we examine our entire history, we, like Clara, are often confused and/or overwhelmed by the multiple losses we have experienced. We may have limited understanding of what the crucial issues are or of what the relationship is between them. Feeling lost in our pasts leaves many of us feeling a pervasive sense of hopelessness and powerlessness to change our lives today.

It is important for adult children of alcoholics to develop a process to sort out what these issues and losses actually are. Clara's history offers an opportunity to do this.

*Loss of Self.* It was not safe in Clara's home for her to relate to the world from her real self. It is likely that no original bonding between Clara and her mother occurred. Clara remembers: *There were six years between me and my next sibling. My mother told me many times that I was not planned. She let me know that she had thought it was all over with babies and then I came along. She used to always say, "You were always one more mouth to feed."*

When Clara was born, her mother was already experiencing symptoms of third stage alcoholism. Bonding is not possible with an alcoholic whose disease has progressed to this state. After the death of Clara's father, she became her mother's primary caretaker and protector. In later years, she stepped into the same role with her alcoholic sister. As a result of the suicide attempts by her mother and sister, and their dependence on her to rescue them, Clara developed a deeper level of codependence. The family situation continually required that Clara focus on others rather than herself.

*Addictions.* Throughout Clara's life, her addictions were those of drugs, alcohol, sexual relationships, especially those that included S & M behaviors. Chemical addiction was a preexisting pattern in her family. She entered treatment through AA and has relapsed several times.

*Family of Origin Structure.* Clara came from an enmeshed family system, one in which blurred boundaries were predominant. Within her family of origin there existed an overall limited level of differentiation between members. Clara was the youngest of seven children. She entered a family of crises. Alcoholism had been deeply incorporated into the family's identity. Severe impairment of the family interactional system existed. Family secrets between various members, kept on such issues as alcoholism, suicide, and physical and sexual abuse, maintained the dysfunctional system of relating.

Sibling interactions were based on survival needs. The siblings were incapable of providing each other with true empathy, nor were they able to protect each other from the abuse. As time went on the psychological cruelty between the siblings reflected the stress and tension within the family.

*Boundary Issues.* The emotional, physical, and sexual boundaries of Clara were repeatedly violated leaving no room for the development of her real self. Boundaries have been violated through incest with both brothers, through witnessing and experiencing physical abuse, and through triangulation within the family. Clara was triangulated by her mother when her mother used Clara for protection against her physically abusive brother. She was further triangulated by her father when he singled her out for special attention.

The following experience that Clara had with her father clearly shows how her boundaries were violated:

The first day of kindergarten, Clara purposefully skipped school and hid outdoors because she was scared. When she was finally found, her father was outraged. She says, *My brothers and sisters knew I'd get beaten. They put me to bed and put books round me to block the blows they knew I would receive from my father. They carefully put covers over me and left my room.*

*When my father came in, he told me that he wanted me to cry and yell as if I were being beaten. He said he didn't have the heart to beat me. He hit the bedposts about ten times and I yelled and cried and acted hysterical. I was really frightened. I was lying on my stomach, facing the bed. He hit the bottom of the bedposts. As he exited my room, in a gruff voice, he said, "You'd better never do that again!" I was not allowed to have supper. No one, no brothers, not even my mother, was allowed to come into my room. I stayed all alone that night and the 'beating' was never discussed.*

Clara's father triangulated her by sending a threatening message to the rest of the family through her. He further violated her boundaries by ordering her to yell as if she were being beaten and by forcing her to keep the secret about the pretense. More importantly, her father's physical and emotional abuse created terror in her.

*Sexual Abuse.* Clara experienced incest with her two brothers and first intercourse abuse. She witnessed physical abuse between her mother and father and all other siblings. She witnessed the physical abuse of her mother by her brother and was herself emotionally and physically battered by him. In her adult sexual relationships, she reports having become addicted to sado-masochistic behaviors.

*Loss.* Experiences of loss in Clara's childhood included: her father's death when she was seven, as well as his long absences throughout the first years of her life; the inability of both parents to connect with her as a result of their own alcoholism; threatened loss through her mother's and sister's many suicide attempts; a loss of control over her body as a result of the physical and sexual abuse; and the betrayal by her trusted brother.

*Family Sexual and Relationship Messages.* Messages that Clara received from family members were "People who love each other abuse each other." "Your body is not your own. Other people can control it." "You can never say no. No means abandonment and rejection." "Nobody can stop someone who is sexually abusive." "Men are not safe to relate to. Women aren't either." "It's not safe to be close to someone because they might not live very long."

*Selection of Unavailable Partners.* Clara reports selecting partners who are not really interested in her. She selected women who enabled her addiction. When living in her family of origin, family members were unavailable to meet her developmental needs. Her father was physically unavailable to Clara as a result of living three weeks out of every month outside the family. His alcoholism made him emotionally unavailable to her, and his emotional outbursts and unpredictable behavior created fear and distance between them.

Clara's mother was physically unavailable as a result of her dependence on alcohol. She did not meet Clara's emotional or physical needs for safety or for bonding.

*Staying in Unhealthy Relationships.* Clara has developed a pattern in her life of entering relationships, discovering that her primary partner is disinterested in her, and then leaving the relationship for an affair. With this pattern of leaving every relationship she is in, Clara avoided being alone and was able to avoid experiencing abandonment depression. If Clara had waited until partners left her, or if she left relationships without having another partner on hand, she would be quite vulnerable to experiencing abandonment depression.

*Sexual Control.* In her previous sexual relationships, Clara has exerted sexual control through her participation in affairs, her unwillingness to allow lovers to touch her sexually, her choice to pretend having orgasms, and through her experiencing S & M behaviors.

*Sexual Orientation Confusion.* Although Clara has engaged in sexual behaviors with men and women, she has exclusively related sexually to women for the past seventeen years of her life. She has experienced orgasms with neither women nor men. During the interview, she expressed no ambivalence or conflict regarding her self-identification as a lesbian.

*Sexual Discrepancy.* Clara rated her current level of sexual adjustment as "unadjusted," her sexual responsiveness rating as "very much below average," her physiological level of sexual satisfaction as "very much dissatisfied," and she rated her psychological level of sexual satisfaction as "very much dissatisfied." Throughout the interview, she gave numerous examples to establish how she made those self-assessments. Her sexual relationship observations appeared quite reality based.

*Desired Change.* Clara wants to find out who she really is. Clara wants no more affairs in her life, no more addictive sex. Nearly all of her desired changes involve learning how to be more intimate in a committed relationship without acting on the need for an affair. She wants to learn how to love, how to be open, and how to be vulnerable in an intimate relationship.

### Assessing the Foundation of Current Strengths

Fortunately, we come to our healing process not only with our losses from childhood, but also with our strengths. *Each of us possesses inner strengths we can utilize and build on as we heal.* It is important for us to look at ourselves and our relationship histories with a gentle eye, seeing both our limitations and our strengths as we begin our journey toward the emergence of self.

Clara has provided her sexual relationship history. She has determined the changes she now seeks. Her history has been broken down into identifiable themes and specific issues within each theme have emerged.

In examining the case of Clara, it is beneficial to assess the particular inner strengths that Clara brings to the goals she has identified for herself. Throughout the three-hour interview with Clara, it was possible to determine specific areas of personal strength that she possesses. Certain segments of her history demonstrate positive characteristics that can provide the necessary foundation upon which her changes can begin.

Clara is currently facing reality in several areas of her life. She has accurately assessed the change in her drinking history, from periodic to daily drinking, and knows that her disease of alcoholism is seriously progressing. She experiences little denial in her observation that her pattern of compulsive sex with S & M and her codependent relationship behaviors have contributed to her previous relapses. She has accurately assessed her level of sexual adjustment and satisfaction.

Clara has the ability to establish goals for herself and the capacity to take effective action toward those goals. After relapsing, she returned to AA and immediately selected a sponsor. Today, Clara is sober and willing to examine those compulsions that cause her harm. Clara also recognizes that she had never examined the issues connected to having been raised in an alcoholic family. She made inquiries about joining an eight-week educational group and then did so. She has attended each meeting.

Clara is willing to risk the anxiety of a new situation in the hopes of gaining something beneficial to her goals. She was notified of the research, phoned to arrange a screening for the interview, and then openly participated in the interview process. She demonstrated courage and perseverance.

During the interview, Clara exhibited an ability to self-disclose, to identify and express feelings in the present, and to show warmth. She has empathy toward others. Clara demonstrates an inquisitiveness, a curiosity about herself and about the world that allows her to ask for information that may be helpful to her. Spiritual development for Clara has already begun.

Of everything noted during the interview, the most positive indicator of Clara's strength is that she is a survivor. Clara wants to live. She survived parental death at an early age, incest, triangulation, physical abuse, suicide attempts by family members, and the developmentally inappropriate demands placed on her to caretake her alcoholic mother and alcoholic sister. She experienced and survived chronic disillusionment and disappointment.

Each of these strengths combine to create the foundation that Clara needs to begin the gradual process of discovering her real self, the real self that was tucked away so many decades ago. As Clara sorts out the issues from her sexual history, she can begin to define a path of healing.

All of us, as adult children of alcoholics, have strengths and skills developed over our lifetime that can serve to provide us the foundation for change. It is beneficial for us to go inside, to take a personal inventory of our strengths before beginning a purposeful step toward self.

## Healing the Self

In order to build a healthy sexual relationship with someone, it is important to develop a healthy relationship with ourselves. As noted in earlier chapters, developing our selves and exploring our childhood family systems can dramatically affect our sexually intimate relationships.

There are identifiable steps to the healing, "self-building" process. Although the timing and the order of these steps may vary considerably from person to person, all the steps are integral parts of allowing the self within us to emerge.

*Who Am I?* The first task in healing the self is developing self-awareness, answering the question "Who am I?" This involves inwardly examining ourselves. How do we feel? What do we think? How do we behave? What do we want and need? Many of us come to this first step, this place of inner examination, only after a serious life crisis, illness, loss or other "bottoming-out" experience. At this point, like Clara, we intuitively know that "things needs to change."

*Facing Addictions/Compulsions.* None of us can achieve self-awareness or a healthy self without facing our addictions and compulsive behaviors. We cannot effectively move toward our selves when we're under the influence of a mood- or mind-altering substance or compulsion. This is particularly true for those of us who grew up in alcoholic families because our families used substances in out-of-control ways. Compulsions are common in alcoholic families and we're particularly vulnerable to addictively using alcohol, prescription or illegal drugs, food, codependency, spending, work, sex, gambling, and exercise. While we've witnessed out-of-control addictive patterns incorporated by family members over several generations, few of us have experienced successful family recovery. We may be the first person in our families for several generations to confront the addiction process and seek change.

When we first begin to confront the unhealthy patterns of addiction and compulsivity in ourselves, relationships, and in our family of origin, it's often the case that we'll receive little or no support from our friends, relationship partner, or childhood family members. This lack of support is due to denial, the need to keep family secrets, and misplaced family loyalty. At this point we must decide to either pursue our own healing or to return to living in denial.

If we decide to confront our addictions and compulsions, we'll clearly need outside support. Primary support is readily available through a variety of Twelve-Step programs of recovery:

- Alcoholics Anonymous for those addicted to alcohol.
- Narcotics Anonymous for those addicted to marijuana, cocaine, heroin, prescription pills, and other drugs.
- Overeaters Anonymous for those who have anorexia, bulimia, or compulsively overeat.

- Alanon for those in relationship with someone who addictively abuses chemicals.
- Gamblers Anonymous for compulsive gamblers.
- Smokers Anonymous for compulsive smokers.
- Debtors Anonymous for compulsive overspenders.
- Sex Anonymous for sex addicts.
- Incest Survivors Anonymous for those who experienced incest.
- Adult Children of Alcoholics for those who grew up in alcoholic families.

Twelve-Step programs offer information about compulsions as well as tools to use in addiction-free daily life. Perhaps more importantly, they offer the support of others who have experienced the same addictions. The no-cost self-help meetings help participants learn from one another's experience, strength, and hope. Confidentiality and anonymity of all members is protected and the only requirement for membership is the desire to recover from the addiction. Although many people are initially reluctant to attend Twelve-Step meetings, most find tremendous identification and support and soon feel they've found the healing community for which they have longed.

Through Twelve-Step recovery programs, many of us can find our first healthy bonding experience for our true selves. We can bond or attach to the group, to individual members, or to "sponsors," members in recovery who serve as direct and personal resources to newcomers and continuing members by sharing the tools and strengths the program offers.

*Feeling and Remembering.* Once we begin to work on our recovery and are no longer acting out our compulsions, our denial usually breaks down and long-repressed feelings and memories begin to emerge. For many of us, it is the first time we've "felt" in many years. These feelings can be intense and confusing for us. An excellent way to work through the emergence of these feelings and strengthen our individual program of recovery is through individual and/or group therapy.

Twelve-Step recovery programs can help confront the physical compulsion. Twelve-Step programs and therapy can provide us with a safe environment in which to form a healing relationship. This therapeutic relationship and the healthy bonding that it entails can help heal the early damage to our selves which occured in our alcoholic families.

As we form bonding relationships with our therapists, we gradually learn how our childhood families functioned as systems and how those systems affected us. We can learn how boundaries between members of our families were violated and how they can be protected. We begin to determine how family rules and roles influenced our development. We can learn to differentiate between healthy and unhealthy ways of interacting and we can acquire new ways to relate to ourselves and others.

However, we cannot sustain our new awareness and healthier methods of relating if we return to chemical abuse or compulsive behaviors. By resorting to our addictions, we almost certainly revert to patterns of unhealthy behavior. It is during this time of reawakening and growth that we are most susceptible to developing new and different compulsions.

During recovery, we often also begin to look more closely at the friends and family who have surrounded us during our addictive years. Commonly, many of these people are current substance abusers or are practicing codependents who do not support our new changes. We may want to reach out and encourage our friends and family to begin their own recovery. Our efforts are likely to be met with resistance and personal rejection. Until we initiate new relationships with people who support our goals of healing, it's likely that we may feel alone and alienated in our recovery.

*Facing Relationship Loss, Facing Fears.* One of the most therapeutic— and at times sad and painful—aspects of healing our selves involves facing the loss of previous relationships that we now identify as unhealthy. Grieving these losses is an integral part of the healing process.

As we begin to develop new and closer relationships with people who support our healing, many of us face our fear of abandonment. Our life in the past has been filled with people who were inconsistent and emotionally unavailable to us. Because of our past experiences, we may begin to "test" and question our newly formed relationships with friends, sponsors, therapists, relatives, and intimate partners. It is through this testing and retesting that we learn our new relationships are becoming solid and that trust is developing.

*Nurturing Self.* Learning to nurture ourselves is essential to the emergence of our true selves. We need to treat ourselves with love and respect. Self-nurturing behaviors are gentle, noncompulsive, and contribute to positive feelings about ourselves. At first, practicing self-nurturing can feel foreign and even painful. As we nurture ourselves, we become aware of the neglect and/or abuse we've suffered from ourselves and from others.

Sometimes facing the memories of abuse can feel overwhelming. Nurturing ourselves and receiving support from therapists and others can reduce our sense of isolation, provide us with the energy and comfort we need to continue our healing journey, and help us work through the issues created by our alcoholic pasts. As we begin to grieve the losses and the abuse, we can begin to release the pain from our pasts.

*Confronting Family Issues.* With support from therapy and self-help groups, we can begin to confront our family issues. We can start to become aware of our numerous early boundary violations and their consequences. With our new awareness, we can start actively sorting out our rights in protecting boundaries in every area of our lives. As we learn and practice assertive skills, we reinforce our ability to define and protect our selves.

It's also likely that actively defending our rights and personal boundaries may feel uncomfortable for us at times. It may bring up old fears of retaliation from others, fears rooted in our abusive pasts. With support from others and through self-assertion, we can work through these fears and learn to assert ourselves without becoming immobilized by them.

*Spiritual Awareness.* Spiritual strength is important throughout our healing process and can develop in many ways. As we begin living from our real selves, we become closer to our spiritual selves. Regardless of whether we connect with our spiritual selves through organized religions, through appreciation of nature, philosophical study, or meditation, access to our spiritual selves, to our sense of "connectedness with life," can bring us calm and can foster hope, serenity, guidance, and the sense of being able to rely on a power greater than ourselves. Awareness of our spiritual selves can be particularly helpful in combating the anxiety and self-doubt that often come as we shift from our false selves to our true selves. It can also help us as we confront the desire to again use addictive substances and engage in compulsive behaviors. As our trust and faith in a spiritual power develops, we often find that our faith and trust in ourselves and others grows as well.

*Affirming Our Right to Healing.* As we move through our journey to self, we develop support systems, learn to use effective tools to feel better about ourselves, and begin to see that healing *is* possible. Often at this point, disturbing questions arise: "Do I deserve to have this healing in my life?" "Am I entitled to feel good about myself?" "Am I entitled to have meaningful relationships in my life?" "Am I worthy of having a life free from chaos and crisis?"

Using affirmations to strengthen our sense of self-worth can help resolve these troublesome questions. As we begin to believe we are truly entitled to all the goodness life has to offer, our healing process can continue.

Developing our selves and exploring and changing our family of origin systems can result in overall changes that affect our sexual identities and our sexually intimate relationships. Expanding the capacities of our real selves can make a wide range of feelings available to us that can help us accept our right to feel sexual pleasure.

Healing our pasts and acquiring a sense of our selves does not come rapidly or easily. We may retrace our steps over the path to healing many times. Each time we face and resolve conflict in our lives, we gain inner strength and increase the foundation of our selves.

Therapist Stephanie Brown, author of *Treating Adult Children of Alcoholics*, says significant change takes time and hard work. It involves making the past real and developing an autonomous sense of ourselves. "Deep changes usually do not occur in a vacuum," she says. "They do not come as a 'fix' from someone else and they are not the result of finding the right formula, manual, or how-to guide. Deep change comes from within."

As our capacity for self-activation increases, our personal goals and wishes connected to sexual relating become more realized. Our ability to form and maintain relationship commitments begins to develop through exploring "middle-ground" sexual solutions. The ultimate benefit of family systems and of "self" work is the recovery and celebration of our sexual selves. We gradually come to believe that our sexual selves are of value.

# The Study

We present this appendix for those of you interested in the study design, participant sample, and research findings.

The primary question Karen Howell, M.A., and I wanted to investigate was: How does growing up with alcoholic parents affect our ability to form and maintain sexually intimate relationships? No one had ever looked simultaneously at the sexual attitudes and behaviors of ACOAs. Several years ago, I designed a pilot study at the Institute for the Advanced Study of Human Sexuality (IAHS) in San Francisco, California. I distributed a sexual behavior and attitudes questionnaire to female adult children of alcoholics attending professional seminars on family alcoholism offered by Author Claudia Black throughout the United States. My findings in this early study suggested that female ACOAs had incredible and similar stories to tell. Many of the women who responded to the pilot study questionnaire wrote in the margins or on the back of the questionnaire expanding their answers and giving personal examples of their sexual experience. These women not only had stories to tell, they wanted and perhaps needed to tell their stories. After years of "keeping the secret" in their alcoholic families, they wanted to be heard.

*Developing the Study.* In response to this initial work, I devised a research tool that combined structured questions with anecdotal open-ended questions that allowed the study participants to describe in their own words their sexual behaviors, experiences, attitudes, and feelings. Collaborating with Family Systems Therapist, Karen Howell, M.A., we conducted three-hour, face-to-face interviews with one hundred female adult children of alcoholics. We wanted to know not only about their sexual experiences and behaviors, we wanted to know if the gender of the alcoholic parent had a particular effect on their subsequent sexual functioning. Was there a difference, for example, if it was the mother who was the alcoholic parent? What if both parents were addicted? We know that children of alcoholics are often passed from adult to adult or to various institutions for caregiving. We wanted to know how these abrupt and frequent caregiver changes affected the future sexual lives of children of alcoholics.

*ACOA Study Participants.* Although the sexual life-histories of the ACOAs presented in this book may appear to be extreme, they are quite typical of the lives of many ACOAs. All the study participants identify themselves as adult children of alcoholics. Each was raised in a home where one or both parents drank alcoholically for a minimum of six years. Thirty-four percent of the women had alcoholic fathers, 33 percent had alcoholic mothers, and 33 percent had both alcoholic mothers and fathers. The women ranged in age from nineteen to fifty-seven years, with the average age being thirty-seven years. Most of the women in the study had completed at least three years of college. Thirty-seven of them had never been married, 31 percent were currently married, 29 percent were separated or divorced, and three were widowed. Forty-four percent were the firstborn in their families. Nearly one-third of the women identified themselves as lesbian or bisexual.

This nonrandom sample came to us from a variety of adult children of alcoholic workshops, from local colleges and universities, from referrals of other therapists, and from other research participants. We screened each woman by phone to make sure she met our criterion of having had parents who drank alcoholically for at least six years from the time of her birth to age eighteen. We excluded women whose parents didn't begin alcohol abuse until after the woman was eighteen, women whose parents were social or recreational drinkers rather than alcoholics, and women with parents addicted to other drugs such as heroin or cocaine, but not to alcohol.

*Sexual Histories.* To draw a complete picture of each woman's sexual history, we asked the women questions about masturbation, intercourse, orgasm, and sexual attitudes taken from questions in a comprehensive questionnaire, "Perceptions of Female Sexual Response Patterns" provided us by Davidson, Conway-Welch, and Darling from the University of Wisconsin—Eau Claire.

Using parts of an incest questionnaire designed in the Department of Social Work at the University of Ohio, we asked about each woman's incest history including questions about the gender and age of the abuser, what specific sexual abuse behaviors occurred, how long the abuse continued, and what the women perceived as the present emotional, social, or sexual consequences they now suffer as a result of the incest.

We asked the women about their drug and alcohol history. Using a standard intake form designed by the medical staff of a southern California drug/alcohol facility, we asked the women to identify their own substance use and abuse and any recovery attempts during their lives.

To ensure each participant was indeed an adult child of an alcoholic, we gave each woman the "Children of Alcoholics Screening Test," a questionnaire designed by John W. Jones. Women who answered yes to six of thirty questions qualified to participate in the study. All of the women in our study answered yes to at least twenty-five of the thirty questions.

Although these four sources of questions gave us objective information about the sex lives of these ACOAs, we also wanted to hear from the women in their own words. We felt their relationships would reveal more about how growing up in an alcoholic environment affects ACOA sex lives than any single objective measure. To elicit these anecdotal stories, we asked each woman open-ended questions which examined her intimate relationships—how she entered, maintained, ended, and assessed relationships with sexual partners. Each face-to-face interview was conducted in a private office with one interviewer and one participant present. We recorded each woman's responses in longhand.

*Study Results.* After Karen Howell and I interviewed each of the hundred women, we read through all of their anecdotal stories watching to see what common themes might emerge. Although details of the women's stories differed, much of what they told us was similar. As we read through their words, the following themes, repeated over and over in each woman's sexual life, emerged:

- Choosing sexually, emotionally, or physically unavailable partners.
- Staying in unhealthy relationships.
- Difficulty defining, maintaining, and receiving intimacy.
- Inability to trust self or others.
- Poor communication in relationships.
- Problems identifying personal boundaries.
- The presence of childhood or adult sexual abuse.
- The need to control sexual relationships.
- Unresolved grief from numerous lifetime losses.
- Inaccurate overt and covert parental sexual messages that affect adult sexuality.
- Using drugs or alcohol to be able to be sexually intimate.
- Confusion about sexual orientation.
- Inability to identify healthy sexual relationships.

# Theoretical Orientation

A theoretical orientation provides researchers and therapists with a system supported by a set of beliefs, from which to observe, understand, predict, and change human behavior. The original research, its analysis, and the clinical interpretation of cases found throughout *Aching for Love* have been deeply influenced by my own theoretical orientation.

In order to provide you with the *base* from which this book has been created, I share with you a brief summary of the theories which combine to form my theoretical orientation. Understanding this personal and political base can add perspective to your understanding of this book and what it may offer you in your healing process.

### Child Development: Who Do We Bond to First? And How?

Over ten years, Psychoanalyst Margaret Mahler closely observed infants alone and as they interacted with their mothers. In her book, *The Psychological Birth of the Human Infant: Symbiosis and Individuation*, she describes the Separation-Individuation theory which identifies how babies progress through a series of developmental stages which eventually lead to the psychological birth of the "self," a separate identity from others, a picture of whom one is in the world. According to Mahler's theory, the quality of the developed self profoundly affects all future interactions the infant has with others.

Mahler focuses her attention on defining those early childhood conditions which foster the healthy development of the self in the newborn. She refers throughout her book to the relationship dynamics between the mother and child. It is important to understand that the primary relationship which develops in the first thirty-six months of life heavily influences the subsequent functioning of the child. Mahler refers to the primary caregiver as "mother." For many children today, the primary caregiver during these thirty-six months continues to be mother. For others, however, the primary caregiver during the first thirty-six months may include relatives, neighbors, other child-care workers, or preschool teachers. The child may bond deeply to any of these individuals, whether they be female or male.

The process through which the self is born is divided into specific phases and subphases: autism, symbiosis, and separation-individuation.

*Autism;* the first developmental stage in Mahler's Separation-Individuation theory, occurs between birth and two months. The newborn has no coherent thoughts, no concept of a discrete self. Physical contact with the mother or primary caregiver comes through holding and feeding and provides important feelings of security. The mother creates a "holding environment" for the newborn. However, a mother who has not developed her own separate self may not be able to adequately attach to her child. A child who is deprived of this early physical closeness may be unable to explore her or his world without feeling neglected or abandoned.

*Symbiosis;* the second developmental stage, occurs between two and six months and begins with the child's first smile of recognition of the mother. The baby now recognizes the mother as different from others but not different from herself. As the baby is rocked and fed by the mother, she molds her body to her mother's and becomes "one" with her. The infant learns to cue the mother with sounds and gestures to respond to her needs for feeding, changing, and rocking. The baby is comforted, develops a sense of safety, and feels powerful when the mother responds to her cues. The baby now follows the mother's movement, listens for her voice, and eventually develops a "confident expectation" that someone is out there for her.

If the mother leaves the baby too long, deprives the baby of touch or resents and rejects her, the baby may return to the earlier autistic stage and become inattentive to her environment. Mothers who themselves did not have these basic needs adequately met often react to the child with frustration, confusion, and sometimes hatred.

*Separation-Individuation;* the third developmental phase, occurs between six and twenty-four months. In this phase, *the psychological birth of the self* occurs as the child proceeds through the three subphases of "hatching," "practicing," and "rapprochement." The "hatching" subphase finds the baby exploring parts of the mother's body, forming a mental picture of the mother, learning to creep. The child can now tell the difference between herself and mother and between her mother and others. A mother who is unable to tolerate her baby's first moves toward "differentiation," developing a separate self, may physically prevent her exploration.

Between ten and sixteen months, the child moves into the "practicing" subphase, actively exploring her environment, periodically returning to her "home base" for emotional refueling. Walking, discovering the world, and playing "catch me" games with the mother create the omnipotent belief in the child that she can control the world. The child darts off across the room, mother chases, scoops her up, and puts her down again. With this developmental game, the baby "practices" escaping from fusion, emotional overinvolvement, and engulfment. Mothers who "catch" the child and do not let her go or mothers who prematurely push the child away, protect *themselves* from feeling abandoned, and interfere with what the child needs to learn in this move toward individuation.

Between sixteen and twenty-four months, the "rapprochement" subphase, the toddler can create symbols and can produce images of her mother in her mind. She can take care of her dolls pretending that she is her mother. With this new cognitive ability, a huge change in her life takes place. She abruptly realizes that she is totally separate from her mother, that her mother exists outside of her. Accompanying this jarring awareness, she becomes acutely aware of her loneliness, vulnerability, neediness, and helplessness. With the recognition of her dependence on her mother, the omnipotence she once felt changes and she feels anger toward her mother. These feelings usher in a confusing period in which she clings to her mother for longer refueling periods and then angrily pushes away from her mother's arms as if she has been wounded.

When the "self" arrives, the child is in conflict. She becomes suddenly ambivalent about exploring the new world. She comes close to the mother for comfort and screams and kicks away. She does not want to lose her new "self" and does not want to lose the earlier "oneness" with the mother. An unhealthy reaction of the mother would be to personalize the child's pushing away as rejection or to cling to the child with a sense of desperateness.

The third subphase, "object constancy," happens between twenty-four and thirty-six months. The child can now hold in her head a relatively steady image of her mother, whether the image of her mother is gratifying or frustrating. As a result of this object constancy, she can now work alone on a task or play without having to "see" or go to the mother as often for emotional refueling. If, while alone, she realizes her mother is gone and she begins to feel insecure or fearful, she can call up the mental image of the "good enough" mother for comfort and reassurance.

If the child has developmentally received what she needed from the primary caregiver to develop object constancy, she now has the capacity to recall good feelings about the mother at the same time that she feels seriously disappointed in the mother. The child also knows that the frustrating absent mother is the very same mother who admires and loves her.

What if the child has not had enough good experiences with her mother, as is often the case in alcoholic families? If she does not have many "good enough mother" images to call up when feeling anxious, she may be overwhelmed by even minor disappointments. She experiences a painful ambivalence. She longs for comfort from her mother, but feels angry at both the feeling of that longing and at herself for having that longing.

## Object Relations Theory: The Real Self and the False Self

According to object relations theory, everyone needs attachment to others and their ability to attach meaningfully to others depends to a large extent on their early childhood experiences of attachment. For most of them, the first "object" to whom they relate is their mother. Their helpless dependence in those early months of life makes them particularly vulnerable to their mother's responses and to whether their early survival needs for food, closeness, and comfort were gratified or frustrated by her.

If each person received "good enough" care during the period described by Margaret Mahler, the birth of her or his psychological self occurs and the conditions of support are sufficient for her or him to develop a "real" self. The real self can emerge when there is a healthy give and take between mother and child, when the child is free to explore the environment and come back for reassurance, and when the adventures of the child are acknowledged and supported by that first caregiver.

When such conditions of safety are satisfied, the real self is permitted to develop the following capacities, described by James Masterson, author of *Search for the Real Self:*

- Experiencing deeply a wide range of feelings.
- Expecting appropriate entitlements.
- Developing skills for self-activating and asserting oneself.
- Developing the ability to soothe one's own painful feelings.
- Developing the ability to make and stick to meaningful commitments.
- Expressing our unique creativity.
- Becoming intimate with oneself and others.
- Developing the ability to be alone.

- Developing a recognition of the continuity of self.
- Developing the ability to find meaning in one's life and a hope for the future.

When one is being her or his real self, one can assess self-doubts, can confront failures and disappointments, can identify and act upon deeply felt wishes and goals, and can adapt creatively to changing roles and life situations. Acting from one's real self can be a guide toward realistic methods of achieving goals and toward experiencing confidence in oneself.

The real self requires an adequate childhood environment in which to grow and thrive. Masterson defines an adequate environment as one which includes caregivers who identify and respond with emotional support to the unique aspects of the child's emerging self, who can produce an environment that is both physically stimulating and safe, and who create emotional and intellectual opportunities for the child that are geared to the appropriate level of development.

What would prevent the creation of this type of environment? A mother who has suffered her own loss and is depressed, physically ill, or emotionally absent may not be able to create these conditions for the growth of the child's true self. Other situations which could interfere with the emergence of the true self might include mothers who are overwhelmingly threatened by the emerging self in the child or mothers who encourage the child to remain dependent on her in order for her to feel secure and protected. Childhood caregivers with impaired selves are most likely to raise children who later become adults with impaired selves.

The real self can be driven into hiding by emotional, physical, and/or sexual abuse, neglect, and childhood deprivation through the process of "splitting." In splitting, people, places, feelings, and things become divided into two extremes. When someone or something gratifies one's childhood need, it is good and loved. When someone or something frustrates one's childhood need, it is bad and hated.

In her book, *Children of Alcoholism, The Struggle for Self and Intimacy in Adult Life,* Barbara Wood describes in detail how infants mistakenly believe that they are dealing with two separate objects. They cannot understand that they have merely experienced two aspects of the same object. They try to keep the good object separate in their mind from the bad object. Abused, young children need to deny the destructiveness and disappointing parts of their parents. Children cannot accept that the caregiver responsible for meeting their basic needs is intentionally and chronically violating them. To do so would create an overwhelming climate of terror and despair. These children are trapped. They cannot survive on their own at this age. They cannot pack their bag and leave in the face of abuse and neglect.

The creative solution to this dilemma comes to the child in the form of an unconscious process of splitting. The child takes on the "bad" qualities of the abusing parents, internalizes the image of the offending parent. This allows the child to see the parent as "all good." The next time the child is abused by the parent, the child convinces her or himself that the abuse occurs as a result of her or his inherent "badness." The child assumes responsibility for the assaults or for the neglect.

With splitting, the abused child feels more in control. "Maybe I can change how I am or who I am and this will not keep happening." To hold the parent accountable for the abuse would be the same as the child admitting that "the badness is in Dad who hits me and has sex with me when he wants; I can do nothing to stop him and I want and need his love." Taking on the destructive traits of the abuser allows the child a chance to reduce her or his terror and discouragement and survive. The self-esteem of the child is sacrificed in the process. Unfortunately, splitting provides only an "illusion" of control.

In the process of splitting, the real self goes into hiding or safe-keeping to protect itself from further damage. The "false" self begins to surface, allowing one to blame others for difficulties, selecting relationships with "unavailable" sexual partners, becoming convinced that unreliable relationships are all that one deserves, and believing that painful feelings can and should be avoided by denial or by participating in self-destructive behaviors. When an ACOA lives from the false self, fantasies, addictions, or clinging/abandoning behavior are substituted for meaningful relationships. Living from the false self means seeking continual reassurances and affection from others, yet sabotaging the goals of the real self with indecisiveness and paralysis.

Object relations theorists believe that the false self is created to protect the real self from childhood annihilation. To heal the splitting requires a favorable environment in which the adult begins the lengthy process of working through the object relations failures of childhood. This theory offers the hope that the protected real self can at this time slowly emerge and grow.

## Family Systems Theory

Family systems theory is based on the concept that the family is a primary and powerful emotional system. Emotional disturbances are thought to come originally from our relationships within the family. Murray Bowen, M.D., family therapist, believes that "emotional fusion" is transmitted from one generation to the next by the family system. Fusion occurs when there is a blurring of psychological boundaries between self and others and when there is an exaggeration of the emotional need of family members for each other. Fusion develops in families in which there are tense interconnections and in which dependent attachments are fostered. In order to differentiate a healthy personality, unresolved emotional attachments to the family need to be worked through.

Key concepts of family systems theory include: *differentiation of self, the family projection process, emotional triangles,* and *emotional cut-off.*

Bowen developed a "Differentiation of Self Scale" which distinguishes people according to the degree of fusion or differentiation between their emotional and intellectual functioning. The more fusion with the family of origin, the less sense of self the person has and the less stable her or his identity. Those who are fused lead lives dominated by intense feelings and are often unable to function effectively under stress. The lower the differentiation of self, the more vulnerable one is to losing oneself in relationships with others. The higher the differentiation of self, the more one has the capacity to interact with others without the loss of self.

Emotional triangulation occurs in a relationship between two persons experiencing considerable anxiety and stress. The partner who feels most uncomfortable will triangulate into the relationship a vulnerable third person. This triangulation will serve to reduce the tension between the original two and will divert the anxiety. The original conflict-producing issues are, however, never addressed or resolved.

Lovers triangulate friends, relatives, co-workers, and even social agencies and courts. Parents in conflict may triangle the most vulnerable child in the family and develop a fused relationship with this child. The triangulating parent may devote exclusive energy and attention to one child, often inappropriately using this child as a confidant. The overly intense relationship results in damage to the child.

Bowen believes that we choose lovers with equivalent levels of differentiation to our own. The relatively undifferentiated lover selects someone who is equally fused to his or her family of origin, someone who manifests extreme dependence or extreme independence in intimate relationships. These two poorly differentiated persons form a relationship that is highly fused. They produce a family with the same unhealthy characteristics. This family emotional system will be unstable and will seek ways to relieve its tensions. Most often anxiety between the spouses will be reduced by: the expression of chronic conflict between the spouses, by the development of physical or emotional dysfunction in one partner, or by projecting the problems onto one or more children.

The child selected for the projection will remain more vulnerable to stress than the other siblings, will have the lowest level of differentiation of self, and the greatest difficulty separating emotionally from the family of origin. The interaction between the parent who projects family problems onto the child and the child may become an intensely close, dependent relationship or may become a highly conflicted, abusive relationship. Sometimes the parents collude to scapegoat a particular child in the family. While the child receives focused, negative attention and begins to develop symptoms of distress, the relationship of the parents survives under the illusion that the family is managing satisfactorily.

The child selected for parental projection may attempt to protect her or himself by moving away from the family as quickly as possible. Some of these children run away to the streets, others marry early, and quite a few attempt an "emotional cut-off" from one or more family members. Emotional cut-off involves breaking contact with the family of origin. The person engaging in cut-off denies the importance of family and prides her or himself on self-sufficiency. Emotional cut-off is a flight from unresolved emotional ties. It involves a "reactive" pulling away from the family of from a particular member of the family. Emotional cut-off does not work in the long run. *Emotional cut-off masks an unexamined fused relationship within the family.* Although it reduces the original anxiety associated with making family contact, the original unresolved fusion with the family of origin remains and is reenacted in the person's adult intimate relationship.

The primary goal of family systems therapy is to increase the differentiation of the self. This involves the reopening of closed family ties, the establishment of individual relationships with selected family relatives, developing skills to detriangulate, learning to define oneself as separate from the family, and achieving a permanent reduction in one's overall emotional reactiveness. The person becomes able to define her or his own beliefs, opinions, values, and feelings, able to express these directly, and able to take responsibility for them and effectively act them out.

# Resources

The encouraging news for adult children of alcoholics is that there is plenty of help available. There are new organizations, self-help groups, books, tapes, and therapists specializing in the identification and treatment of ACOA issues. Throughout *Aching for Love,* we've discussed relevant research from the fields of alcoholism, codependence, adult children of alcoholism, eating disorders/body image, sexuality/sexual abuse, and object relations and family systems therapies. We have arranged the following resources accordingly and hope you find them useful.

## ORGANIZATIONS

The addresses and phone numbers listed are for national offices of selected organizations. You can contact these organizations to find the local chapters nearest you.

*National Association of Children of Alcoholics (NACOA)*
31706 Coast Highway
South Laguna, CA 92677
(714) 499-3889

NACOA offers bibliographies of publications and informational materials free of charge. They also hold an annual convention and regional conferences.

*Al-Anon Family Group Headquarters*
P.O. Box 182
Madison Square Station
New York, NY 10159
(800) 245-4656; in New York area (212) 302-7240

For family members of alcoholics, Al-Anon provides listings of local groups.

*Alcoholics Anonymous (AA)*
468 Park Avenue South
New York, NY 10016
(212) 686-1100

AA provides referrals to local chapters, a free catalog of literature, and low-cost books, pamphlets, and videos.

*Incest Survivor's Anonymous (ISA)*
P.O. Box 5613
Long Beach, CA 90805-0613
(213) 428-5599

ISA is a Twelve-Step self-help peer program for incest survivors.

*Narcotics Anonymous (NA)*
P.O. Box 9999
Van Nuys, CA 91409
(818) 780-3951

NA provides referrals to local chapters and low-cost addiction literature.

*National Cocaine-Abuse Hotline*
(800) 262-2463

This 24-hour cocaine-abuse crisis line is operated by the Fair Oaks Hospital in Summit, New Jersey, and offers general information about cocaine addiction and referrals to therapists and treatment centers throughout the country.

*Cocaine Anonymous*
P.O. Box 1367
Culver City, CA 90232
(213) 559-5833

Hotline gives referrals to Twelve-Step groups.

*Overeaters Anonymous (OA)*
4025 Spencer Street, Suite 203
Torrance, CA 90504
(213) 542-8363

OA offers free introductory literature and referrals to local meetings.

*Victims of Incest Can Emerge (VOICES)*
Voices in Action, Inc.
P.O. Box 148309
Chicago, IL 60614
(312) 327-1500

VOICES offers a free referral service, listing therapists, agencies, and self-help groups that have been recommended by other survivors.

*Women for Sobriety*
Box 618
Quakertown, PN 18951
(215) 536-8026

Women for Sobriety provides referrals to local area support groups.

## BOOKS/ARTICLES

### Adult Children of Alcoholics

Ackerman, Robert. *Growing in the Shadow.* Pompano Beach, Flor.: Health Communications, 1986.
———. *Children of Alcoholics.* Holmes Beach, Flor.: Learning Publications, 1983.
Bepko, Claudia, with Kreston, Jo Ann. *The Responsibility Trap: A Blueprint for Treating the Alcoholic Family.* New York: Free Press, 1985.
Black, Claudia. *It Will Never Happen to Me.* Denver, Colo.: M.A.C. Publications, 1981.
Briggs, William. *Transitions: Making Sense of Life's Changes.* Reading, Mass.: Addison-Wesley Publishing Co., 1980.
Brown, Stephanie. *Treating Adult Children of Alcoholics: A Developmental Perspective.* New York: John Wiley and Sons, 1988.
Cermak, Timmen, L., M.D. *A Time to Heal.* Los Angeles: Jeremy P. Tarcher, Inc., 1988.
Covington, Stephanie, and Beckett, Liana. *Leaving the Enchanted Forest: The Path from Relationship Addiction to Intimacy.* San Francisco: Harper & Row, 1988.
Curtin, Paul H. *Tumbleweeds: A Therapist's Guide to Treatment of ACOAs.* Rockaway, N.J.: Quotidian, 1985.
Deutsch, Charles. *Broken Bottles, Broken Dreams: Understanding and Helping the Children of Alcoholics.* New York: Teachers College, 1982.
Fossum, Merle A., and Mason, Marilyn J. *Facing Shame: Families in Recovery.* New York: W.W. Norton, 1986.
Friel, John, and Friel, Linda. *Adult Children: The Secrets of Dysfunctional Families.* Pompano Beach, Flor.: Health Communications, 1988.
Gravitz, Herbert L., and Bowden, Julie D. *Guide to Recovery—A Book for ACOAs.* Holmes Beach, Flor.: Learning Publications, 1985.
Kritsberg, Wayne. *The Adult Children of Alcoholics Syndrome: From Discovery to Recovery.* Pompano Beach, Flor.: Health Communications, 1985.

Marlin, Emily. *Hope: New Choices and Recovery Strategies for Adult Children of Alcoholics.* New York: Harper & Row, 1987.

McConnell, Patty. *A Workbook for Healing: Adult Children of Alcoholics.* San Francisco: Harper & Row, 1986.

Middelton-Moz, Jane, and Dwinell, Lorie. *After the Tears,* Pompano Beach, Flor.: Health Communications, 1986.

Porterfield, Kay Marie. *Keeping Promises: The Challenge of a Sober Alcoholic.* San Francisco: Harper/Hazelden, 1986.

Rosellini, Gayle, and Worden, Mark. *Here Comes the Sun: Dealing with Depression.* San Francisco: Harper/Hazelden, 1987.

Scales, Cynthia G. *Potato Chips for Breakfast.* Rockaway, N.J.: Quotidian, 1986.

Sexias, Judith S., and Youcha, Geraldine. *Children of Alcoholism: A Survivor's Manual.* New York: Harper & Row, 1985.

Steinglass, Peter, M.D. *The Alcoholic Family.* New York: Basic Books, Inc., 1987.

Wegscheider, Sharon. *Another Chance: Hope and Health for the Alcoholic Family.* Palo Alto, Calif.: Science and Behavior Books, 1981.

Wegscheider-Cruse, Sharon. *Choicemaking.* Pompano Beach, Flor.: Health Communications, 1985.

———. *Coupleship: How to Build a Relationship.* Deerfield Beach, Flor.: Health Communications, 1988.

Woitiz, Jane Geringer. *Adult Children of Alcoholics.* Pompano Beach, Flor.: Health Communications, 1983.

———. *Struggle for Intimacy.* Pompano Beach, Flor.: Health Communications, 1985.

Wood, Barbara L. *Children of Alcoholism: The Struggle for Self and Intimacy in Adult Life.* New York: New York University Press, 1987.

Wuertzer, Patricia, and May, Lucinda. *Relax, Recover.* San Francisco: Harper/Hazelden, 1988.

### Alcoholism

*Alcoholics Anonymous.* New York: Alcoholics Anonymous World Services, Inc., 1976.

Bratter, Thomas E., and Forrest, Gary G. *Alcoholism and Substance Abuse: Strategies for Clinical Intevention.* New York: The Free Press, 1985.

Brown, Stephanie. *Treating the Alcoholic: A Developmental Model of Recovery.* New York: John Wiley and Sons, Inc., 1985.

Finnegan, Dana G., and McNally, Emily B. *Dual Identities: Counseling Chemically Dependent Gay Men and Lesbians.* Minneapolis: Hazelden, 1987.

Fitzgerald, Kathleen Whalen. *Alcoholism: The Genetic Inheritance.* New York: Doubleday, 1988.

Gorski, Terence T., and Miller, Merlene. *Counseling for Relapse Prevention.* Independence, Mo.: Independence Press, 1982.

Jellinek, E.M. *The Disease Concept of Alcoholism,* New Haven, Conn.: Yale College and University Press, 1960.

Kaufman, Edward, M.D. *Substance Abuse and Family Therapy.* Orlando, Flor.: Grune and Stratton, 1985.

Kirkpatrick, Jean. *Goodbye Hangovers, Hello Life.* New York, Ballantine Books, 1986.

Metzger, Lawrence. *From Denial to Recovery.* San Francisco: Jossey-Bass Publishers, 1988.

Miller, Merlene; Gorski, Terence T.; and Miller, David K. *Learning to Live Again: A Guide to Recovery.* Independence, Mo.: Independence Press, 1982.

Milan, James, and Ketcham, Katherine. *Under the Influence: A Guide to the Myths and Realities of Alcoholism.* New York: Bantam Books, 1981.

Schwartz, Tony. "Acceleration Syndrome: Does Everyone Live In the Fast Lane Nowadays?" *Utne Reader,* Vol. 31 Jan.-Feb. 1989, 36–43.

Wilshack, Sharon C., and Beckman, Linda J. *Alcohol Problems in Women.* New York: Guilford Press, 1984.

### Codependence

Beattie, Melody. *Codependent No More.* San Francisco: Harper/Hazelden, 1987.

Cermak, Timmen, L., M.D. *Diagnosing and Treating Co-Dependency.* Minneaplois: Johnson Institute, 1986.

Lerner, Harriet Goldhor. *The Dance of Anger.* New York: Harper & Row, 1985.

Schaef, Anne Wilson. *Co-Dependence Misunderstood—Mistreated.* Minneapolis: Winston Press, 1986.

Schaeffer, Brenda. *Is It Love or Is It Addiction?* San Francisco: Harper/Hazelden, 1987.

Subby, Robert. *Lost in the Shuffle: The Codependent Reality.* Pompano Beach, Flor.: Health Communications, 1987.

### Eating Disorders/Body Image

Bill, B. *Compulsive Overeating.* Minneapolis: CompCare Publications, 1981.

Hirschmann, Jane R., and Munter, Carol H. *Overcoming Overeating: Living Free in a World of Food.* Reading, Mass.: Addison-Wesley, 1988.

Hollis, Judi. *Fat is a Family Affair.* San Francisco: Harper/Hazelden, 1985.

Hutchinson, Marcia Germaine. *Transforming Body Image.* Trumansburg, N.Y.: The Crossing Press, 1985.

*Overeaters Anonymous.* Torrance, Calif.: Overeaters Anonymous, Inc., 1980.

### Object Relations and Family Systems Therapy

Bowlby, John. *A Secure Base, Parent-Child Attachment and Healthy Human Development.* New York: Basic Books, Inc., 1988.

———. *Attachments.* New York: Basic Books, 1982.

———. *Loss: Sadness and Depression.* New York: Basic Books, Inc., 1980.

Bridges, William. *Transitions.* Reading, Mass.: Addison-Wesley Publishing Co., 1985.

Briere, John. *Therapy for Adults Molested as Children—Beyond Survival.* New York: Springer Publishing Co., 1989.

Curran, Dolores. *Traits of a Healthy Family.* Minneapolis: Winston Press, 1983.

Edward, Joyce; Ruskin, Nathene; and Turrini, Patsy. *Separation and Individuation.* New York: Gardner Press, 1981.

Hamilton, N. Gregory. *Self and Others.* Northvale, N.J.: Jason Aronson, Inc., 1988.

Jesse, Rosalie C. *Children of Alcoholics: Their Sibling World, Siblings in Therapy, Life Span and Clinical Issues.* New York: Norton, 1988.

Johnson, M. Stephen. *Characterological Transformation.* New York: W. W. Norton, 1985.

————. *Humanizing the Narcissistic Style.* New York: W. W. Norton, 1988.

Kahn, Michael D., and Lewis, Karen Gail. *Siblings in Therapy.* New York: W.W. Norton, 1988.

Kaplan, Louise J. *Oneness and Separateness: From Infant to Individual.* New York: Simon and Schuster, 1978.

Kerr, Michael E., and Bowen, Murray. *Family Evaluation.* New York: W.W. Norton, 1988.

Krestan, Jo Ann, and Bepko, Claudia. "The Problem of Fusion in the Lesbian Relationship," *Family Process* (September 1980): 277–89.

Lerner, Harriet Goldhor. *Women in Therapy.* Northvale, N.J.: Jason Aronson Inc., 1988.

Mahler, Margaret S. *The Psychological Birth of the Human Infant.* New York: Basic Books, 1975.

Masterson, James F. *The Search for the Real Self.* New York: The Free Press, 1988.

McGoldrick, Monica, and Gerson, Randy. *Genograms in Family Assessment.* New York: W.W. Norton, 1985.

Miller, Alice. *For Your Own Good.* New York: Farrar, Straus & Giroux, 1984.

Minuchin, Salvador. *Families and Family Therapy.* Cambridge, Mass.: Harvard University Press, 1974.

Napier, Augustus Y. *The Fragile Bond.* New York: Harper & Row, 1988.

————. "The Rejection-Intrusion Pattern: A Central Family Dynamic," *Journal of Marriage and Family Counseling* (Winter 1982): 20–27.

Nichols, Margaret. *The Treatment of Inhibited Sexual Desire (ISD) in Lesbian Couples, Women and Therapy,* Winter, 1982.

Nichols, Michael P. *The Self in the System.* New York: Brunner/Mazel, 1987.

Scarf, Maggie. *Intimate Partners.* New York: Random House, 1987.

Viorst, Judith. *Necessary Losses.* New York: Simon and Schuster, 1986.

Williamson, Don S. "New Life at the Graveyard: A Method of Therapy for Individuation from a Dead Former Parent," *Journal of Marriage and Family Counseling* (January 1978): 93–99.

### Sexuality and Sexual Abuse

Apter-Marsh, Mickey. "The Sexual Behavior of Alcoholic Women While Drinking and During Sobriety," Ph.D. diss., Institute for the Advanced Study of Human Sexuality, San Francisco, 1982.

Armstrong, Louise. *Kiss Daddy Goodnight: A Speakout on Incest.* New York: Pocket Books, 1978.

Barbach, Lonnie Garfield. *For Yourself: The Fulfillment of Female Sexuality.* New York: New American Library, 1975.

Bass, Ellen, and Davis, Laura. *The Courage to Heal.* New York: Harper & Row, 1988.

Beckman, L. "Reported Effects of Alcohol on the Sexual Feelings and Behavior of Women Alcoholics and Non-Alcoholics," *Journal of Studies on Alcohol* 40, no. 3 (1979): 272–282.

Berzon, Betty, Ph.D., *Permanent Partners—Building Gay and Lesbian Relationships That Last.* New York: E.P. Dutton, 1988.

Blixseth, Edna D. *Uncharged Battery.* Portland, Oreg.: Portland Entertainment Publishing, 1987.

Brady, Katherine. *Father's Days.* New York: Dell Publishing Co., 1979.

Brecher, Edward M. *Love, Sex, and Aging.* Boston: Little, Brown, and Co., 1984.

Butler, Sandra. *Conspiracy of Silence: The Trauma of Incest.* San Francisco: Volcano Press, 1984.

Calderone, Mary S., M.D., and Johnson, Eric W. *The Family Book About Sexuality.* New York: Harper & Row, 1981.

Carnes, Patrick. *The Sexual Addiction.* Minneapolis: CompCare Publications, 1983.

Clunis, D. Merilee and Green, G. Dorsey, *Lesbian Couples.* Seattle, WA: Seal Press, 1988.

Courtois, Christine A. *Healing the Incest Wound.* New York: W. W. Norton.

Covington, Stephanie S., *Misconceptions About Women's Sexuality: Understand the Influence of Alcoholism.* Focus on Family, March/April, 1986.

Davidson, J. Kenneth Sr., Darling, Carol S., Conway-Welch, Colleen. *Perceptions of Female Sexual Response Patterns.* University of Wisconsin-Eau Claire, ___.

————. *Self Perceptions of Female Sexuality.* University of Wisconsin-Eau Clair, ___.

Densen-Gerber, J. "Addiction and Female Sexuality," *Journal of Addictions and Health* 2 (1977): 94–115.

Drews, Toby Rice. *Sex and the Sober Alcoholic.* Baltimore, Md.: Recovery Communications, 1988.

Evans, S., and Schafer, S. "Why Women's Sexuality is Important to Address in Chemical Dependency Treatment Programs." Paper presented at the National Council on Alcoholism Annual Meeting, Seattle, Wash., May 1980.

Federation of Feminist Women's Health Centers. *A New View of a Woman's Body.* New York: Simon and Schuster, 1981.

Finnegan, Dana G., and McNally, Emily B. *Dual Identities: Counseling Chemically Dependent Gay Men and Lesbians.* Center City, Minn.: Hazelden, 1987.

Gil, Eliana. *Outgrowing the Pain.* San Francisco: Lauch Press, 1983.

————. *Treatment of Adult Survivors of Childhood Abuse.* Walnut Creek, Calif.: Launch Press, 1988.

Heiman, Judith Lewis. *Father-Daughter Incest.* Cambridge, Mass.: Harvard University Press, 1981.

Heiman, Julia; LoPiccolo, Leslie; and LoPiccolo, Joseph. *Becoming Orgasmic: A Sexual Growth Program for Women.* Englewood Cliffs, N.J.: Prentice-Hall, 1976.

Hill, Eleanor. *The Family Secret.* New York: Dell Publishing, 1985.

Kinsey, A.C., et al. *Sexual Behavior in the Human Female.* Philadelphia: Saunders, 1953.

Klausner, Mary Ann. "Sexual Behavior and Attitudes of Female Adult Children of Alcoholics: A Descriptive Study." Paper submitted to The Institute for Advanced Study of Human Sexuality, San Francisco, 1983.

Klein, Fritz, et al. "Sexual Orientation: A Multi-Variable Dynamic Process," *Journal of Homosexuality* (Spring 1985).

Loulan, JoAnn. *Lesbian Passion: Loving Ourselves and Each Other.* San Francisco: Spinsters/Aunt Lute Book Co., 1987.

————. *Lesbian Sex.* San Francisco: Spinsters Ink, 1984.

Malatesta, V., et al. "Acute Alcohol Intoxication and Female Orgasmic Response," *The Jornal of Sex Research* 18 (1982): 1–17.

Maltz, Wendy, and Holman, Beverly. *Incest and Sexuality: A Guide to Understanding and Healing.* Lexington, MA: Lexington Books, 1987.

Morris, Michelle. *If I Should Die Before I Wake.* Los Angeles: J.P. Tarcher, Inc., 1982.

Murphy, W., et al. "Sexual Dysfunction and Treatment in Alcoholic Women," *Sexuality and Disability* 3, no. 4 (1980): 240–255.

Neidig, Peter H., and Friedman, Dale H. *Spouse Abuse: A Treatment Program for Couples.* Champaign, Ill.: Research Press, 1984.

NiCarthy, Ginny. *Getting Free: A Handbook for Women in Abusive Relationships.* Seattle, Wash.: The Seal Press, 1982.

Pinhas, V., "Sex, Guilt and Sexual Control in Women Alcoholics in Early Sobriety," *Sexuality and Disability* 3, no. 4 (1980): 256–272.

Powell, D. "Management of Sexual Dysfunctions in Alcoholics," Chap. 12 in *Practical Approaches to Alcoholic Psychotherapy.* New York: Plenum Press, 1985.

Russell, Diana. *The Secret Trauma: Incest in the Lives of Girls and Women.* New York: Basic Books, 1986.

Sgroi, Suzanne, M.D. *Handbook for Clinical Intervention in Child Sexual Abuse.* Lexington, Mass.: Lexington Books, 1983.

Smith, A. "Treatment Issues for Addicted Adult Children of Alcoholic Families," *Focus on Family* (March/April 1988): 15–17, 35.

Swallow, Jean. *Out from Under Sober Dykes and Our Friends.* San Francisco: Spinsters Ink, 1983.

The Troops for Truddi Chase. *When Rabbit Howls.* New York: E.P. Dutton, 1987.

Weber, E. "Incest-Sexual Abuse Begins at Home." *Ms.,* April 1977.

Weinberg, Jon R. *Sex and Recovery: Straight Talk for the Chemically Dependent and Those They Love.* Minneapolis: Recovery Press, 1977.

# Index